**SAGE** was founded in 1965 by Sara Miller McCune to support the dissemination of usable knowledge by publishing innovative and high-quality research and teaching content. Today, we publish over 900 journals, including those of more than 400 learned societies, more than 800 new books per year, and a growing range of library products including archives, data, case studies, reports, and video. SAGE remains majority-owned by our founder, and after Sara's lifetime will become owned by a charitable trust that secures our continued independence.

Los Angeles | London | New Delhi | Singapore | Washington DC | Melbourne

## Advance Praise

Anjali writes with passion, knowledge, and experience. Her book is a must-read for professional women—and men. Achieving true gender equality isn't an impossible dream. This incredible book shows us how. From the role of government and civil society to actionable steps corporate leaders can take today, the book is a crucial, definitive read.

**Marshall Goldsmith**
The author of the #1 *New York Times* bestseller
*Triggers* and *What Got You Here Won't Get You There*

Though half a century has passed since women first forced open the boardroom doors, it is indeed disappointing to see gender stereotypes hampering the recruitment, promotions, and succession process for women in the corporate world. An expert on leadership development and organizational change, Anjali Hazarika in her book provides priceless insights into how a truly inclusive and empowering organizational culture allows merit to be recognized irrespective of gender.

**Kiran Mazumdar-Shaw**
Chairperson and Managing Director
Biocon, Bengaluru

From demanding electoral reservation in the Parliament to assisting victims of sexual violence on the streets and homes, the women's leadership has played a significant role in increasing women's visibility, voice as well as validity of their economic participation. However, it is a long way to women's leadership building a constructive peaceful society. Anjali has done well in articulating possibilities of filling this gap. I hope this book will draw more women into active leadership roles at all levels of the society. The book gives hope that the civil society and public sector will play a positive and partnership role in making this possible.

**Ela R. Bhatt**
Founder
Self Employed Women's Association (SEWA), Ahmedabad

Anjali Hazarika's book is a meaningful effort in sensitizing all stakeholders to sit up and take notice of the lacunae in achieving gender neutrality at workplaces. A book like this if read by all members of the civil society could start a revolution. Women's role in the growth of organizations has largely been unheralded and I think it's about time that we acknowledge and embrace the idea of women empowerment in all walks of life.

**Dinesh K. Sarraf**
Chairman and Managing Director
Oil and Natural Gas Corporation Limited (ONGC), Dehradun

The book *Walk the Talk: Women, Work, Equity, Effectiveness* by Anjali Hazarika navigates through the challenges and stereotyping faced by women at their workplaces. Drawing attention to deep-rooted patriarchal mindsets, monocultural paradigms, and complexities women face in their leadership roles, the book provides insights and strategies to help women in their career progression.

The quantitative data and the qualitative material of the book provides a way forward to nurture an ecosystem to enhance collaboration among various stakeholders for achieving equity and efficiency. Scouting through the years of development of women empowerment in the country, this book is no dry academic treatise or self-help book but referral material to sustain women's development in the country.

**U. D. Choubey**
Director General
Standing Conference of Public Enterprises (SCOPE), New Delhi

# WALK
## THE TALK

# WALK THE TALK

## Women, Work, Equity, Effectiveness

### Anjali Hazarika

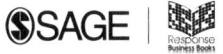

Los Angeles | London | New Delhi
Singapore | Washington DC | Melbourne

Copyright © Anjali Hazarika, 2017

All rights reserved. No part of this book may be reproduced or utilized in any form or by any means, electronic or mechanical, including photocopying, recording, or by any information storage or retrieval system, without permission in writing from the publisher.

First published in 2017 by

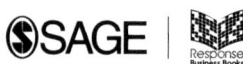

**SAGE Publications India Pvt Ltd**
B1/I-1 Mohan Cooperative Industrial Area
Mathura Road, New Delhi 110 044, India
www.sagepub.in

**SAGE Publications Inc**
2455 Teller Road
Thousand Oaks, California 91320, USA

**SAGE Publications Ltd**
1 Oliver's Yard, 55 City Road
London EC1Y 1SP, United Kingdom

**SAGE Publications Asia-Pacific Pte Ltd**
3 Church Street
#10-04 Samsung Hub
Singapore 049483

Published by Vivek Mehra for SAGE Publications India Pvt Ltd, typeset in 11/14 pt Garamond by Diligent Typesetter India Pvt Ltd, Delhi, and printed at Saurabh Printers Pvt Ltd, Greater Noida.

**Library of Congress Cataloging-in-Publication Data**

Name: Hazarika, Anjali, author.
Title: Walk the talk : women, work, equity, effectiveness / Anjali Hazarika.
Description: First Edition. | Thousand Oaks : SAGE Publications India Pvt Ltd, [2017] | Includes bibliographical references and index.
Identifiers: LCCN 2017021634 (print) | LCCN 2017035639 (ebook) | ISBN 9789386446930 (E pub 2.0) | ISBN 9789386446923 (E Book) | ISBN 9789386446916 (pbk. : alk. paper)
Subjects: LCSH: Women executives. | Sex discrimination in employment.
Classification: LCC HD6054.3 (ebook) | LCC HD6054.3 .H395 2017 (print) | DDC 331.4/81658—dc23
LC record available at https://lccn.loc.gov/2017021634

**ISBN:** 978-93-864-4691-6 (PB)

**SAGE Team:** Manisha Mathews, Sandhya Gola, and Ritu Chopra

*To my mother*
*for telling me*
*"Be there for others but never leave yourself behind."*

*And to my husband*
*for making that possible.*

Thank you for choosing a SAGE product!
If you have any comment, observation or feedback,
I would like to personally hear from you.
Please write to me at **contactceo@sagepub.in**

**Vivek Mehra,** Managing Director and CEO, SAGE India.

**Bulk Sales**

SAGE India offers special discounts
for purchase of books in bulk.
We also make available special imprints
and excerpts from our books on demand.

*For orders and enquiries, write to us at*

Marketing Department
SAGE Publications India Pvt Ltd
B1/I-1, Mohan Cooperative Industrial Area
Mathura Road, Post Bag 7
New Delhi 110044, India

*E-mail us at* **marketing@sagepub.in**

**Get to know more about SAGE**

Be invited to SAGE events, get on our mailing list.
*Write today to* **marketing@sagepub.in**

This book is also available as an e-book.

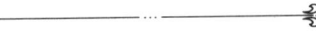

# Contents

| | |
|---|---|
| *Preface* | xi |
| *Acknowledgments* | xiii |

**1. Equality with a Difference** — 1
   A Complex Scenario with Vast Contradictions — 8
   Two Models Based on Two Assumptions — 13
   Why Differences Will Make a Difference? — 25
   Redefining Leadership — 26

**2. In the Shackles of Stereotypes ... Even Today** — 29
   Gender Stereotyping and Its Impact on
      Women's Careers — 30
   Encountering Glass Ceilings and Walls — 31
   Myths About Women Executives — 34
   Implications for Corporate Performance — 55
   A Virtue of Necessity — 76

**3. The Tyranny of Invisible Barriers** — 84
   Will She Fit in? Challenges of Fitting in
      the Organizational Culture — 89
   Career by Chance — 91
   Is "Ambition" a Bad Word? — 94
   The Tightrope Circus — 102
   How Can Dreams Be Realized? — 104

## 4. Networks as Catalysts for Change — 109
Reflections on Formative Years of Women's Network — 114
Fundamental Interventions That Made an Impact — 115
Collaboration with Other Agencies — 120
The Struggle for Sustainability — 127
The Power of Intercorporate Network for Change — 132
Lessons from the Intercorporate Initiative — 137

## 5. The Skills for All Seasons — 141
Is the "Cream" Being Pushed to the Top? — 143
The Strategies for Success — 145
    Understanding the Culture and Politics of the Organization — 146
    Seeking Mentors and Role Models in the Organization — 147
    Being Open to Constructive Feedback — 150
    Developing Ability to Take Initiatives — 153
    Building Resiliency and Change Readiness — 156
    Honing Influencing Skills — 158
    Dealing with the Challenge of Being Yourself — 161
    Defining "Work–Life Balance" for Yourself — 164

## 6. Coaching in the Rush Hour of Life — 173
Leadership Transitions — 175
Five Signature Themes in Live Action — 178
    Managing Emotions — 178
    Standing Up to Be Counted — 183
    Ability to Deal with Trouble — 188
    The Pitfalls of Overcommitment — 191
    Developing a Strategic Mindset — 194

## 7. When the Boss Is a Woman — 198
Ambivalence Is Everywhere — 201
    What Is It Like to Work for a Woman Boss? — 204
Resistance to Women's Leadership, Authority, and Expertise — 209

| | |
|---|---|
| Reclaiming One's Own Power and Authority | 212 |
| Crystallizing Leadership Identity | 215 |
| Developing Leadership Brand | 216 |
| Is It Worthwhile Being on a Board? | 218 |
| A Case for Diversity on Boards | 224 |

## 8. Creating Sanctuaries in Workplaces — 232

| | |
|---|---|
| Jumping Off the Career Ladder the Only Option? | 236 |
| Level the Playing Field | 240 |
| The Power of Small Change | 242 |
| Making a Business Case | 244 |
| Different Strokes for Different Organizations | 248 |
| The Best Practice Organizations | 253 |

## 9. The Ecosystem of Empowerment — 276

| | |
|---|---|
| Harnessing the Ecosystem | 280 |
| How Can Government (Policy-makers) Make a Difference? | 281 |
| How Can Employers Make a Difference? | 297 |
| How Can NGOs Make a difference? | 317 |
| How Can We—Men and Women—Make a Difference? | 319 |
| How Can Civil Society Make a Difference? | 322 |

*Index* — 329

# **Preface**

Sometimes, a change of mindset can happen in the most unexpected way. A friend of mine narrated the following incident to me. At work, she was discussing with her senior colleague the prospective employment opportunities for his daughter. They hammered out the reputation and brand of every company under discussion. Then, she asked him, "Would you want her to work for a company that treats her differently? That has lower expectations for women?" Suddenly, sitting across a table from a respected colleague, hearing her talk openly about an invisible organizational pattern of a certain company, he became acutely aware of two things: the invisible pattern of gender bias in most organizations and his own unconscious mindset. As she effectively summed it up for me, "We have not only narrowed the gender gap but we have narrowed the gap between who we think we are and who we truly are."

Small interventions such as these encourage people to behave in slightly different ways at critical moments. The simple act of talking about taboo subjects at work as if they were acceptable topics of discussion can make the subconscious conscious. So women need to do this more often. It is like doing their bit for the cause.

If you take away one simple truth from this book, I hope it is this: gender bias is real. It is real, it is persistent, and we all have to do our bit to fight it, because it is undermining gender diversity and economic security. If we recognize that economic growth requires the efficient allocation of resources, then how can half of the world's population be prevented from making a full contribution?

So who can make a difference? The answer is: all of us—men and women, businesses and governments, not-for-profit organizations, and the civil society. How can years of discrimination with deep-rooted systemic patterns vanish overnight? It requires deeper dialogues with all the stakeholders to ensure we are part of the solution, as surely we are all part of the problem.

It is time men got engaged too, many of whom care about gender equity as much as women do. They must play an active role in women's advancement. Organizations need to make a top-level commitment and then act in accordance with their words. By changing inflexible/unfair work standards that end up penalizing working mothers. By creating hospitable environments where the unique contributions of men and women are rewarded.

Governments need to practice what they preach. They need to develop necessary infrastructure, legislation, and policy architecture to fight visible barriers.

The civil society needs to move away from social norms that hold women to impossible standards and stigmatize men who share childcare. All this must begin from the individual level where men and women are aware of gender discrimination at workplaces and at home, and each works at his/her level to make workplaces more equitable and the society more open and fair.

True equality can only be achieved when we all fight the stereotypes that hold us back and "walk the talk" in order to achieve true equity with effectiveness.

# Acknowledgments

The project of officially writing this book took shape over a couple of years. However, it seems to me that I have been writing this book in my head all my working life. Many people have contributed to this project. I am grateful to Mr J. Ravichandran and Mr C. Mukherjee of the National Stock Exchange; Mr Srirang of ICICI Bank; Ms Sunita Cherian of Wipro; and Mr Ajay Mukherjee and Ms Ritu Anand of TCS for providing data on their best practices. I would like to thank Mr Dileep Ranjekar, CEO, Azim Premji Foundation, for supporting the project in more ways than one. I am also indebted to all the women leaders who shared their experiences that form much of the qualitative material of this book. I would also like to thank the participants of my workshops, whose insights have made a lasting difference to my understanding.

A special mention must be made of Shri Srinivas Chary, Assistant Librarian at the Administrative Staff College of India Library, for his support in sourcing reference material throughout the course of writing this book.

It has been my privilege to work with SAGE. I would like to convey my appreciation to the whole team at SAGE—from commissioning to editorial and from production to marketing, and everyone else, for creatively collaborating on the project.

Last but not the least, I would like to to thank my family—Antara, Abhishek, and Amitabh—for providing invaluable support throughout the course of writing this book.

# 1
# Equality with a Difference

Sitting around a conference table in a beautiful resort overlooking the panoramic and magnificent view of the Rocky Mountains in Colorado, I am reflecting on the corporate simulation exercise we have just finished. I marvel that even in the month of July the Rockies are snow topped and offering a great visual treat. It is a class size of 20 participants, of which the majority represent the crème de la crème—the top two or three percent of executives—from the US business and industry community, and the minority represent governmental and non-governmental organizations.

The dynamic corporate simulation exercise effectively replicates typical business challenges. It serves as a laboratory, a practice field for us to learn in a very safe environment about how one can improve strategic leadership through embedding a high-performance culture across the organization. To that end, an atmosphere of candor is created where participants can challenge group decisions and each other, and pose differing opinions and questions in a collaborative and constructive way. In our table group, we have identified key business issues and have discussed the implementation of certain strategies for achieving critical business goals. In the process, we get so deeply involved in the future business prospects of that simulated global company that, in fact, the simulation ceases to be an abstract game. It gets too real for comfort. The frank and candid discussions throw up many questions, such as:

- Would a joint venture with one of the major European companies serve as a long-term strategic direction?
- What products will add more customer value?
- Is the product quality world-class?
- Does the corporate mindset need to shift from an operational focus to customer focus?

And many others.

The corporate simulation mainly focuses on the operational and financial aspects of business restructuring through quantitative parameters. Therefore, it has well-defined competencies and performance metrics on financial/business strategy. But it has none of the qualitative parameters related to leadership issues—the competencies that would facilitate organizational restructuring and transformation. If people are any organization's most important asset, then how is it that people metrics or leadership strategy do not even find a place in the simulation? As we know, what is captured is measured, and what is measured is managed.

I share this observation in my table group during the discussion and the group wholeheartedly endorses it. It also acknowledges the common fact that most people often tend to only "think" about people issues. But when it comes to actually "acting" on or "influencing" precisely those issues, they do not *do* enough to create awareness in their respective organizations. So when my turn comes in the feedback session, I give a gist of the discussion in our table group and request the faculty to consider introducing specific qualitative parameters related to "leadership issues" in the forthcoming review of the simulation exercise. At the same time, although I recognize that mere introduction of qualitative parameters would not guarantee instant people orientation, at least it might succeed in making a beginning—in focusing a spotlight on the "invisible" issues.

As I am mulling over the group discussion, I hope that the future will witness an increasing shift from quantitative parameters with focus on mere financials to qualitative parameters with emphasis on people issues not only in the simulation at that institute—considered one of the very best for executive education—but also in the practice of management itself. That feedback seems to have struck a chord because a few participants as well as an adjunct faculty member come up to me during the coffee break and express agreement and resonance with the sentiments shared in the class.

Next morning, in the program evaluation session we discuss everyone's overall participation in the training program and provide constructive feedback to each other in small groups about how one can further enhance one's effectiveness. In the process, I am told that the group was a little surprised by my feedback about the simulation of the program. While the group members appreciated my engagement and commitment during the discussion on various issues, they were also surprised by my frankness, because they had not expected an Indian woman manager to be so articulate and forthright! One of my peers even wondered aloud if reticence, submissiveness, and passivity were the hallmarks of Indian women. Indian culture and tradition govern that women should be silent and submissive.

In short, I departed from the stereotype of the Indian woman. At the same time, they also cautioned me that in my enthusiasm for taking up issues and causes, I must not leave anyone behind and as a woman must make an extra effort to take everyone on board.

Later, I was also given to understand that though the faculty admired my courage of conviction in offering an honest feedback, I must also remember not to be so upfront and direct and must never forget the fact that I am a woman after all and that too an Indian!

When I heard that feedback, everything was a blur for a moment. Can this possibly happen in this day and age? Am I living in the 18th century? What does that feedback have to do with my being a woman or an Indian, I wondered. Again, expectations about my behavior were defined in a manner that was forcing me into a limited, stereotypical category.

I cannot quite figure out why and how this feedback can be influenced by the stereotype of how an Indian woman manager should behave or express herself. Frankly, it was one of the most unlikely places in the world to be confronted with such stereotypical thinking. Neither was I prepared for it nor expected it.

Stereotypes, as we know, are used as cognitive shortcuts to process information or to make initial assessments or to guide our judgments about people belonging to specific groups [1]. They include expectations about what members of a certain group are actually like (descriptive beliefs) and what they should be like (prescriptive beliefs). But they do not tell us how these specific people actually are or how they act.

For most of us, most of the time, stereotypes operate under the surface, hiding away from conscious awareness. As a result, we are unaware of their presence. So the prescriptive stereotype about how a woman manager should behave can be unconscious, invisible and can manifest itself in myriad ways. It can color the way we process information because we interpret new information in order to fit our stereotypes. Often, we are so accustomed to using these cognitive shortcuts that they can even become our second nature.

To be fair, perceiving people accurately is hard. No one is truly an "open book." I also recognize the fact that our words and behaviors are subject to interpretation. Although each one of us is uniquely different, stereotyping can prevent people from seeing the full picture. So the feedback was not meant to hurt me or to exclude me, nor did it harm me directly. But it was a subtle yet powerful bias that drew an invisible circle around me, suggesting limits based on cultural assumptions and patterns of interaction.

Then, I was hit by another contradiction. How is it that we preach candor in the class but do not like it when we see it in the real world? How can a simple observation about the simulation of the program be seen as challenging or even threatening, simply because it is coming from me—a woman?

What is the purpose of an evaluation session after all?

I have always believed that those of us who consider themselves to have benefited from any program have a responsibility, if not an obligation, to contribute to the design or content of the program at an appropriate time, should such an opportunity present itself. Am I wrong in holding this assumption?

At the same time, I do realize that by raising the issue of stereotypes I am not providing an easy excuse or defense to overlook the constructive criticism which is meant for my own development. I do recognize that perceptions of people and colleagues form a part of the reality at work, regardless of whether those perceptions are accurate. Just as I recognize the partial validity of this feedback, I also recognize that it's loaded with a certain bias. At that moment, it also struck me that although I acted out of my professional identity as a human resource professional during the course of the program, I was actually being predominantly perceived as an Indian woman. Would I have been better off by being silent and making myself invisible? For the first time I also became acutely aware that I was the only South Asian in that group (leave alone Indian) and one of the very few women participants.

Was that a celebration of difference or a condemnation of it?

Does that mean I had hit a "double glass ceiling" within the program—as a foreigner *and* a woman?

Does that mean this program, which at one level imparts training to analyze strategic issues, sharpen skill sets, and motivate the best and the brightest, also reflects societal patterns at another level, that acquiescent and subservient behavior is rewarded and associated with a certain gender, and therefore, outspokenness and assertiveness can result in sanctions?

With that complex feedback, I also realized that the transformation of culture depends on gradual shifts in perception and that cultural or corporate assumptions about people change only one person at a time. It was a reminder that cultures can only change when people do. In fact, often people's lives change more quickly than institutional practices or, for that matter, even individual mindsets. This in itself is not in the least surprising. What is surprising, and more than a bit depressing, is that in this day and age I have to be reminded of my gender and the expected norm of behavior associated with that gender from the faculty of an institution known for its feedback-rich programs.

When I was a young girl in the 1970s, I was brought up to believe that by saying what you know is true or right at an appropriate time and in the right way, you begin to slowly change your world, making it possible for others to change and evolve. One does not always have to join a cause or take on a giant, for that matter. You have to say what needs to be said, what is true for you, wherever you are. Sometimes, this is welcomed as a contribution, and sometimes, this is seen as challenging the old ways of doing things, as Gandhi did when he took on the government of South Africa on behalf of its Indian population. A "No" uttered with the deepest conviction is better than a "Yes" merely uttered to please or, worse, to avoid trouble. Small acts of courage on the part of ordinary people can be a source of inspiration to others. Depending on the circumstances, one has to be ready to accept any of these outcomes.

As a young girl, I was also mesmerized by the vision of the future—that distant time at the end of the century and beyond—where the purpose of our existence, as I thought then, would be to express our untapped potential for building a new and better world.

Forty years later, I am living in "that" future, which seemed so distant in the imagination of that young girl, making myself often wonder: have the times really changed at all for women, anywhere in the world? What have countries, companies, and women themselves done to improve their status? Is the future going to be a repeat of the past? If yes, why?

Memory of another time flashed by. In 1991, I attended a tripartite program on "Women's Issues at Workplaces," jointly organized by the US Department of Labor in Washington and the Clark Atlanta University. The program was attended by 26 delegates from 12 countries in Europe, Asia, Africa, Latin America, and the North

America comprising teams of representatives from the labor sector, employer's organizations/management, and the federal government of each country.

In that program, each country group narrated its stories about what was breaking down in its society, how advancement opportunities for women were limited, and how institutions were crumbling around them, and expressed a deepening sense of anxiety about the future. But I could not help notice that within those external differences, there were profound commonalties between countries, cultures, and companies.

What became clear through the discussions and presentations, though, was that in country after country, the proportion of women in leadership positions falls woefully short of men. In some countries, a small percentage of women are found in high positions, but in none have they approached a significant number. With continuing change, the obstacles that women face have become surmountable at least by some women some of the time. Women have also become more publicly visible than in the past, and, therefore, assumptions about equality between men and women probably reflect people's observations of women in many high-visibility leadership roles and lack of awareness and insight into the subtle and not-so-subtle processes that continue to produce discrimination. But the pattern prevails in the Oriental and Occidental cultures; in communist, capitalist, and socialist systems; and in both economically developed and developing countries.

If proven effectiveness is not the reason, what is? Why are there so few women executives in significant positions worldwide? Why has the progress been slow? If not because of the individual shortcomings of women then apparently because of other factors, such as dual responsibilities at home and at work, cultural norms, stereotypes associated with gender roles, entrenched practices, and a traditionally masculine work environment which tends to favor and attract men and discriminate against the participation of women. These are some of the questions now that, as Rilke said, "perhaps even without knowing it, you will along some distant day into your answers" [2].

It was amazing to find out that in some sense, no one played solitaire in their respective corner of the world. The concerns facing women at work in the 1990s and even now, several years later, are similar in nature the world over. They are only different in degree, impact, and the conditions in which women operate, with only the relative importance of each of these factors varying from society to society. Clearly, the differences between the sexes are undervalued or even devalued altogether everywhere, and this phenomenon knows no boundary of nationality, religion, or race. It is this story that has united all women as one. In that sense, it tied my story to the larger narrative of women.

This was a defining moment for me. I "stepped back" from whatever identity I was in and viewed myself and all women—as a collective identity—from a larger perspective. Disidentification enabled me to begin to see the universality of experience and to take my own "stuff" less personally.

## A Complex Scenario with Vast Contradictions

There has been some progress since world leaders agreed on the 30 percent target in 1995 at the landmark Fourth World Conference on Women in Beijing, where the Platform For Action blueprint was adopted. At that time, only 11 percent of the world's legislators were women. That figure had doubled to 22 percent in 2015, according to the report of the Inter-Parliamentary Union [3,4]. Gender-based quotas for political parties and national legislatures are credited with lifting women's representation. Yet in many countries, quotas have been ignored or unenforced. As a result, representation of women has begun to slow down, prompting the Inter-Parliamentary Union to wonder in a report released in 2015 whether the world has hit a glass ceiling when it came to women in parliament. This is not only with regard to the world parliaments; it is equally true for the corporate sector, the healthcare sector, the police force, and academia, as well as for enrollment in business schools [5,6,7,8]. It is the same story everywhere. Because there are so few women at the top, not only are they visible, they are also seen as representative of their whole gender. Progress, therefore, cannot be taken for granted. It requires constant effort, action, and political will.

Women's equality is a complex scenario defined by vast contradictions. The past few years have seen a surge in coverage and awareness of workplace discrimination and inequality as well as several paradoxical trends. The growing recognition of women's rights and gender equality is now juxtaposed against new and persisting forms of violence against women such as rape, trafficking, online abuse, etc. Availability of new work opportunities for women coexist with weak bargaining power in the labor market. An increasing number of educated career women enter workplaces, while large sections of women remain illiterate and engaged in the low-paid informal sector. Climate change can leave a significant impact on women, but women have not been invited to constructive debates about managing natural resources. Deep-rooted patriarchal mindsets continue to affect women, leaving them powerless and vulnerable.

At the same time, there has been slow but welcome change in the last two decades. A small number of women have become CEOs of large corporations, presidents of universities, members of parliaments, ministers, governors and heads of states. For example, women represented 3 percent of Standard & Poor's 500 companies CEOs and less than 15 percent of corporate executives worldwide in 2010, but in 2017, they represent 5.8 percent of S&P 500 companies CEOs and 25.1 percent of corporate executives in the US [9]. It is definitely encouraging. But the proportion of senior roles held by women varies enormously by industry. Women tend to be over-represented in service industries such as education, healthcare, hospitality, and banking, while the leadership teams of more traditional industries such as manufacturing, transport, construction, real estate, mining, and petroleum are overwhelmingly made up of men.

After all, women make up 40 percent of the global workforce. They are earning advanced professional degrees. Some companies are sensitive to this issue and have implemented programs to fix structural biases against women and support their full participation in the workforce. These statistics demonstrate considerable social change and show that women's careers have been far more successful than they were in the past. Many, therefore, believe that gender inequality is a thing of the past, and the fight for women's rights is over. What is the problem?

The problem is that despite a decade of aggressive efforts to create opportunities for women, inequity remains entrenched. For every woman achiever who makes headlines, there is a huge number of women languishing in the pipeline. The percentages quoted before are only the tip of the iceberg. It is a classic case of a glass half filled with water. How would you describe it? Half full or half empty? It depends on your perspective. Those who see the glass as half full say that so many women have gained access to leadership. Those who see it as half empty say women are held back because many inequities still remain. Therefore, we have to be thankful to have a glass in the first place.

But to see real progress we need business bosses to stop talking—even though they are saying the right things—and take action. Across all of these areas, there is a common truth: talking about the issue does not necessarily equate to doing something about it. We need to walk the talk.

Having a diversity program is fantastic, but it doesn't solve the problem. Such initiatives must be supported with top-down leadership and concrete change, on everything from pay transparency to flexible working hours, shared parental leave to real action on harassment. Part of the problem is that it tends to be mainly women who are involved in diversity projects and mentoring networks, while men at the top are busy making the decisions that have the greatest impact. All the brilliant women's networking in the world can't help female candidates if the opportunity to reach the executive board is decided by a group of men calling on those they already know and socialize with. This psychology is subtle. There may not be deliberate, conscious gender bias. Few people actually intend to discriminate. But the status quo does suggest an unconscious bias in recruitment, a lack of proactive consideration of women for major assignments, a lack of gender consideration in succession planning, and an unwillingness to mentor women at the leadership level. The subsequent lack of female role models at the senior level magnifies the perception among women that advancement opportunities are limited.

Many of the women leaders I have spoken with do not like to think about women's issues as women's issues. They think of themselves as professionals, not as *women* professionals. They want to be known not as female business leaders but simply as business leaders, successful in their own right, not because they happen to be women. In fact, they have worked hard to take gender out of the equation, to simply be recognized for their skills and talents. Therefore, they do not want concessions. They do not want reservations or quotas, and certainly not at the cost of competence. Everyone would agree that women should not be brought on as tokens simply because they are women. To serve organizations well, women need high-level corporate experience or the knowledge, skills, and abilities needed to contribute effectively. It is possible that these women have not experienced bias yet, so they cannot empathize with the issue. Strangely, many women are unaware of having personally been subject to gender discrimination and deny it when they see that women in general experience it. Even when situations contain unfairness, they prefer to see the world as just. They seem to have internalized the portrayal and representation of women by men. As a result, they can be perpetrators of bias without realizing it.

No wonder there are debates about whether discrimination still limits women's opportunities to lead. Opinions differ on whether women themselves opt out of employment because it conflicts with their family obligations. Apart from these work-life issues, questions are raised about whether organizations suffer from a lack of qualified women or that they embody masculine culture that hinders women from networking. In these settings, preferences of executives to work with people similar to themselves, along with beliefs that management positions require masculine qualities, compound women's difficulties in advancing. So as you can see, for the majority of women all the questions are not answered yet. The debates, therefore, are likely to continue ad nauseam, stands are likely to be taken only to be changed later, and a complete consensus over an important, complex, and multifaceted issue such as this would always be elusive. However, as the saying goes, half a loaf of bread is better than no bread.

It needs to be recognized that diversity is not only about differences but simultaneously about differences and similarities. We are so accustomed to thinking of diversity in terms of workplace demographics and equating it with minority groups in a particular organization, we tend to assume diversity means qualities that are different. The definition here actually includes not only differences but also similarities.

This is a critical distinction, because management is not about making assumptions. It is all about taking critical and inclusive decisions to meet certain objectives. It means that when making managerial decisions, you no longer have the option of dealing only with the differences or similarities present in the situation. Instead, you must deal with *both* simultaneously. Diversity is also to be understood as the variety of approaches and perspectives that members of different identity groups bring to work. When allowed, they bring relevant knowledge and perspectives about how to actually do work: how to design processes, reach goals, frame tasks, create effective teams, communicate ideas, and lead. They can help companies grow and improve by challenging basic assumptions about an organization's functions, strategies, operations, practices, and procedures. In doing so, they are able to bring more of their whole selves to the workplace and identify more fully with the work they do, setting a virtuous cycle in motion. Unfortunately, this is far removed from reality.

## Two Models Based on Two Assumptions

When one reviews the status of women in management in different countries, fundamentally different assumptions are made that shape up different models and create and feed different organizational cultures and systems. Each assumption has its constituency and its defenders.

The first is the *equality* model, based on the assumptions that men and women are equal as professionals and therefore need to be treated in the same way, and that gender does not matter, differences do not exist, and if they do, they are of no consequence. It is also expected, therefore, that men and women are capable of contributing and competing in the same measure.

A woman is equal to man all right, but she is definitely not the same as man. Also, if two things are same, or similar, they are identical, not "equal." Right? In mathematics, the "equals" sign is used to indicate that two expressions are equivalent in value, not that they are the same. Champions of this model have the unreasonable expectation that men and women should think and act in the same way, engage the world of work and relationships in the same way, and approach their careers in the same way and for the same reasons. Effectiveness, then, is understandably measured against male norms. The burden of adjustment, of fitting into the corporate culture, lies squarely on the shoulders of women. Moreover, by placing the onus on the individual alone, the company is lulled into a false comfort, perhaps believing that everything is fine and it does not have to change what may be termed exclusive practices. However, an organization can never obtain the best efforts from employees who do not feel valued and respected.

I have come across successful businesspersons and educators who, out of fear of stereotyping, purposefully ignore or discount any gender differences and even ridicule anyone who suggest otherwise. More than any other blind spot, this is the one that contributes most to making uneducated assumptions about the motivations behind the behavior of others. Some organizations also adopt a casual or careless attitude towards the fact that men and women actually have different work experiences in the same workplace. They put forth policies and programs of equality and are reluctant to examine behaviors and systems that are not in sync with the long held assumption of equality. As a result, they actually fail to explore and take advantage of gender differences. The potential of women to make a unique contribution remains outside the realm of the equality model and therefore invisible. However, this position of "gender neutrality" can be more accurately termed as "gender blindness." It is like turning a blind eye to the reality and to relieve oneself of the responsibility to make a difference or to make things right.

This monocultural paradigm was most prevalent in the previous decades when most members of the workforce were men—more similar than different. Those similarities enabled corporations to design and implement policies, procedures, and benefit packages that met the needs of the majority of the workforce while still meeting corporate objectives.

Moreover, in recent years, there has been a push to eradicate bias and discrimination against women by adopting a competency-based approach which actually hides the gender-blind mindset. Believing in everyone's capacity and right for equal opportunity, everyone is treated the same. While in some respect this has helped, there has been an unintended negative consequence. Real differences are rarely acknowledged, leave alone addressed out of fear of stereotyping or engaging in discrimination. In such a culture, there is no tolerance for debate and members do not feel comfortable in taking the initiative to apply their skills and experiences in new ways to enhance their job performance.

There are also big gaps between what woman can deliver and what they are actually paid. Even when women do the same or, in most cases, much more work, they typically receive 30–40 percent less on average than men worldwide. Worse still, much of women's work is not paid for, as it is not recorded or recognized as economically productive. These are some of the deep-rooted prejudices that block their advancement.

The gender pay gap reflects this reality as there is a gap between beliefs and actual practice. The assumption of equality actually hides the reality of inequality. Women and men have always participated in the workforce in different ways—and have been treated differently by employers—and, though those differences have shrunk over time, they still contribute to women being paid less than men. For instance, the persistent wage gap between men and women is mainly due to the consequences women suffer when they decide to have children mid-career. Such income losses persist and get carried over time. Women who take significant breaks from employment never catch up to those who do not take breaks [10,11]. Even with the same level of education and in the same occupation, women earn just three-quarters of what men earn.

In one early study, economists Susan Harkness and Jane Waldfogel [12] compared the wage gap across seven industrialized countries and found that it was particularly wide in the US. To illustrate, in France, women earn 81 percent of the male wages; in Sweden, 84 percent; and in Australia, 88 percent, while in the US, women continue to earn a mere 78 percent of the male wages. If you compare that with the recent OECD data on gender wage gap of 2015 [13], it merely shows a variation of 1–5 percentage points in so many years. In fact, since the establishment of Equal Pay Act in the US in 1963, the gap has barely budged, with women making 77–79 percent of what the men make. This clearly suggests that unless the passage of such legislation changes attitudes and social mores, the gender wage gap is likely to persist.

Direct discrimination may explain only a small part of gender wage differences. The wage gap is due to a variety of reasons, such as differences in education choices, differences in preferred jobs and industry, differences in types of jobs and positions held by men and women (for instance, men's preference for highly paid high-risk jobs), breaks in employment, and women's lack of willingness and ability to negotiate salaries. But closing the wage gap would certainly create economic equality. Yet according to recent studies, an increasingly large part of the wage gap can only be attributed to childbearing and child-rearing, which impact women's—but not men's—careers, permanently restricting their earning power. Research reveals that mothers receive a 4 percent wage penalty for the first child and a 12 percent penalty for each additional child [14].

If the gap between what men and women earn in the US is wider than elsewhere, then it could be because, despite the best of intentions, it has failed to develop policies in the workplace and support systems in society as a whole that would facilitate working mothers.

The National Organization for Women (NOW) has spent 50 years fighting for a wide array of equal rights, ranging from educational and job opportunities to equal pay and access to credit. It was believed that once all discrimination against women is dismantled, the playing field becomes level and women can assume a free and equal place in society by simply learning the masculine model. But consider the high cost women have to pay to practice this model. It simply means for many women working is like encountering a series of hurdles and tests and a burning need to continuously prove oneself.

In Europe, as the study indicates, various groups of social feminists have viewed the problem for women quite differently. For them, it is not a woman's lack of legal rights that constitutes her main handicap, or even her lack of reproductive freedom. Rather, it is her dual burden—taking care of a home and family as well as holding down a job—that leads to her second-class status. The gender pay gap between men and women is the worst in Europe, with female workers earning on average 17–18 percent less than their male counterparts even after equal pay legislation was introduced in 1970. It is a long enough period to do better. In fact, it is too long. So much for the assumption of equality!

Women in India earn about 72 percent of men's annual pay [15]. However, this picture is changing. A recent study found that talented women are ahead of the curve. For instance, 42 percent of highly educated Indian women earn as much as or more than their spouses [16]. Even in the US, it has become far more common than before for wives to have higher income than husbands. In about 29 percent of families in which both spouses are employed, the wife now earns more. This situation changes the debate from career versus family to more equal contribution by mothers and fathers in both domains [17]. Leaving aside these recent, exceptional trends in the US and India, even highly industrialized societies are far from reaching the goal of equality. It is, therefore, crucial that people understand why equality has not been reached despite substantial improvement in the status of women.

The second model is visible throughout Asian countries. It is based on the assumption of *difference*—different not in the positive sense but with a question mark on the right kind of attitude or competence. Proclaiming the difference between the personalities of men and women has been used as a traditional excuse or argument to deny leadership opportunities to women for long. This assumption of difference has given birth to a constellation of traits or characteristics that uniquely describe women and limit their advancement in organizations. Such an assumption creates an organizational culture where women will be expected to underperform—a negative assumption that too often becomes a self-fulfilling prophecy.

It is sometimes said that as women and men can never be "the same," it goes against common sense to require employers to treat them "equally." This is a misunderstanding. Just as there is evidence that women managers are different, psychologically and socially, from men, there is enough evidence about similarities in the personality traits of men and women. If women are different in ways that account for variances in managerial performance, special considerations are probably warranted. If, on the other hand, they are not different in these ways, then they need to be effectively utilized as valuable human resources. The whole idea of equality assumes that the two people or two things being compared are clearly different. If they were the same, there would be no point in comparing them. They would be automatically treated the same. Study after study reveals that women are considered different not in the positive sense; they are considered to be intellectually inferior, less assertive, authoritative, or even emotionally unstable and therefore unsuitable for management positions. The traits that are considered desirable to succeed in management (aggressive, tough, analytical, risk-taking, independent, competitive, decisive) are generally associated with men in large, traditional, control-and-command type organizations. Women who joined the management ranks in initial years learnt to develop these characteristics or code of conduct that spelled success for men. Failing which, despite all things being equal, they would be deprived of important, impact-making assignments, challenging postings, and overseas or cross-cultural training opportunities, which are necessary for advancement. This is downright unfair because an important objective of any organization is to ensure that each job in the company is being done by the best available person to do the job. The objective is not that the *unsuitable* candidates should have a right to jobs which they are *unable* to do but that the *suitable* candidates should have a right to be considered for jobs which they *can* do. This comes from the recognition of the fact that effective leadership does not come from a set mold. It depends on the organizational context.

Psychological research has illuminated sex differences as well as similarities in personality traits and the relevance of these traits to effective leadership. These findings suggest female advantage as often as male advantage. The new generation of women, therefore, given the opportunity to work for fast-changing organizations would demonstrate that they can achieve results in different ways: by finding new solutions, new systems, and new ways of leading. As Christine Lagarde reminds us, women then need to "dare the difference." To "dare" means to take risks, to step out of cozy, comfort zones, to let hope extinguish fear and courage conquer timidity. Ultimately, daring the difference means wedging open the door to the contribution of women and their *leadership* [18]. For that to happen, women have to walk the talk too.

However, in the final analysis, both these models are unipolar or one-dimensional. Reality demands a bit of both. The realities of the workforce today are as multicultural as the realities of yesterday were monocultural. Corporations that fail to build a workplace that is attractive to the talented segment of the emerging, diverse workforce (including men) will lose in creativity, productivity, quality, and customer satisfaction. Business is what makes economies run and flourish, but talent is what runs business. And talent comes in both genders.

In fact, leadership roles are in flux because of broader changes in the economy and society. The drivers that are accelerating these changes are workforce diversity, intense competitive pressures, and breaking of geopolitical boundaries. In fact, the CEO role of today is vastly different from the CEO role of yesterday and is still going through transition. The role needs to be humanized if the CEO wants to connect with the millennials. As a result, company boards are increasingly looking for CEOs who must deal with multiple stakeholders and exhibit superb people skills externally and resemble a good coach internally. In such environments, the control and command style of management would be dysfunctional in negotiating the complex stakeholder relationships. It is for this reason that there would be greater emphasis on developing democratic relationships, participatory decision-making, delegation, and team-based leadership—qualities that are more associated with women than men. In many organizations, effective leaders manifest both traditionally masculine and traditionally feminine qualities. It is, therefore, recommended that men and women take on the qualities of the other gender. Women not only need to become more like men, but men also need to become more like women. In fact, leaders who have an extremely masculine or extremely feminine style of leadership are likely to be at a disadvantage in most contemporary organizations.

It may, therefore, be appropriate to view women as *equal but different*. Equal in value, not that they are the same. It is also because they bring a different set of qualifications, experience, competence, perspective, and skills to the workplace. They contribute just as much as men to the complex world of business. They need the same kind of opportunities as men for career progression and to give their best to the job.

At the same time, they are different. This comes from understanding the natural differences between men and women that go beyond the biological and cultural to include physiological differences in the male and female brain structure, chemistry, and functions that influence memory, emotion, hearing, and spatial orientation [19,20].

Advances in neuroscience have convincingly shown that the variations that occur throughout the brain influence in different ways how men and women communicate, listen, solve problems, make decisions, handle emotions, deal with conflict, and manage stress. These differences are first shaped by nature and then nurture (family, education, culture, and environment). These differences add variety and beauty to transactions and imply the unique advantage of both genders.

Women are also different as they have different needs in different stages of their lives. This is primarily due to the nurturing roles they are entrusted with. Their styles of functioning and patterns of working are distinctly different from men. They also approach the corporate world from uniquely different perspectives and social positions. In fact, they are succeeding because of, not in spite of, certain characteristics generally considered to be "feminine"—understanding, accommodating, nurturing, sharing information, encouraging interaction and participation, collaborating, and empowering. In fact, women will be inspired to make specific contributions if they have backgrounds, personalities, and behaviors that are different from men, and if they are perceived and treated as different from men.

Men and women have unique talents and skills that can complement each other and improve the productivity and innovativeness of an organization. To that end, men and women play uniquely important roles as "agents of change," both as contributors to economic growth and recipients of benefits from public expenditure. We have to deal with this paradoxical model-keeping in view of both these dimensions. It is interesting that differences have to be acknowledged in order to reach the goal of equality. From this perspective, the strategies of change in enlightened/multicultural organizations would revolve around:

- Identifying unique contributions of both men and women
- Creating the right environment for both types of contributions to be made, facilitated, and rewarded within organizations
- Promoting work–life balance and integration for both men and women

The challenge then is to achieve and maintain balance with both these models, without abandoning one for the other. At a deeper level, this paradigm is a reflection of life itself. We have to recognize that the differences between men and women are naturally designed to complement and not compete with the opposite gender. The differences add purpose, meaning, and value to life. Everywhere, life displays itself as a complex, tangled web of relationships. From these relationships, life creates systems that are interdependent and offer greater stability and support than life lived alone. If you look at life as integration, inclusion, and collaboration, then without these two dimensions, there is no existence. The blending and integration of masculine and feminine energies are the basis of our entire existence. The similarities shared by men and women are more universal and fundamental than the differences that separate them. Those differences shaped up by culture, learning, and education play out in communication, problem-solving, and decision-making processes so diversely that intelligent and sensitive companies can benefit from both styles and leverage them to their advantage. Every organization reflects this naturally occurring phenomenon arising from the interactions and needs of individuals who have decided to come together for uncharted levels of contributions and innovation. From this perspective, adapting to any one model would be counterproductive.

I, therefore, have a hope and a dream that the future years would be able to transcend the boundaries that hold women back with only one assumption—either they are "equal" or they are "different"—and that we will move from a unidimensional, hierarchical paradigm to one governed by a multidimensional, circular, interdependent paradigm with an all-inclusive assumption that women are equal but different. Earlier, it was believed that equality means treating everyone the same, but it is now recognized that it actually requires treating genders differently. We cannot equate men and women but we can certainly create equal opportunities. This is the only way to simultaneously achieve equity with effectiveness and to go beyond boundaries.

But how can that happen? Most importantly, when will that happen?

Obviously, there is no single or simple solution. It requires a concerted effort on the part of all the stakeholders—women professionals, corporate managements, governments, non-governmental organizations, and civil society—to address these complex issues at the workplace. We all have to walk the talk—practice what we preach or only preach what we practice.

That is precisely the theme of this book. This book grows directly out of the personal challenges I have grappled with over the years, conversations with women in a variety of settings, and constructive debates with corporate representatives and policy planners on how we might begin the process of change. Change is the only constant. No matter what has been achieved earlier, we need to do more.

I have also referred to a broad range of other sources—research from management science, psychology, sociology, economics, as well as journalist's reports, biographies, and individual anecdotes and recollections. In the process, I have benefited from the insights that have emerged across the social sciences. Quantitative data was gathered through surveys of organizations known to be standout employers, with an enduring reputation to attract and retain the brightest and best right from the entry level to top leadership positions. A substantial amount of qualitative material was collected through in-depth one-on-one interviews, much of it consisting of statements by women leaders. In some cases, names and affiliations have been protected on request. (When only first names are used, they are pseudonyms). These illustrations substantiate the principles presented. This is not to say that I know exactly how to do it, although I do discuss the various dimensions in each chapter and suggest, in broad strokes, the path I believe we could take for a more inclusive workplace. These are based on personal reflections as well as assessment based on my experience as a practicing woman manager, trainer, facilitator, executive coach, and a change agent at work, and as a daughter, wife, and mother at home.

Let me be more specific about how the book is organized. Looking at all the progress we have made, many would like to claim it as a "gender-blind" society and that the fight for equality has been won, or the problems related to gender today are largely imaginary or self-inflicted. But we know the statistics. On almost every single socioeconomic indicator from infant mortality to life expectancy to enrollment in educational institutions to employment, women continue to lag behind their male counterparts in general and at every career stage in particular.

In corporate boardrooms or in leadership positions, women are grossly underrepresented. To suggest that our attitudes play no role in these inequities or to say that prejudice does not exist is to turn a blind eye to both history and present reality and to relieve ourselves of the responsibility to make things right. None of us—men or women—is immune to the stereotypes that our culture continues to feed us, whether it be about women's intelligence, women's emotionality, or women's competence. It is, therefore, unrealistic to believe that these stereotypes don't have some unconscious and cumulative impact on the often snap decisions of who is recruited and who is promoted or who is retained or who is groomed for a leadership position. After all, organizations mirror the prevalent societal patterns and, therefore, unexamined attitudes and stereotypes can leave a lasting impact. In fact, there is a tendency to oversimplify things or to dismiss a single experience by calling it just that: a single experience. But a single experience can serve as a telling commentary on deeply entrenched myths. The huge challenge is to topple invisible barriers—mindsets widely held by managers or leaders, men and women alike, that are rarely acknowledged but are potent forces that block the way. Chapter 2, therefore, explores the power of these subtle stereotypes that doubt women's abilities—suggesting women are not equal—and their devastating implications for corporate performance, from recruitment to placement and from promotions to succession.

At the same time, it is not enough for women to merely rail against the corporate world. Some of the onus must fall on women themselves. Chapter 3 invites women to take an honest look at themselves, at the stereotypical behavior even they subject themselves to in order to get approval and to get along, and at the boundaries women unconsciously draw around themselves to feel safe and secure. Chapter 4 is about what women can learn and do through a networking platform to collectively sensitize corporate managements and contribute towards their own growth and development. Networks—whether at the corporate, industry, or national level—such as the ones I discuss in this chapter, provide a great learning opportunity. Just as joining and participating in networks create social capital, developing skills creates intellectual capital. Chapter 5 is about the need to develop skills and the ability to set priorities in order to enhance a sense of individual well-being and organizational productivity, and explore the choices and trade-offs women face while juggling personal and professional lives, and the sacrifices they are called upon to make at the altar of equality. One needs continuous learning and development and an enhanced ability to recognize the challenges that lie ahead in every phase of development. In response to the challenges, successful women leaders often cultivate a skill set that overcomes the hazards they encounter in the workplace. Complimentary to this theme of development is executive coaching as a technique to provoke greater performance and unlock deeper potential in business leaders. In Chapter 6, therefore, I deal with certain themes that I repeatedly see in coaching women leaders that can be effectively addressed for further advancement. Chapter 7 describes how women in most leadership roles face complexities not encountered by men because of continuing uncertainties about their ability to lead and use power and influence in the organizational context.

There is more turnover of women throughout the ranks of the industry the world over. The primary reason for leaving is for not being valued or in having difficulty in balancing career and family due to the organizational cultures that are designed by men for men. Chapter 8 looks at what four best-in-the-class organizations—ICICI, WIPRO, TCS, and NSE—have done to tackle the issues of attrition and how they can serve as models to others.

Chapter 9 suggests a partnership model between all the stakeholders to implement sustainable change towards achieving equity with efficiency and effectiveness. It recommends a way forward by creating, nurturing and enriching an ecosystem that can enhance collaboration among institutions, such as governments, the corporate sector, NGOs, men and women employees, and civil society. This is because, when the stakeholders of any system operate in isolation, they are less effective. They add greater value when effectively networked. Initiatives, therefore, need to be taken in each part of the ecosystem. The ecosystem builds an advantage where the power of partners is successfully harnessed by simultaneously creating and capturing value.

## Why differences will make a difference?

This then is a slow march towards reaching the milestone of equality while celebrating difference all the way.

We have come a long way since the time when men saw women as lacking the kind of intelligence that would allow them to contribute to business. What was even worse, women carried this unspoken burden that they could not make it because they could not be like men and nothing else mattered. But now that women have shown themselves the equals of men in all walks of life, we can all venture to examine the fact that men and women are different.

While doing so, there may be a temptation to take the beaten path, when you see that the world is treating you differently in a negative sense. At a minimum, it can grant you social sanction and approval and the security of staying in a comfort zone. But what if you would like to exercise your right to ask questions, to challenge the status quo, to demand your entitlements and privileges, to expect to be validated as individuals and, most importantly, to realize your fullest potential?

It requires hard work with systems and organizations, individually as well as collectively. It is also hard work with oneself to continuously examine where one unconsciously colludes with the stereotypes and, therefore, perpetuates them, or the boundaries one inadvertently draws around oneself in order to feel safe or when one needs to take a stand to be treated differently in a positive sense. It is all about feeling good about ourselves, feeling equal to men in organizations, not sacrificing feminine behavior, and balancing the mindset of equality with the enjoyment of difference. This is how we can make the field different for those who come after us.

## Redefining Leadership

In ancient Indian texts, there is an interesting concept of *ardhanarisvara*, a composite form of Lord Shiva presented as half-male and half-female—Shiva and Shakti [21]. In fact, the term *ardhanarisvara* translates as the "lord who is half woman." The apparent paradox that exists within the form of *ardhanarisvara* represents the wholeness and completeness of human existence. The principles of masculinity or femininity are not mutually exclusive. They act as interchangeable identities, distinct and in unison. Excessive and obsessive identification with any one is the root of all problems. By their opposite yet complimentary attributes, they act in symmetry and harmony and provide synergies. They represent the profound dualism present in nature: day and night, summer and winter, heat and cold. The masculine and feminine principles exist in each one of us. One cannot exist without the other. Only when they are nurtured in balanced proportion that a complete human being is born again. The understanding of *ardhanarisvara*—the human potential that is within each one of us—paves a way for going beyond the limitations of gender or even the transcendence of gender itself.

In the future, as the socialization of boys and girls and the experiences and expectations of young men and women steadily grow more androgynous, the differences in workplace behavior will begin to fade.

All over the world, good leadership is in short supply. No industry, no organization, no nation can afford to ignore the losses that follow from underutilization of the human capital that includes women, or unfairly blocking their access to leadership roles. New models of leadership are, therefore, required in the current business environment, where men and women are expected to complement, and not compete with, each other.

An effective leader is someone who can bring out the best in people. The best includes both masculine as well as feminine skills—an integrated set of skills that are more androgynous than either masculine or feminine. Men and women need to take on the qualities of the other sex. Opposite qualities need to be blended. Take, for instance, an ability to improve operational excellence while transforming culture. That would require blending competence with compassion, agency with reflection, adventure and risk-taking with adaptability, collaboration with task orientation, execution with empowerment, communication with authenticity, and creativity with complementarity. In short, being both mindful of tradition and effective in leading innovation. Excellence emerges from leaders who transcend the limits imposed by masculine or feminine stereotypes. To that end, men need to access, connect, and harness the "inner woman," just as women need to access, connect, and harness the "inner man." In fact, men and women need to be released from the old polarities of gender that force them into limiting roles. Finally, while accepting and committing to develop the physical/mental attributes of gender to one's fullest potential, it is important to go beyond, to transcend gender itself, and to embrace limitless possibilities.

In one sense, therefore, it is beyond doubt that we have come a long way. However, it is equally true that we have a long way to go.

## References

1. Northhouse, P. G., *Leadership Theory and Practise,* Thousand Oaks, CA: SAGE Publications, 2007.
2. Rilke, Rainer Maria, *Letters to a Young Poet,* New York: Dover Publications, 2002.
3. IPU, *Women in Parliament: 20 Years in Review* (Report), Geneva: Inter-parliamentary Union (IPU), 2015.
4. Sengupta, Somini, 'Most Nations Miss a Goal for Women in Leadership', *New York Times,* September 1, 2015, https://www.nytimes.com/2015/.../most-nations-miss-a-goal-for-women-in-leadership.ht (accessed on May 9, 2016).
5. Bhattacharya, Soumya and Devina Sengupta, 'Top B-schools, IITs Fail to Impress Corporate India on Gender Diversity', *Economic Times,* March 6, 2012, www.im4change.org/.../iims-iits-fail-to-impress-india-inc-on-gender-diversity-recruiters (accessed on August 12, 2014).
6. Eiser, B. J. and P. Morahan, 'Fixing the System: Breaking the Glass Ceiling in Health Care', *Leadership in Action* September–October 2006; 26, no. 4: 8–13.

7. Mukherji, Anahita, 'Dire Lack of Women in Police—National Average a Mere 6%', *Times of India*, August 30, 2015, www.epaperbeta.timesofindia.com/Article.aspx?...Dire-lack-of-women-in-police-national-aver (accessed in June 2017).
8. Basu, Sreeradha, 'Glass Ceiling Intact for Women in Academia', *Economic Times*, December 1, 2015, www.itbhuglobal.org/chronicle/archives/2015/11/index-news.php (accessed on June 12, 2016).
9. Catalyst Pyramid, 'Women in S and P-500 Companies', *N. Y. Catalyst*, July 1, 2016, www.itbhuglobal.org/chronicle/archives/2015/11/index-news.php (accessed in December 2016).
10. Waldfogel, J., 'The Family Gap for Young Women in the United States and Britain: Can Maternity Leave Make a Difference?' *Journal of Labour Economics*, no. 16 (1998): 505–45.
11. Arun S. V., T. G. Arun and V. K. Barooah, 'The Effect of Career Breaks on the Working Lives of Women', *Feminist Economics*, 10, no. 1 (2004): 65–84.
12. Harkness, Susan and Jane Waldfogel, *The Family Gap in Pay: Evidence from Seven Industrialised Countries* (CASE Paper No. 29), London: Centre for Analysis of Social Exclusion, London School of Economics, November 1999).
13. OECD, 'Data: Gender Wage Gap 2015', https://data.oecd.org/earnwage/gender-wage-gap.htm
14. Chang, Mariko Lin, *Short Changed: Why Women Have Less Wealth and What Can Be Done About It*, New York: Oxford University Press, September 2010.
15. Biju, Varkkey, Rupa Korede and Leeja Anand, 'Gender Pay Gap in the Formal Sector: Preliminary Evidence from Paycheck India Data', *Wage Indicator Report*, Wage Indicator Foundation, Amsterdam, Netherlands, series 2 (2012).
16. Hewlett, S. A. and R. Rashid, 'The Battle for Female Talent in Emerging Markets', *Harvard Business Review*, May (2010).
17. US Bureau of Labor Statistics, 'Employment Characteristics of Families, 2006C', *press release*, 2006, http://www.bls.gov/news.release/pdf/famec.pdf
18. Christine Lagarde, 'Daring the Difference: The 3 Ls of Women's Empowerment', address at the National Democratic Institute, Washington, DC, May 19, 2014.
19. Gurian, Michael and Barbara Annis, '*Leadership and the Sexes: Using Gender Science to Create Success in Business*', San Francisco, CA: Jossey–Bass, 2008.
20. Gurian, Michael and Annis Barbara, *Gender Intelligence: Breakthrough Strategies for Increasing Diversity and Improving your Bottom Line*, New York: HarperCollins, 2014.
21. Doniger O' Flaherty, Wendy, 'Ascetism and Sexuality in the Mythology of Siva–Part 1', in *History of Religions*, University of Chicago Press, Chicago, series 8, no. 4 (1969): 300–01.

# 2
# In the Shackles of Stereotypes … Even Today

A few years ago, as we came out of a meeting called to discuss the proposed reorganization of some departments at the corporate headquarters of Oil India Limited, two of my colleagues from other functions and myself, all women, lingered near the elevator discussing the ramifications of the action plan proposed in the meeting before heading out to our respective offices. Just then the elevator stopped and our Chairman stepped out, looked at the three of us and smilingly said, "I can see that a great shopping expedition is getting planned." He laughed and walked off. We all joined him in laughter as his comment was meant to be light hearted. However, after the laughter died down, we all had a similar reaction. We looked at each other, and we were thinking the same thing. We felt crushed, wondering if that's all a group of women is supposed to be talking about. Does our bandwidth begin and end with shopping, babies, and domestic issues?

At the end of the day, it did not matter what we were actually talking about. What mattered was our Chairman's assumption: the casual assumption which was not acknowledged or even examined. In all fairness, he is not the only one. We do it all the time, because we are not even conscious of how we evaluate and judge others or what assumptions we hold about them. It can, therefore, be manifested in a variety of ways, sometimes functional and sometimes dysfunctional.

Admittedly, this kind of stereotypical thinking is not limited to gender, but extends to age, community, disciplines, etc.

Such thinking is based on certain assumptions. Assumptions, in turn, are based on certain ideas or biases that we hold about others who are different from us and which affect our behavior towards them. It is often easier to see this bias in others than being conscious of the bias we ourselves hold. Often, being different from the majority group automatically implies an inability to perform; a difference not in the positive sense, but as a question mark on one's attitude, competence, exposure, etc.

Interestingly, however, we think of them as facts, not assumptions or stereotypes. They can simply be subconscious and subtle prejudices deeply ingrained in our psyche about how certain groups of people act or think, without the necessary validation of how they actually act or think! These prejudices are sometimes so subtle that their impact on our behavior is not recognized by us. Impulses that trigger reaction or overreaction are the offshoots of our prejudices. It is not as much the provocation from the other side, but the reactions we have due to our own prejudices.

Although it is true that such prejudices are far more loosely held than they once were, they have certainly not vanished. If anything, they have become less visible. They cause old, traditional forms of behavior to surface time and again. Understanding and recognizing one's very beliefs and how they affect one's behavior and decisions, is a transformational process that cannot help but positively affect how one works through other issues of diversity.

## Gender Stereotyping and Its Impact on Women's Careers

In the last two decades, women's improved education and increasingly delayed marriage and childbearing have created a pool of qualified women available for professional and managerial jobs worldwide. At the same time, the growth of the public sector and services and the introduction of equality laws and policies in many countries have provided opportunities for qualified women to occupy lower- and middle-level management posts. These changes have paved the way for their taking up and aspiring for more management positions. However, women's professional training and the predicted shortages of highly qualified managers have not resulted in women obtaining top executive positions in significant numbers.

## Encountering Glass Ceilings and Walls

Large companies and organizations mirror societal patterns. It is a common observation that where women have managed to reach high-level managerial positions, these are often restricted to those in areas less central or strategic to the organization such as human resources, administration, public relations, or corporate social responsibility.

"Glass ceiling" is a term coined by the *Wall Street Journal* in the 1970s in the United States to describe the invisible artificial barriers created by attitudinal and organizational prejudices which bar women from top executive jobs or other leadership positions [1]. Governments, enterprises, labor and women's organizations have provided much impetus, analysis and plans of implementation for overcoming attitudinal and institutional discrimination that hinder women's career development. Yet for many the results fall far short of expectations. The glass ceiling is still encountered depending on the extent to which women's entry into organizations is permitted: it may be higher or lower, closer to the corporate head, or at the middle management level, or even below them. If the term "glass ceiling" well illustrates the point that there is no objective reason preventing women from rising to the very top like men, other than the inherent discrimination in organizational structures and processes, it is also equally difficult for women to move laterally into strategic areas such as product development, marketing, corporate finance, and then upwards through the central pathways to key executive positions in the pyramidal structure characteristic of large corporations. These

## The Glass Ceiling and the Glass Wall in the Organizational Pyramid

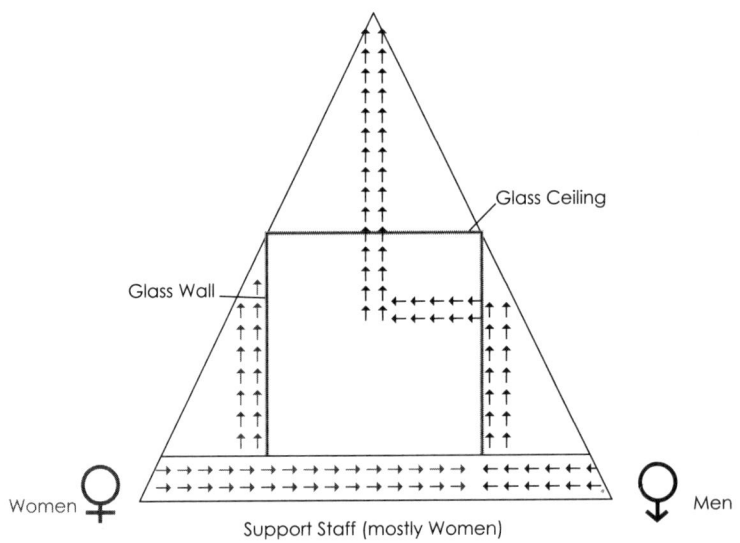

*Source:* Adapted from Wirth, Linda, *Breaking Through the Glass Ceiling: Women in Management*, Geneva: ILO, 2001.

barriers can be called "glass walls," through which you can see but cannot enter without creating a great deal of noise and a good deal of mess.

The glass wall can be encountered anytime, anywhere, and in any profession. It could be encountered at the entry point, even when women graduates possess the necessary qualifications as advertised and required by the job, but are not taken due to unspoken assumptions about lack of mobility, the prospect of marriage, etc. After selection and completion of probation, they can be encountered once again when assignments or placements are given (She is good but will company clients accept a woman engineer?) Having managed to go through these walls, women encounter another wall when it comes to promotions. In dual-career families, often women have to decide to stay put in the same place of posting for one or two years due to family responsibilities such as children undertaking critical examinations, etc. Then, the question arises: "How can I promote her if she cannot move to another city?" In fact, occasionally a senior manager may learn his first lesson about equality or lack of it when his daughter does not get a promotion despite good performance, or when he does not want her to work for a company that has lower expectations for women.

These walls that eventually become the glass ceiling, whether in the workplace or in politics, are essentially a reflection of social and economic gender inequality. With the achievement of educational parity along with changing social attitudes, it was somehow assumed that women would quickly move up the career ladder. This is proving hard to achieve, especially close to the top where the sheer prevalence of male executives tends to perpetuate the glass ceiling. Women, at times, also find themselves without the right mix of corporate experience required for top executive positions.

Breaking through the glass ceiling is not an event at a fixed point in time or a designated level in career, beyond which progress is impossible. In fact, it is a series of events in the careers of women professionals, from recruitment to placements to promotion to development. It is, in fact, a cumulative outcome of attitudinal, cultural, and organizational biases at work. Women and organizations, on occasion, may take a long time to understand this. Once understood, a systematic enterprise-level approach addressing all existing barriers is necessary for women to break through them. As examples show, some women have broken the glass ceiling at least some of the time. A small number of women have become CEOs of large corporations, presidents or deans of universities, ministers in cabinets, and governors or secretaries of states. However, women in powerful positions are still rare. The glass ceiling seems to exist even today, because our cultural norms concerning the proper role of women in society have colored the organizational norms. The traditional roles associated with men and women have walked into corporate life.

## Myths About Women Executives

By and large, management is widely perceived as a male occupation, requiring male traits. This perception poses a major barrier to women who otherwise qualify and excel in positions of leadership. This perception is based on long-held myths. There are several myths, which, over time, have evolved as stereotypes that act in distorting perceptions of male and female performance and potential.

Let's examine five such myths in the section below:

## Myth 1: A "woman" is not right for that role

Here, the emphasis is not on the 'role' but on the woman. Let it be any role, from entry-level as a management trainee, to middle-level role as a manager, to one of heading a function. The first question asked is, "Is a woman right for that role?" "Does she have the 'take–charge' quality associated with men?" The assumption is that she is not right for the role, because she lacks the necessary skills.

Organizations consider candidates for a role on the basis of a candidate's personal qualifications and experience, not on the basis of gender. Any decision made about women, without considering individual factors such as background, education, experience, personality, and potential, are likely to be unfair. Considering that many educated women have already entered non-traditional functions from sales to technology, and banking to aviation, and even defense, such mindsets set women up for failure. Attending a technical institution or a business school is a reasonable indication of intelligence, talent, ambition, and promise.

In many countries, there are now more women graduates than men, however, despite their educational achievement, women face multiple barriers to equal access, participation, and progress in the labor market [2].

The *All India Survey on Higher Education* indicates that the estimated enrollment for postgraduate courses across India for men was 1.8 million and for women, 2.1 million in 2015–16 [3]. Obviously, women have reached that level by competing in various examinations.

But an increasing number of female graduates has not yet translated into increasing participation in the upper echelons of the business world. The increasing number of educated women also addresses the deficit of the right kinds of skills and competencies required to fuel the growth engine of any economy. Keeping them out of the workplace would hurt the economy. India is expected to gain significantly from its demographic dividend and the share of women as its potential productive workforce will be critical. The new millennium and rapidly changing global and national scenarios have ushered in fresh opportunities and possibilities for women's empowerment. They will grant women what they value most—the freedom to make choices. The snap judgments about women are based on a stereotype of what women should be like (prescriptive beliefs). For example, that women are not suited for management and they are not good at management [4] (See for description of prescriptive and descriptive stereotypes about men and women). Underneath this assumption is a myth that women are intellectually inferior to men, and inherently less assertive and more risk averse—characteristics required for success in organizations.

About the only testable difference between men and women seems to be women's greater ability in interpersonal relationships [5]. Based on brain scan studies, many scientists have concluded that the female brain is designed to quickly access the thoughts, beliefs and intentions of others based on the smallest hints, intuitive gut feelings, and hunches. If women are attributed to a finer sense of emotion, intuition, and empathy, then it is actually grounded in biology [6, 7; see for comparisons of men and women on emotional intelligence.].

This finding should augur well for business. Even earlier research comparing men and women on a variety of aptitudes does not support the perceived intellectual superiority of men. In fact, the most consistent finding has been that women surpass men on tests of verbal aptitude, memory, and scholastic achievement [8]. Scientists previously believed that the relatively low numbers of women in higher mathematics could be due to biological differences between men and women.

Take, for instance, the furor surrounding the statement made by Dr Lawrence Summers, the then President of Harvard University, one of the most elite institutions of higher learning in the United States, in January 2005. His remarks, to the effect that women are so little represented in the ranks of senior faculty at Harvard and other major research institutions, because they would not make the necessary sacrifices and maybe did not have the intellectual or intrinsic aptitude to do first-rate science and mathematics, created quite a stir on the campus and beyond. Summers was condemned by the mass media and many faculty at his own university. However, he was voicing views widely shared by many. It is interesting to note that Harvard waited until 1945 to admit women to its medical school; until 1950 to admit women to its law school; and until 1963 to admit women to its business school [9].

However, a new, international study done in schools from 86 countries, including those in non-western countries, concluded that the perceived differences were due to a complex variety of sociocultural factors rather than intrinsic differences, that is, due to unequal societies and attitudes towards women, and not due to biology [10].

One of the possible reasons for this stereotype could be that there is a silent disapproval when a woman makes a statement about her abilities. People may accept self-promotion in men but, as demonstrated by research [11] (See for discussion of the double bind), they dislike self-promoting women more often and consider them less deserving of recognition or support than modest women. In fact, modesty is expected even in highly competent and accomplished women. As a result, many intelligent women, unfortunately, act "dumb" to fulfill the expectations of male superiors and to fit in. Even the most competent and intelligent woman is often torn between the desire for approval by authorities (often male) for whom she must play the role of the naïve, uninformed person, and the need for an outright demonstration of competence for which she might risk ridicule or isolation by departing from her stereotype: that she has only beauty not brains.

Indeed, men perceive their general intellect as well as their intelligence to be higher. Moreover, parents perceive their sons' intelligence to be higher than their daughters'. This gets perpetuated when children perceive the intelligence of their fathers to be higher than that of their mothers. How gender and parental status influence judgements! Is there a motherhood penalty at home too? [12,13,14].

The good news is that these perceptions have been invalidated by a survey conducted by the National Council of Educational Research and Training (NCERT) in India in 2015. The survey of more than 2.7 million students of Class X (O level) following different educational boards in 7,216 schools across 33 states and union territories in India, indicate that girls performed on an equal footing with boys in mathematics, science, and social sciences; and outperformed in English and other languages. The notion that girls are not good with numbers and science is just a myth [15].

What about assertiveness, a trait related to exercising power in organizations? By and large, women are brought up to be passive and docile by nature and men are innately more assertive than women. No wonder, women do tend to score lower on personality measures of dominance because of cultural values and not basic biological differences in the sexes [16]. When women choose to express dominance or assertiveness, it is to support a team or to facilitate group activity, not to promote themselves over others. By and large, women tend to think of power as cooperative, as well as interdependent, rather than competitive. However, evidence indicates that women assimilate and learn the skills required for assertive/leadership roles as effectively as men, if the need arises.

It is for this reason that a woman attempting to assert herself or to exert leadership in a male environment may face certain problems which do not exist for the average male. She'll be caught in a double bind. If she demonstrates assertiveness, many men, and even women, will see her as aggressive and over-controlling. However, if she fails to fulfill the role of an independent, assertive and self-reliant manager, then her peers and direct reports will perceive her as weak and passive, more capable of being led than leading.

Most of the time, organizations marginalize women in a subtler manner. A senior manager tells of her frustration at being part of a management team but finding her input limited on all issues.

Her strategic skills and business acumen is constantly questioned. Another woman leader, promoted into a senior management role in an organization dominated by technical personnel, notices that her colleagues listen to her only when the topic of discussion concerns information technology, her particular field of expertise. Unlike the rest of the senior managers—mostly men—her views are not taken seriously when she strays beyond her defined field of competence.

In social transactions, men seem to prefer women who do not challenge them intellectually. While discussing intelligent women, I have heard many men mentioning, "I am scared of her! She is so intelligent, competent and so much in control." As if these are all negative attributes!

When people hear about a woman succeeding in male-dominated fields, such as engineering or petroleum, they assume that the woman is less likable, less socially desirable, less attractive than a woman who succeeds in a typically feminine career. For some reason, high-flying, high-achieving and high-earning women are also seen as more likely to be unfaithful or having affairs by the dozen. An early study by Hollander found that, as the grade points average of high school males increased, so did their self-esteem. On the other hand, the self-esteem of women *decreased* with increases in their grade point averages, so that women with A averages had lower self-esteem than those with C averages [17]. When it comes to interpersonal attraction, how do people respond to being outperformed? Are they more (or less) attracted to potential partners who outshine them in important domains? Let's take a look at the new study carried out by researchers from University at Buffalo, California Lutheran University, and the University of Texas at Austin. Men find the prospect of dating intelligent women intimidating. Divided into two parts, the men were asked to rank women who outperform them in an English or Math course. Then, they were asked to imagine them as romantic partners. The study stated that men formed favorable impressions and showed greater interest in women who displayed more intelligence than themselves. However, the second part of the study—where men were asked if they would date such women in real life—showed the men getting cold feet. They distanced themselves more the women, tended to rate them as less attractive, and showed less desire to exchange contact information or plan a date with them [18, 19].

General intelligence, which is associated with management and leadership, is equal in men and women. Intelligence and commitment are gender-neutral qualities. This has been consistently shown by the earlier research using psychological tests to the latest research on personality traits such as the Big Five personality traits that affect leadership. On the Big Five personality tests, men exceed women on assertiveness and excitement seeking, while and women exceed men on warmth, gregariousness, and activity [20]. Therefore, neither men nor women have an overall advantage. This myth is slowly being shattered, if you consider the steadily growing number of women enrolled in tertiary education worldwide. But watch out! It does survive in a vestigial form.

## Myth 2: Women cannot deal with tough feedback

Over the years, it has been observed that senior leaders (mostly male) are hesitant or nervous about having a conversation with their female direct reports about performance issues. "I don't know how to talk to her" "or "I don't know how she will receive the feedback" (Will she feel intimidated?). Men probably feel they would prefer to work with someone they did not have to be "careful" with or with whom they share a few common interests.

In fact, women need more feedback than men because they have not still gathered a critical mass and, therefore, are part of a minority. While working in a male-dominated environment, women require more support and guidance in order to feel comfortable at least in the beginning. Women need reassurance that their behavior, actions and decisions are appropriate because the environment is less familiar to them. However, exactly the opposite is true. Male managers tend to shy away from giving direct feedback to women, thinking the women will have an emotional response. There appears to be a fear by men in leadership of "taking a risk" on women. It is a different matter that women are held to a higher standard of performance. Yet the apprehension is that any minor thing will knock them out of contender status.

The McKinsey and Lean In researchers confirmed, for example, that while both men and women recognize that face time with leaders and informal feedback are important to getting ahead, men get more such feedback and more chances to interact with top leadership [21]. Please note that they're not asking for less feedback; they're *getting* less feedback. The bad news is that women state that they're 30 percent less likely to receive it.

This stems from the commonly perceived notion that women are more erratic, emotional, sentimental, temperamental and therefore vulnerable to drastic swing of moods than men. Women tend to take temperamental decisions and are ready to cry at the drop of a hat. Crying in response to normal work situation is considered taboo so if you must cry, talk and cry at the same time. This last piece of advice is also supported by Atwood's work [22].

Women's first reaction to feedback is to personalize it. They internalize it and try to make sense of the situation and the issues around it, and seek greater understanding. Men, on the other hand, may treat the whole feedback business in a detached manner and simply seek solutions. The difference in approach can lead to discord and disharmony.

One reason for this stereotype may be that, traditionally, a woman's expression of emotions like fear, anxiety, grief, disappointment or pain has been more socially acceptable than it has been for men. Since women may express a greater variety of emotions than men without fear of disapproval, it is easier to assume that they are temperamentally unstable. In fact, stereotyping is accentuated by emotions. Any legitimate expression of anger, disappointment or frustration can prompt people to conclude that women are weak and unsuitable for leadership roles. In case of a female professional who is crying, it would simply reinforce the negative stereotype.

The paradox for women is that they may be condemned for crying but also disliked for any toughness they show. However, the same range of emotions exists in men, even though the emotions are less likely to be expressed. It is not unusual to see men losing temper at work or even using unparliamentary language. In those cases, they may be seen as either sensitive or powerful. Some female leaders can also have problems with anger and be resistant to criticism. However, the corporate environment—and society as a whole—is much less tolerant of these characteristics in women than in men.

Then again, expressing emotions or feelings and losing one's cool and getting unduly upset are two different things. Being able to function normally under stress without losing composure is a critical requirement for success, irrespective of gender. Similarly, a personal and social definition of a "male role" requires men to appear tough, subjective, striving, achieving, unsentimental, and emotionally unexpressive. So, if a certain man acts out of his role and shows emotion, weakness or vulnerability of any kind, then he is likely be viewed as unmanly or inferior by others.

Misconceptions concerning biological cycles such as menstruation affecting mood and temperament have also contributed to this stereotype. Evidence reveals that women react individually to biological cycles and, most importantly, these cycles exist in both men and women. There is no evidence to support the contention that the effects of emotional cycles on the performance of women are any greater than the effects of similar cycles on the performance of men.

But the real issue here is that, if men do not know how to talk to women, then they will find it hard to build relationships with them as members of their team. It will be harder still to mentor or coach them; a clear advantage younger men will have over younger women in advancing their careers. Very few managers realize that they have to play a much more active role in developing people from diverse backgrounds. To that end, women need additional support in the form of mentoring, greater access to formal organizational information, and support from management in providing appropriate job experiences.

## Myth 3: Women do not value achievement, promotion, and meaningful work as much as men

Nothing could be farther from the truth. A comprehensive survey of Harvard Business School graduates—men and women—suggests that the conventional wisdom about women and leadership needs to be rethought. The findings of the survey suggest that women want more meaningful work, more challenging assignments, and more opportunities for career growth [23].

Women have long been perceived as interested in what Frederick Herzberg called the hygiene factors: money, security, clean working conditions, social relations and other extrinsic factors of work. In comparison, men value intrinsic motivators such as the desire to achieve, to be promoted, to use their skills and competencies, to have an impact on the organization, and to have power, authority, and significance. It is for these alleged differences in motivation that women are thought less committed to work itself. Conventional wisdom expects women to scale down or forgo opportunities, projects, and jobs. The very premise seems to be that women value careers less, or that those who have become mothers do not value high profile, challenging work, and finally a woman's primary career obstacle is herself.

There are several reasons for the creation of this stereotype. First, women are often traditionally socialized from an early age not to express their aspirations, desires, and needs, but to focus instead on the needs of others. These messages, whether given directly or indirectly by significant others—parents, teachers, media, and society in general—can be so powerful that they become ingrained from an early age. This conscious as well as subconscious bias may affect women's willingness to negotiate. Most women tend to secretly hope that their hard work would be seen, recognized and rewarded by their superiors. Unlike men, they do not know that they can ask for more.

So what happens if they ask for meaningful work, a raise or a promotion? The probability that a woman is going to be perceived as bossy, aggressive, intimidating—words that the McKinsey research specifically asked about—versus men who ask for the same thing is almost 30 percent more likely.

Women are already behind so women need to ask for it. But when they ask for it then there's clearly a hidden penalty here for women. On top of that they never get to know about this perception, because they do not get critical feedback. Is it any wonder women are stalling in the pipeline of production? [24]

Second, any organizational culture—just as family cultures do—penalizes women when they do express what they want, further discouraging them from doing so. Women who openly and actively pursue their own ambitions are considered self-serving and pushy. They frequently see their work devalued and find themselves ostracized from access to important information or networks. Not only that, if they ask for more resources for their department or unit, they are considered unduly competitive and aggressive. Many women find it easier to accept prevailing organizational practices than to lobby for change.

As a result, women in the corporate world learn to keep quiet when they should speak up and often watch their male colleagues get better assignments, good training and timely promotions, more resources, more manpower, whatever .... In several studies [25], it has been demonstrated that men place themselves in negotiation situations more often than women do and regard more of their interactions as potential negotiations.

Several studies dispute the notion that women are less intrinsically motivated. A study conducted by the Center for Work-Life Policy on 4,350 college educated men and women in the BRIC countries and the UAE in 2010 completely shatters the myth [26]. The report states that, although highly educated women are ambitious the world over, the degree of ambition and aspiration among BRIC and UAE women is very high: 85 percent in India, 92 percent in the UAE, 63 percent in Russia, and 65 percent in China, while only 36 percent of women in the US consider themselves very ambitious and aspire to hold a top job. In fact, women can be as dissatisfied as men with work which fails to utilize their abilities. When chances of promotions or utilization of abilities are minimal, commitment to the job decreases for both men and women because commitment has nothing to do with any gender.

Third, there are widespread assumptions about how women leave mid-career to start families and, therefore, do not aspire to upper management. It is true that women may take a break to tend to family commitments but it is not true that it is because they do not aspire to higher management. Those who take a break do so after soul-searching introspection and long debate about how that break will impact their career plans. There are heavy costs associated with this decision: the psychological investment that comes from education and long-term preparation, the blocked career growth, depreciation of skills, insecurity about reestablishing one's career, and the lost income. None of these consequences are easy to deal with. At least 25–28 percent quit at this level, creating a dip in the middle [27].

The crux of the problem lies at the dip in the middle or, more appropriately, the hump in the middle. Talented women can reach the top if they jump the hump. A typical female career path which is moving steady up to 30–32 years of age, hits the first roadblock between the ages of 30 and 40. Just as this is a perfect age to launch the career, it also coincides with the perfect time to launch a family. Maternity is one factor that limits the progress of a professional career, because there are many women who ask for a reduced workday that involves less time to the company and more time to the family. Less time does not necessarily mean less work or less commitment but it is perceived to be so.

Does that mean women are less career-focused? No, it simply means women want to be both: engaged, committed employees as well as active, responsible parents. However, because of their gender role, women are perceived to be family focused, while men are seen as career-focused. Many surveys reveal that both categories of women—whether predominantly family-focused or career-focused—although smaller in number, are found at both ends of the spectrum. This finding reflects a universal trend. The family focused group may not be available to sacrifice part of their personal life and free time, may not want to travel as much, and may not want to relocate to another geography during the critical period of child bearing or rearing. The career-focused group may decide to remain single for the sake of career or postpone childbirth if married. They are willing to travel, relocate and naturally expect exposure to a wide range of functions. They must be treated as well as the best of male executives.

However, there is a vast majority of women in between who would like to balance both career and family. Such women, when they return from their maternity or child-rearing phase, become very career-oriented and are raring to go. Instead of assigning easy tasks to women returning from a break in their career, organizations need to refuel their ambitions by involving them in challenging and complex assignments. Women will ensure that they make a success out of it as a return on the organization's faith in their talent and potential. With support and proper mentoring, they can also become ideal mentors in turn for the younger women coming after them. Instead, they get branded as employees not committed to work.

For that matter, gender is a poor predictor of commitment, turnover and absenteeism, contrary to the popular notion that absenteeism and turnover rates are higher among women than men. Women tend to show slightly high absenteeism than men and slightly higher turnover during the child-bearing or child-rearing phases in their lives. When the children are young, a working mother tends to take more sick days. In fact, one study shows that women make greater use of sick days compared to men but not for their own sicknesses [28]. Her absence, in fact, reflects her family responsibility which actually confirms the expectation as well as stereotype that mothers should take care of sick children. These differences can be further explained by lack of childcare support at home, and by the restriction of women to routine and low-status positions within organizations.

For instance, as per the World Development Report [29], Indian women clearly aspire to work outside their homes. Assumptions about life and career choices, are challenged. But over 50 percent of the women surveyed said there was no help to share their household duties. And 33.73 percent said that they would accept work in addition to domestic work. Further, a study [30] conducted among professionals holding entry-level to senior positions by the recruitment firm Michael Page India in 2014–15 on employee intentions, has shown that a higher percentage of women (73 percent) compared to men (68 percent) have asked for promotions and career progression. This is a welcome change.

## Myth 4: Women do not like to travel, relocate, or take international assignments

In a borderless world, global experience is considered increasingly important as a requirement for advancing in higher management positions. Yet, women have to continuously fight cultural stereotypes that prevent them from plum job opportunities, only because it is assumed that a woman's primary responsibility is to her family: her home, her husband, and her children. Her career is secondary. No wonder, literature suggests that companies have traditionally been hesitant to send women on global assignments in particular, because of the assumption that women do not want to disrupt family life or are not willing to relocate to new locations. This is increasingly changing. Research from a 2000 Catalyst survey [31] belies that notion, suggesting that, contrary to the traditional myth, women are willing to accept, relocate for, and ultimately succeed in such assignments.

The key question is: are the employers willing to give them the choice? Are the employers willing to treat each individual woman and her situation as an exclusive case? Are the employers and the male managers willing to first examine and then challenge their own cultural beliefs and assumptions?

There is a general assumption that women do not like to travel because women do not want to disrupt work-life concerns or women have difficulty adjusting to different cultures. It is for the same reason they are not interested in global assignments. We often misinterpret one another or generalize one situation as a representative of the entire gender. For instance, just because one woman declines a promotion that involves relocation because of her family, does not mean all women with families would not want to relocate ever. It is to be understood that, if women make that choice, then it is during certain phases of their life, such as child-bearing or child-rearing phases. That choice is personal and cannot be considered valid for her entire life and is not representative of women who want to travel, hold, or aspire to responsible positions.

By and large, working mothers are considered primarily responsible for childcare. It is, therefore, assumed that she is more committed to her home, husband, and children than to her career. Conversely, men are perceived more committed to career. For them, long working hours and travel are not only a possibility, they are considered a necessity.

The issue of mobility becomes problematic for a working mother when family is involved, and children have to be taken out of and readmitted to schools in a new place of posting. At times, this means terminating arrangements with trusted childcare providers. Most employed women also have employed husbands who may not be in a position to move to the new city. Leaving a spouse behind is not the best of solutions. Finding a new job for him is not easy either. The prospect of disruption can appear overwhelming and, therefore, not worth the relocation effort. But times change and difficult times pass. Companies need to have a candid conversation with working mothers before thrusting management decisions on them.

I have made choices in my career and have accepted the consequences of making those choices. For instance, during the final years of my daughter's school graduation, I had declined an opportunity for relocation and a consequent promotion. At another time, when I got the challenging assignment of heading the National Petroleum Management Program—a knowledge network of all the oil and gas companies in India—I decided to stay put in New Delhi and did not join my husband in his place of posting. It meant that we lived in different cities and accepted the challenges a long-distance marriage would bring. At yet another time, I went on an overseas developmental program for a month after making elaborate arrangements at home. I know of several women who would perhaps make similar choices.

As you can see, women's priorities change with age, a certain stage of life, and career goals. Just as one solution does not fit all, one assumption cannot define all women in all the phases of their life. Women are well aware of the professional price they have to pay for lack of mobility. But empowerment, after all, is about having the freedom to make those choices.

In one study [32], sponsored by the International Personnel Association (IPA) in the US of 60 American and Canadian multinational corporations which were also member companies of IPA, the findings suggest that sex-role stereotyping may still be a problem for women on international assignments. It is also seen that managers discourage women, however tacitly, from accepting international assignments. The findings also suggest that, in general, women are interested in, and likely to accept, International assignments. Women in dual-career relationships accepted slightly fewer international assignments than single women or women who lived with non-working partners. Finally, women with children are less likely to accept international assignments than women without children. But women will not hesitate to accept global assignments if relocation benefits include support for spouse and children. Organizations have to also be sensitive to the fact that cultural concerns, gender norms, employment laws, healthcare services, and views on work–life balance vary from culture to culture and country to country. When executives decide to travel or relocate, it is after due consideration to all the above factors.

New research in the BRIC nations and the UAE by Hewlett and Rashid [33] indicates that 60 percent of the women in their sample expressed strong interest in an international assignment and also considered them critical for career progression. How about giving them a chance?

## Myth 5: Women and leadership do not go together

There is an implicit expectation that if you must lead, then "lead like a man," because leaders in general are viewed as possessing more masculine, agentic characteristics than feminine characteristics. This "think leader, think male" phenomenon transcends geo-cultural boundaries and is universally found across all nations [34]. There seems to be perceived incompatibility between requirements of feminine behavior and those of leadership. For many, women and leadership seems like a contradiction in terms. For many women, therefore, it is a challenge to reconcile being feminine *and* being a leader, when the leadership paradigm is driven by the masculine gender.

Everywhere leadership in general and management in particular are seen as masculine domains. Popular beliefs about what is required of management are socially constructed from stereotypically defined masculine traits and from the collective interest and experience of men. After all, the business environment was designed with male leaders in mind. This is mainly because entry of women into management only happened in recent decades. No wonder, women fill up a minority of management positions and, in most cases, remain invisible in senior positions.

Men and women are also evaluated differently in leadership roles. The position of leader has been a male-dominated role for many years. As a result, there is still some evidence today to shows that men more than women feel that good leaders have more masculine characteristics such as crisis-management abilities, tough-mindedness, emotional stability, and ambition, and fewer of the traits valued in women, such as empathy, sensitivity, ability to nurture and develop others, team spirit, etc. [35]. However, evidence indicates that, if required, women assimilate and learn the skills required for assertive/leadership roles as effectively as men. Other than those small percentages of women who are assertive by nature, most women do require assertiveness training or need to develop conscious role-playing behavior that would be seen as active and powerful.

Many a times, instances are quoted in assertiveness training workshops about how women, despite their position or authority, are taken advantage of. But, if and when a woman demonstrates assertiveness, initiative, or ambition, she is viewed as aggressive, hostile, and power crazy. Too often, positive traits in a man are judged as negative traits in a woman.

As one female executive once told me, "If you take a stand, if you stick your neck out, you are dead." In fact, it is a great dilemma, since a successful manager is seen as assertive and self-reliant. Failure to fulfill this role would cause a woman's peers and juniors to perceive her as weak and passive, more suited to be led than leading. Is it not strange that the same leadership qualities in men are judged as traits of aggression and hostility in women, even if they consciously develop them as required for their leadership roles?

Clearly, there are contradictory expectations associated with managerial roles. Because women are stereotyped as less competent than men, they are expected to keep quiet about their own abilities, strengths, and accomplishments. Yet, the paradox is such that, if they legitimately promote themselves, they invite disapproval. However, men who promote themselves do not invite the same mixed outcomes. In fact, self-promotion by men is associated with higher levels of competence and acceptability. How is it that we subject men and women to contradictory expectations and evaluations of performance standards?

This stereotype also breeds another one which expects women not to demand higher compensation, promotions, or other relevant work opportunities, despite the fact that they amply deserve them. Even at the entry level, women tend not to negotiate salary in the same fashion, or as directly, as men. Since women tend to think of it as a confrontation, it seems inappropriate to them to enter into a disagreement with one's employer just as the relationship is beginning. Research indicates that, when offered a job, only 7 percent of women will negotiate their incoming salary, while more than 55 percent of men will negotiate for as much compensation as they can get [36]. At the same time, employers regard women who ask for a raise in salary as overly demanding and, therefore, less hirable than women who do not make such demands. They prefer women to use more indirect tactics. Although these traits produce approval otherwise, they do not produce respect in a leadership role, because, as a leader, one is expected to use more direct and assertive influence tactics. As you can see, on the one hand, women leaders are expected to fulfill the female gender role by being warm, supportive, and selfless, and, on the other hand, they are also expected to fulfill the leadership role by displaying assertiveness and competence. How does one deal with this double bind?

A senior vice-president from an Indian bank once explained to me how she had to be extremely vigilant and alert when she confronted employees. "The situation demands that you have to be strong and assertive. At the same time, you have to try not to get angry and confrontational, and must not be seen as using your power to attack people. So, you push a little and wait to see its impact and how far you can go without offending people. Then push some more to see a desired outcome. However, it gets increasingly difficult at higher levels."

> The gender stereotype in leadership is still active for female leaders even though the actual experience of subordinates with female leaders does not fit this stereotype. Since these stereotypes have been around for so long, it is not surprising that they would be highly resistant to change [37].

This stereotype was clearly visible when Hillary Clinton decided to contest the US Presidential Elections in 2008. Without even considering the merit and eligibility of the candidate, poll after poll indicated that US citizens preferred a male candidate [38], and about 70 percent of American voters did not think Hillary Clinton would win a presidential election in 2008. She lost the democratic nomination to Obama then, but she created history by winning the Democrat Party presidential nomination, the first for any woman in America's electoral history, in 2016. However, the US Presidential Elections were able to shatter the race stereotype in 2008, but not the gender stereotype in 2016.

But the findings from the latest survey [39] of 7,280 leaders on leadership effectiveness from 360 evaluations on the 16 competencies, confirm some eternal truths about men and women leaders, while also holding some surprises. The first finding confirms that the majority of leaders (64 percent) are still men, just as 78 percent of top managers are all men. The second confirmation is that women excel at "nurturing" competencies, such as developing others and building relationships, engaging, self-development, and exhibiting integrity. Specifically, in this survey, women are rated at all levels higher in 12 out of 16 competencies that define outstanding leadership. The other two traits where women outscored men—taking initiative and driving for results—have long been thought of as particularly male strengths. Men outscored women significantly on only one management competency—the ability to develop a strategic perspective. Top leaders always score significantly higher on this competency. Since top leaders are mostly men, men score higher here in the aggregate.

However, as we know, a good leader/manager is situational. The new leader motivates, empowers, and collaborates, irrespective of gender. The most important quality of a good leader may be the ability to change his or her style of management according to the situation. Unfortunately, some managers, men and women alike, lack this flexibility, rigidly adhering to the stereotype of the good leader as a tough, unemotional and dominating individual. Leaders who have the ability to reflect and self-correct often ask themselves, "How is my behavior affecting the people around me?" They always ask the question in the context of any situation or any form of difference, whether it's gender, culture, community, or country.

## Are these myths or facts?

When the number of women in industry was miniscule, the impact of these assumptions was not felt much. But, as the number of women in business and industry grows steadily, new processes need to be introduced into traditional management systems which have primarily been male oriented till now. As men and women work closely together, subtle issues of gender insensitivity and discrimination have also emerged, posing new challenges for employers and employees alike.

The number of studies on gender stereotypes show how deep rooted these stereotypes are in organizations. According to the executive women surveyed in the US, Catalyst found out that among the top five reasons why women are not advancing to the senior ranks are male stereotypes and perceptions about women's roles and abilities [40].

**Top Barriers to Women's Advancement**

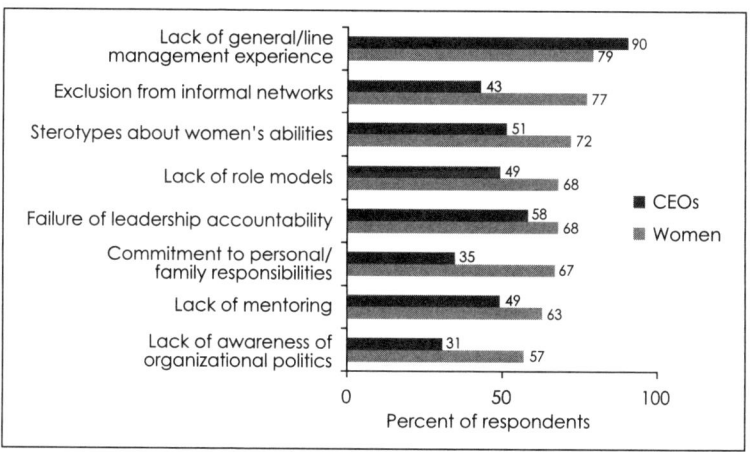

*Source:* Catalyst: Women in US Corporate Leadership (2003).

If this is considered dated, then consider the findings of the study conducted by the Center For Work-Life Policy in the BRIC countries or emerging markets in 2011 [41] and the 2013 McKinsey Global Survey of 1,421 global executives on gender diversity [42]. The study conducted in the BRIC countries or emerging markets in 2011, indicates that 45 percent of both men and women in India, 36 percent of men and women in China, 32 percent women and 18 percent men in UAE, 25 percent women and 23 percent men in

Brazil, and 19 percent women and 13 percent men in Russia believe that women are treated unfairly because of their gender. Together, the findings of these three reports suggest that attitudinal/cultural factors continue to play a central role in missing diversity goals.

Could it be that our biases are so deeply ingrained that our actions still haven't caught up with our enlightened views? Most educated people *claim* to hold equitable views—they know these are the right views to have, much like most people will certainly say they are not racist. But converting such views into practice is another matter entirely.

Even with equal skills and qualifications, women have much more difficulty in reaching top management positions. What's worse, few men recognize the challenges women face. The women are almost twice as likely to cite gender bias as their male peers (19 percent versus 10 percent), although there is significant variation between the regions of the world [43].

The strength and shackles of these stereotypes suggest just how difficult it can be for women to be effectively active and agentic in organizations. This, in fact, is an invisible barrier, the so-called glass ceiling.

Several studies on the lack of women in senior management [44] and the gender pay gap [45] indicate that women are disproportionately underrepresented in top management and paid less than men are when they do reach the top [46]. In their analysis of executive officers of Fortune 1000 companies, Helfat et al found that there were more than twice as many male executives as compared to female executives in HR management. Given these trends, what kinds of stereotypes must be in operation [44]?

For instance, gender stereotypes have consistently been found to portray men and women as opposites, with men perceived as masculine and achievement-oriented, and women as being nurturing and facilitative. Translated to employment-related decisions, such portrayals can lead to biased evaluations of women's performance and qualifications in selections, placements, retention, and promotion decisions [47], especially for managerial jobs.

There are two kinds of stereotypes: descriptive and prescriptive. Descriptive stereotypes are constellations of traits thought to uniquely describe men and women [47]. In contrast, prescriptive stereotypes describe how men and women should behave, i.e., what behaviors are and are not appropriate based on one's gender. When women demonstrate masculine behavior or succeed at male type jobs, then that behavior is seen as violating the prescriptive stereotype. They are greeted with hostility and disapproval, ultimately resulting in downwardly biased performance evaluations [48]. When a woman exhibits stereotypically feminine behavior, she is considered a poor fit for most managerial jobs.

Let's take a look at the question of whether stereotypes limit women's opportunities as leaders using an occupational lens in the section below.

## Implications for Corporate Performance

Beyond meeting immediate recruitment and succession planning needs, the most successful companies use talent management as a tool to drive strategic change, innovation, and long-term organizational health. Interventions at all stages of the talent life-cycle—including recruitment, development, rotation, evaluation, reward, and recognition—not only deliver business outcomes, but develop great leaders. But what happens in the case of women?

The stereotypes can be a huge limiting factor. Not just unconscious biases, but conscious biases, too, can be quite pervasive at the workplace. Let's hold that mirror up and see what those biases are driving us toward.

## Talent acquisition and placement

Times may have changed but the stereotype of women as lacking the abilities and character traits required of managers is widely held. One of the findings of the Randstad Workmonitor Survey indicates that 55 percent of the overall respondents from India favored men over women when two candidates are equally qualified for the same set of responsibilities. Globally, the figure stood at 70 percent. This survey covers 33 countries around the world [49]. As a consequence, there is an unstated resistance to bringing in people with a background that is very divergent from the current group [50; a research conducted by Innovisor in 29 countries found that when men and women select a work colleague they are likely to choose people of the same gender].

Evidence continues to mount for the power and pervasive nature of unconscious bias, in both men and women. In a 2012 Yale University study, researchers asked 127 scientists at six universities to review identical applications for a lab manager position, with the resumes randomly assigned male or female names. The researchers found that staff consistently judged male candidates to be more competent and deserving of an extra US$4,000 pay on average. They were also willing to provide male applicants with mentoring and were more likely to hire them.

Notably, women in the study were just as likely as men to make these judgments. Even scientists, those guardians of objectivity, responded no better than control groups. The best policies alone will not address these issues—change will only come if interviewers and decision-makers become aware of their unconscious biases [50].

While the business environment has changed dramatically over the last two or three decades, the recruitment practices of the organizations have not changed at all. They are based on a male definition of what a successful candidate would look like, by describing a role or a profile in very specific terms and frames of reference. Often, recruiters, especially for larger companies, do not recognize transferable skills. They only consider a candidate for a certain position if one has worked in a particular specific role, or completed specific industry training. This limits the talent pool.

For instance, computer science programs are still populated by men. The talent pool of women pursuing technology as a career option is fairly small globally. Young girls need to be encouraged to take up mathematics and science, and stick to these subjects till the post-graduate level, if interested [52]. It is for this reason that, if IT firms want to hire more women for their IT departments, they will have to widen their search. New trends suggest that IT or IT-enabled service organizations are becoming less about building technology and more about providing services and building better relationships with internal as well as external customers.

In a recent, thought-provoking study, chief information officers were asked where women had the most positive impact on IT. Their responses indicate that it is not the women's technical skill so much as their ability to build alliances with business partners and stakeholders, and bring diverse ideas to the domain of programming, that is considered valuable [53].

But the first course of action of HR from any organization would be to dip into the same pool of candidates, looking for degrees in technology, ignoring the changing and more diverse needs of the company. HR professionals, therefore, need to understand how their talent management or recruitment processes contribute to the problem. There can be inherent bias in the selection process itself at the entry level. The interviewers need to be sensitized on their approach towards hiring women candidates. Senior women officers need to be placed on recruitment panels, so that they can bond with the fresh women candidates better. This is really important regarding women's first jobs, as they set the stage for all inequities to follow. Assumptions about life and career choices can become handy justifications for women's inequity in the management ranks. The other assumption is that men are qualified and ready, but women have to prove themselves first. Despite genuine efforts to ensure fairness, some managers may be inadvertently overlooking bias that creeps in at initial job placements, postings, and simply in evaluating women for promotions. When done right, as was the case with Hinduja Global Solutions [54], the ratio of women could go up from 20 percent in the workforce to 35 percent, and the retention rates can get better too.

These assumptions are not sector specific but universal.

Back in the mid-1990s, we were recruiting management trainees in technical disciplines for Oil India Limited. The recruitment officer had thoroughly evaluated the employment suitability of male and female candidates for entry level positions. This was a panel consisting of two senior executives from technical departments and myself representing human resources function. Although all individuals were identical in grade point averages and other qualifications, men were consistently rated more suitable than female candidates. Two smart young women engineers made it to the shortlist based on merit demonstrated throughout the written examination as well as interview. However, when it came to actually making an offer, one panelist expressed, "All said and done, the boys would be better." The other readily agreed.

I was taken aback. "Why so?" I asked.

"There are a whole lot of issues you see—nightshifts, working on the shop floor, traveling, dealing with mainly male colleagues and workers, etc. The girls would find it difficult."

"Let's not make any assumptions about what they would find difficult. Shall we ask them?" I suggested.

"No harm," they echoed, "But make it fast as we might lose an extra half hour. As you know, there are a large number of interviews yet to be conducted."

We had one more round of conversation with both the girls independently. The girls said that they went in to study engineering fully aware of the employment opportunities or challenges (depending on how you look at it) in the future. They were fully prepared to deal with all the challenges such a job would throw up. "Please give us a chance to prove what we can do," they said. Their enthusiasm and optimism were infectious.

"What will you do once you get married?" the Chairman of the selection committee asked one of the candidates. I could clearly hear an unspoken question. "Would you compromise your work for family considerations?"

There was a long pause.

Then the girl said, "Sir, have you also posed the same question to the male candidates?" I admired her boldness.

Now, there was a longer pause at our side of the table, accompanied by some nervous shifting on the seat. However, the silence turned out to be positive. Both the girls got the job and have overtime made good advancement in their respective careers.

How often are such options presented to deserving women candidates? That's when I realized that the 30 minutes allotted for each interview were not enough for women candidates to do their best. Such a short time often forces the panelists to rely on first impressions which are so often a function of perceived similarity. It was all about who would fit the mold? The interviewers could not see beyond the technical abilities for which the jobs were advertised. The candidates could not connect with or impress the interviewers just as the interviewers could not effectively assess the candidates. This picture could change only when there was a female manager—in this case me—on the interview panel. The brief to the interview panel was the same, but the understanding and implementation in the second instance was different.

In short, women candidates face a challenge at the interview level even if they get shortlisted. But the general assumption prior to developing a shortlist is that companies would be able to hire more women if more women were simply invited for interviews during campus recruitment. Such examples prove how invisible, even unintentional, gender inequity thrives in today's companies.

A study conducted by a well-known management school in India shows another perspective. Even if women are recruited in larger numbers than before, there continues to exist a bias in the kind of jobs that are allocated to them. Not getting an opportunity to handle challenging jobs implies that women do not get a chance to prove their worth and move up. They get stuck in soft dead-end jobs that come to be labeled as "female" in due course of time. The exclusion of women from policy formation and decision-making relegates them to peripheral, supportive, infrastructural jobs such as general and personnel administration, public relations, healthcare, and retail segments, or mostly the hospitality industry. By clinging on to stereotypic beliefs about women, such as "women prefer secure low-risk jobs", which may be true of some women but cannot be generalized to include all women, the corporate sector underutilizes the potential of many women managers. No wonder, one survey in India found out that companies have policies which exclude women from certain posts, such as manufacturing, production, shop floor, sales and marketing, and top-level positions [55; In this survey of 149 companies in India by the Confederation of Indian Industry (CII), about half of the medium-level companies said there were departments where they did not prefer women. Companies are also wary of sexual harassment cases]. This robs women managers of a chance to prove themselves and stretch their capabilities.

Even when recruitment at the entry level is commensurate with graduate profile, anecdotal evidence suggests that this is not so at the middle level. A pathbreaking study by PWC in 2008 [56] called the attrition of women talent with 5–15 years of experience, the "leaking pipeline" and noted that it was prevalent across industries and countries. The Leaking Pipeline report indicated that the percentage of working women in the 30-plus age group is significantly lower than that of women in their 20s, indicating that this is the stage when women tend to leave the workforce. This is true across the world just as this is true of India as well, where women often leave the workforce due to the tug of war between work and family. Women who choose to take a break at this stage typically miss the critical step that takes them to the next level of management. And when they do choose to return to their careers, they find that they have lost leadership roles to their peers who remained in the workforce. We need to recognize the fact that internal processes for identifying high-potential employees often focus on managers between the ages of 28 and 35. HR policies need to broaden the parameters for women by taking into account the time spent on maternity leave (typically up to two years) to ensure that evaluation processes do not overlook qualified women.

## Need to redesign recruitment practices

Corporations which genuinely want to increase the number of women in their workforce need to introspect as to what blocks their way—is there a bias against women or is it lack of qualified candidates? They also have to think about how they would overcome systemic limitations. In times of mergers, acquisitions, and downsizing, corporate policies need to protect women from insensitive treatment by a male-biased corporate culture.

For that to happen, the HR leaders in organizations may consider the following:

- Communicate recruitment opportunities and selection criteria transparently.
- Reconsider the composition of recruitment selection teams; include at least one female member on panels where subconscious bias can affect decision making.
- Encourage women to communicate interest in and apply for leadership positions.
- Identify the motivational factors that drive employees early in the recruitment process. Understanding what candidates want out of their careers during job interviews will allow hiring managers to better assess the resources and training required to help empower them within the organization. This may lead to a lower attrition rate and better employee satisfaction.
- Set performance targets for female retention, promotion, and leadership development improvements, with clear personal and team accountabilities.
- Commit to including a target number of female candidates for each leadership appointment.
- Monitor performance on intended advancements. Are set guidelines being followed and producing results?
- Finally, employers reinforce social norms through their policies and practices and they can change social norms through the same mechanisms. HR practitioners need to be mindful of

these dynamics when examining the hiring and compensation policies. Awareness and fair policies can assist in making better meritorious recruitment decisions, with the help of objective tools and techniques. But it does require a constant vigilance over systems, processes, and organizational mindsets.

Creative recruitment techniques executed with women in mind will also help attract more women. Tapping into women's networks and using positive role models to give speeches at schools and universities will help to encourage more women to enter the corporate sector.

## Talent maintenance/retention

What happens when women are selected for managerial or staff positions? It seems that their superiors are less committed to retaining them, than they would be to the career of their male counterparts; and their male colleagues would prefer to select another male colleague over an equally qualified female colleague when asked to choose a participant in a management development seminar.

## Conflict between work and family obligations

A survey [57] asked 1,500 managers about decisions regarding hypothetical male and female subordinates faced with a variety of conflicts and problems. One problem involved a conflict between job demands and family obligations. Most of the respondents indicated that they would expect the male employee to put his job above his family, but they would expect a woman in the same situation to sacrifice her career. Another situation involved personal misconduct which threatened a valued employee's job. The managers indicated that they would make more exceptions and go to greater efforts to retain a male employee than they would a woman with equal qualifications.

I have also seen this happen several times in my career. Once, a very competent and qualified mid-level female executive got unwittingly caught up in a departmental feud that was blown out of proportion. In a fact-finding enquiry all four people involved—three male officers along with her—were interviewed. They all had more or less an equal role to play in that situation. But the woman officer was given two choices. She was asked to either resign or to proceed on leave while her male colleagues were asked to be more careful. That's all! However, she demonstrated more guts than everyone expected. She did not choose either of the options, and decided to stay put and brave the storm. But in the process she had to stand completely alone. More often than not, women do not get any support when they find themselves in the eye of the storm.

According to the 2013 Catalyst *First Step: India Overview* report [58] 48 percent of Indian women drop out of the pipeline before reaching mid-career, compared with Asia's average of 29 percent. The Asia-Pacific region continues to lose between US$42 and 47 billion a year in GDP due to the lack of participation of talented women in the workforce, according to the 2012 report *India's Economy: The Other Half* by the Center for Strategic and International Studies [59].

## Excessively long hours

A study of women who had quit their high-level managerial and professional jobs found that 86 percent cited work-related factors as coercing their decisions, especially norms dictating extremely long hours [60]. Also, given that men often earn more than women, when couples decide that one parent should take major responsibility for childcare, they typically select the mother, in part because of her less earning power besides the maternal role.

At one time, women provided all the support system that enabled men to devote their time and energy to a 35–40-hour work week. But, as women begin to join the workforce in greater numbers, there is no one around to do family errands. Working families are faced with daily dilemmas such as who will take care of the car repair, who will attend the Parent-Teacher Meeting at school, who will stay back to let the plumber in, etc.

There are many ways progressive companies can address the issue of retention of talented women. These are highlighted in the last chapter. But, one of the initiatives taken by many companies, is to stay connected with employees who are on maternity leave. This is to address the issue of attrition, with companies realizing that many such women will seek a change in role on their return to work. It is important to create a conducive environment for returning mothers, so they stay connected, relevant, and inspired.

It would, therefore, be important to undertake studies to assess the effectiveness of women in business and industry. The study on performance effectiveness of women in different sectors would help, at least to an extent, in reducing the doubts and stereotypes associated with effectiveness of women in management. It is also important to conduct a cost-benefit analysis of the return on company's investment in high-performing women. Once it is established that women's value is greater than the cost to recruit, and develop them, then women will be seen not as a cost but as an investment, an investment worth safeguarding and nurturing.

## Talent development and utilization

Ten years ago, we came to grips with the fact that, by and large, women in the petroleum industry do not get nominated an equal number of times as their male counterparts for overseas training. This came to light when a specific request was made in seeking nominations for an overseas program. Their superiors made assumptions about what is good for them. "Travel puts too much pressure on women" or, more common, "Her family will not put up with her long absence from home." In fact, as is always the case, most often the superiors were not even conscious of making such assumptions. Neither did they feel it necessary to check whether their assumptions were right.

Take, for instance, my own case. In the middle phase of my career, two of my male colleagues were nominated for a six-week course in Canada. Despite my eligibility, I was not even considered.

The overseas training was very relevant to my role and I would have benefitted from the developmental exposure. Then why did I not get the nomination? What was the criterion that was used for making the selection decision? I felt crushed. After a sleepless night, I mustered enough courage and decided to ask my senior manager.

But it was not easy. "Will I be seen as promoting my own interests? Will I be penalized for asking for what I want?" I had a load of questions with no ready answers. For that matter, nobody working for him had any answers. He was new to the organization. He had fixed ideas and an inflexible, arrogant attitude towards everyone. On top of that, he was a bad listener. It was difficult working with him. I know "challenging" will sound politically correct, but it was just very hard.

So, when I went up to him, my superior was surprised that I thought it fit enough to even ask him. He felt questioned and challenged by a junior to whom he owed no explanation. However, he explained that he had to take this decision in my best interest!

What would I do about my children for six long weeks? A ray of hope flickered when I heard that concern!

"My husband is extremely supportive. In addition, I have full-time domestic help and my mother would come to support and look after my children," I said.

"My friends are there too .... Women support each other all the time," I thought to myself. But I was not prepared for what I heard.

"Call me old fashioned if you like, but a woman's place is at home. As a wife and a mother, you must be self-sacrificing. Certainly not globe-trotting with male colleagues for six long weeks! Period," my boss said.

I never felt so unheard in my entire career as I felt that day. I had hit rock bottom. I had to settle for what I did not get. The only consolation was that it had nothing to do with my work or quality of my work. It had everything to do with my being a woman.

Did I feel good about asking? Yes and no. Not all happiness is created equal!

## Limited developmental exposure

Evidence suggests that women get limited exposure to challenging assignments and committee experiences that can prepare them for senior positions. This also suggests that, although women and men may be promoted to similar organizational levels, men actually get more significant learning and developmental opportunities. One wonders whether it is due to the stereotype associated with women that implicitly expects them to fail [61], or the reluctance to assign them problem-solving, risk-taking assignments that require preparation, exposure, and relevant professional opportunities. In fact, compared to men at the same level of management, women experience their job as less critical and less visible to the organization.

What's more, even at the executive level, women have less authority than men, as indicated by a number of direct reports [62]. In another study, organizational psychologists Lyness and Thompson [63] found that women experienced greater difficulty in getting important assignments and opportunities to relocate to a new location for a better position. They also performed fewer functions dealing with products, customers, and markets critical for the growth of the organization. Meeting the challenges inherent in tough assignments and being recognized for having overcome these challenges are very critical for advancement to senior positions. However, women do not get access to high-stake assignments. The proportion of women in management roles has increased more in human resources than in any other field due to perceived stereotypical abilities such as social sensitivity or interest in people. But women's representation in top management has remained essentially unchanged over the last ten years [64]. Even in HR, as we saw earlier, there were more than twice as many male executives as female.

## Challenging assignments

What role do these gender-based assumptions about women's careers and aspirations play in the process of assigning plum assignments to high-performing and deserving women?

A typical scenario would have superiors evaluating two promising young professionals, a woman and man, with identical skills. Of the woman, the superior would say, "She is really good, but I just can't see her interacting and dealing with that tough CFO. She can always work on her presentation skills."

The conversation about the man would vary slightly but significantly. "He is good. He has tremendous potential. I am taking the CFO golfing next week. He can join me and learn one or two things about being combative. I know he can grow into it." Seemingly harmless conversations such as these could send careers in very different directions. A woman is found a bit wanting and the male superiors cannot see how she will get to the next level. The thought of helping her does not even occur to them. Despite the fact that women get evaluated on their performance, they have to prove their worth over and over again before they are even considered for critical, visible, transformative assignments. However, the process of assigning these plum assignments remains largely unexamined. Too often women are passed over for such assignments. Often men get evaluated on their *potential* while women get evaluated on their *performance*. What use is training a woman to negotiate fiercely and put herself forward for a senior role if the top jobs are being handed down from a mostly male boys' club to their mostly male circle of acquaintances? What use are good personal presentation skills if you never get the chance to present your candidacy because the position isn't advertised in the first place?

However, there are positive instances when seniors are willing to look beyond titles or designations on visiting cards and CVs and lack of previous experience. One senior manager I interviewed from a FMCG company said she would not have gotten where she is today if past decisions had been made only on the basis of her previous experience. Instead, her Chairman saw her potential for success in that role, even though she had not done the exact job before. This is an important criterion when considering prospective women directors, since many will not possess prior experience as a director. In those industries, such as retail, financial services, etc., where women have held leadership roles, bringing women into the board is a natural step. However, in many industries where women have not been at the helm, a proper education and sensitization process needs to be undertaken.

## Nomination on executive committees

What about other opportunities like nominations of competent women on high-level committees which take decisions on important policy matters? Lack of general management or line experience is often cited as the greatest impediment to selecting women to board-level positions. But, even at middle level, women have difficulty in obtaining developmental assignments, because they are mostly serving staff functions.

The fact that gender determines career experience is central to the issue of women's advancement. Women are not considered fit for revenue generating, line or high-visibility, international assignments. At the root of this assumption is the stereotype that their abilities, skills, and interests match staff functions more than line functions. Such low-stake assignments do little to advance their career. As a result, men are often assigned line functions that provide opportunities to get into senior leadership [65]. There are glorious exceptions, of course, but they are just that—glorious exceptions!

McKinsey and Company conducted a series of "Women Matter" studies [66] of 441 companies from the local reference stock index of six European and BRIC countries from 2007 to 2010. The 2010 report confirms that women are barely present in executive committees. In fact, one interesting aspect of the study points out that the representation of women in corporate governing bodies as well as executive committees varies by industry.

No wonder then that a much smaller number of them make the leadership transition from senior manager to an executive position, and even fewer reach the executive committee of large organizations. In 2011, women held 21 percent of the seats on executive committees in Sweden, 15 percent in Norway, 14 percent in the United

States, 12 percent in Australia, 11 percent in the United Kingdom, 9 percent in China, 8 percent in France, 3 percent in Germany, 3 percent in India, and 1 percent in Japan [67].

## Even in the world of science

This sad scenario also exists in the world of science. The findings of the World Science Report [68], released by UNESCO, highlighted gender discrimination as a worrying, continuing trend in the world of science. The report attributes gender imbalance in science and technology to two reasons. First, review committees in governments and research institutions basically do not encourage studies on gender issues. Second, women are virtually absent on high-level science and technology committees which advise or take decisions on national and international policy matters. Further, these problems remain invisible as there is little data on such issues.

In the Indian context, Abha Sur [69] critically examines the issues related to caste and gender in areas of knowledge production and institution building in science, and wonders why even those who have suffered discrimination continue to reinforce and project institutions of science as gender-blind entities committed to excellence and meritocracy, where caste and gender discrimination are seen as individual rather than systemic actions.

No wonder that Russian scientist Anton Nemilov [70] once stated that the concept of inequality between men and women is so deeply rooted, not only in lesser educated people but also in the highly educated as well as in women themselves, that, if on occasion women are treated as equals of men, this is attributed to men's weakness and impotency. "If we pursue the thoughts of any scientist, writer, student, businessman ... we shall soon realize that he does not in his heart of hearts regard woman as his equal."

## Talent recognition and evaluation

When I was in charge of talent management at Oil India Ltd, two young women having MBAs with pedigrees dropped in to say

"Hello." They had completed three years of service and updated me informally on what they had been doing. But the real reason for the meeting gradually became clear. They felt underutilized and bored. They spent two years doing insignificant assignments which they knew had no impact on anything. There were big projects being handled, but they did not get staffed on them, which meant no exposure, no recognition, nothing. Of course, they were given the responsibility of organizing birthdays and Christmas parties in the department, but that marginalized them even further. When they joined, they had dreams of making it big and rising quickly to the next level based on their performance. Three years and one promotion round later, that had not happened. Does anyone aspire for this kind of life in the pipeline? I made it a point to talk to their senior. He seemed to appreciate their performance but had no specific plans to utilize them gainfully. So he was not even aware of the set of perceptions and unconscious beliefs that had shaped his decision, or the impact of his decision. He promised to rectify this at the next available opportunity.

Women in the Workplace, a study conducted by LeanIn.Org and McKinsey, suggests that women are less likely to receive the first critical promotion to manager—which is why far fewer end up on the path to leadership—and they are less likely to be hired into more senior positions [71].

- Women remain underrepresented at every level in the corporate pipeline. Corporate America promotes men at 30 percent higher rates than women during their early career stages, and entry-level women are significantly more likely than men to have spent five or more years in the same role.
- Women negotiate for promotions and raises as often as men do but face more pushback when they do. Not surprisingly, women are almost three times more likely than men to think their gender will make it harder to get a raise, promotion, or chance to get ahead.

The NES Global Talent Survey 2015 found that 45 percent of the women who responded to the survey said that they do not get the same recognition as men [72]. It's not just a talent gap; it's a gender gap.

Studies have been long indicating that promotions come more slowly for women than men. Women have to wait much longer than men to be considered for managerial roles, and wait longer for promotions between managerial levels [73]. Not only does a woman have to convince her seniors that she is worthy of advancement, but she is often held to standards that are set higher than men [74].

Gender stereotypes can also distort performance evaluation. In one study, raters were asked to evaluate the quality of a professional paper with half of them believing that the author was male and the other half believing the author was female. Those who thought the author was female judged the paper poorer in its professional quality than those who believed the author to be male. In another study, raters attributed the good performance of a man in traditionally male tasks to intelligence, while the success of a woman on the same tasks was attributed to luck, looks, and contacts [75]. However, reactions to failure can be different. Because leadership or managerial activity is commonly perceived as masculine, their failures are attributed to their being overwhelmed by the difficulty or challenges of work. Being different can cause women to be assessed unfairly, according to stereotypical notions, rather than demonstrated skill or actual behavior. In the beginning, being different helps women to get noticed, but it can cause them to be overly or critically evaluated as their superiors consciously or unconsciously expect them to be less than competent. Such inaccurate assumptions can leave women feeling over-challenged, driving them to work twice as hard with a burning desire to exceed expectations over and over again. But, once things start going even slightly wrong, then the superiors are less forgiving and a lot more intolerant compared towards men with similar mistakes or errors of judgment. The whole problem starts with the difficulty of recognizing competence and excellence in women. That is why small imperfections, or any imperfections for that matter, become magnified. As if that is not enough, even when men and women receive evaluation of their performance at the same level, those evaluations can have different meanings on the same performance norm.

For instance, when superiors describe a woman and a man as "competent in their team," they may not necessarily mean that the woman and man are equal in abilities, but rather that a woman is competent for a woman and the man for a man. So, the man receives a challenging assignment while the woman continues to do the same job but at a higher level. In fact, more often than not, women are held to a higher standard of performance to be seen as equal to men with a different behavior set. People expect male leaders to speak assertively, challenge decisions, initiate action, take risks, and influence others. In contrast, people expect female leaders to speak tentatively, accept others' suggestions, give credit to others, support and empathize with others, and solve interpersonal problems.

To ensure fairness, the evaluation of candidates for promotion should be based on explicit, transparent performance evaluations that leaves no scope for the influence of the members of the selection committees' conscious or unconscious bias. The members of the selection committee must be held accountable for basing their evaluation on demonstrated abilities and accomplishments. In fact, if open personnel processes are employed with greater fairness, from recruitment to promotions, within the organizations, then the number of women in managerial roles will increase [76]. It is important to refine "up or out" promotion system that exists in most companies to allow people to stay in the same roles for longer periods of time, with no impact on their eventual advancement, if they need flexibility at that stage in life. Recruitment and promotion is a complex outcome of organizational practices interacting with market forces. Nonetheless, specific policies and practices that have a discriminating impact on women, such as the requirement that managers relocate to advance, can be reviewed [77].

Another conscious bias is the general tendency of people to associate with others who are similar to themselves. This leads to men's natural preference to work with other men than working with women, fill positions with individuals who are similar to them, and, other things being equal, give more favorable evaluations to juniors who are similar to themselves in race and gender [78]. However, awareness about the influence of stereotypes on their personnel decisions, and carefully monitoring them through diversity committees or affirmative action plans, will ensure fairness in the systems. In fact, there is evidence to show that such programs have been effective in increasing the number of women in management [79].

A recent study also found that scientists of both genders favorably evaluated the male applications for a lab manager position, despite all other things being equal. Even with similar qualifications, women applicants were offered a lower starting salary and less mentoring [80].

Clearly, steps need to be taken to increase women's participation and visibility in formal/informal scientific expeditions, and to increase sensitivity to invisible discrimination.

Autumn Stanley, in her masterpiece, *Mothers and Daughters of Invention* [81], lamented the share of women patent holders, which was less than one percent from 1809 to 1985 in the US. She demonstrated how many times men were given credit for the inventions of their wives. This number has increased to about 4–8 percent (by different estimates). Stanley's contention is that women do invent, but they are not recognized as inventors. Her book is an extraordinary study of women's creativity and inventiveness. And, yet, despite the fact that the author spent 13 years to write the book, and provided unassailable evidence of how women invented new technologies during the last 200 years in the US, the work has remained obscure. It would not be wrong to state that, not only has women's creativity been ignored and devalued, but even the evidence of their creativity has been ignored and devalued.

Given that managers have a tremendous impact on their employees' commitment to the team and the organization itself, managerial objectivity in performance-management activities such as performance evaluation, needs to be increased. This will go a long way in retaining talented women.

## Succession planning

Progressive companies recognize the importance of devoting time to identifying future leaders and then providing them with assignments that challenge them. They owe it to all the stakeholders to plan a smooth succession. Succession planning is a complex process that takes into consideration multiple factors.

Do women figure in such planning? One of the major challenges women face is the lack of gender consideration in succession planning, or lack of proactive consideration for major assignments. Building a diverse succession plan means looking beyond issues of race and gender. Martha Frase-Blunt [82] defines a phenomenon where executives choose successors who are similar to themselves, in age, style, industry experience, and, importantly, gender. Men who hold the majority of leadership positions are not even aware of this subconscious filtering of candidates. Women are more often perceived to be "on the bench" rather than "ready now."

Current leadership teams in organizations, who are serious about tackling this problem, need to examine existing succession plans with a focus on improving three aspects. First, through conscious inclusion. The unconscious bias of senior leaders needs to be evaluated in order to constructively address the gender imbalance. Second, effective succession management involves more than just the identification of qualified candidates. It must also include on-the-job training, coaching, mentoring, and relevant skill development around the career path of high potential people. Third, the regular monitoring of the status of the gender pipeline is important as leadership is not readily able to see the full range of talent, skills, and interest available, just as employees do not know what jobs are available or the criteria for eligibility and selection.

CEOs surveyed in McKinsey and LeanIn.org's study on leadership [83] report that, when looking to appoint successors, they typically seek individuals with high-level profit and loss experience. Further research suggests that global experience is increasingly important as a requirement to advance to higher management positions. However, organizations typically promote high-potential women into staff roles such as human resources or corporate communications, rather than as line officers responsible for profits and losses (e.g., research and development). The organizational pyramid narrows as people move up. If women are not groomed or selected for the top jobs—despite evidence of their effectiveness—they start to fall off the ladder quickly, considering that, at the higher levels of organizations, women are greatly outnumbered by men.

Succession planning is not about who will be the next CEO. It is about developing a leadership bench strength-ready and prepared to operate and engage together to address complex challenges. It is, therefore, not about a certain leader walking on a specially created path to reach the top, but about the entire ecosystem. When it comes to preparing all leaders, including competent women executives, for the filling of managerial posts, the key is in preparing women for such jobs and ensuring a better gender balance in management. In particular, organizations need to monitor and track the developmental assignments of women executives, because succession plans are almost unheard of with regard to them. No wonder, limited variety in career assignments is one explanation given for lack of advancement of women managers.

To that end, novel succession strategies can be devised. Top managers with few years of service can be requested to indicate the three most suitable persons to replace them. The first is a manager who could fill the job in an emergency. The second is the person who would require three to five years of grooming. The third must be a woman or any member of a minority. This means also employing more than one woman at a time, especially in functions where there are few or no women. The organization is then expected to give that third person the necessary environment to gain the required experience [84].

Many of the senior women managers I had interviewed stated that, typically, the obstacles increased with the management level. There were fewer measures for senior than junior managers. This is mainly because this is the first generation of women to move into senior management positions. This suggests that new approaches in dealing with the problems at this level may need to be developed. Organizations need to prepare women for board-level positions if they mean business.

Leaders must let go of the belief that men and women executives are the same and make efforts to embrace the value diversity can bring. They need to consciously work towards removing potential blind spots based on assessing people on the principle of sameness, and create a gender mix and diverse slate of candidates.

The checklist for change would then include:

- Building cultural awareness of the subconscious gender stereotypes that exist in succession planning.
- Formalize succession planning objectives and processes for leadership roles.
- Provide transparency to potential leaders on criteria, selection process, relevant experience, and attributes, for succession planning and leadership appointments.
- Identify and communicate relevant career paths and stepping stones for leadership roles.
- Undertake, and transparently communicate, career potential analysis for all female leaders.

## A Virtue of Necessity

This whole case about conscious and unconscious stereotypes is argued to emphasize the fact that decisions made about women on the basis of their gender, without considering such individual factors as background, education, experience, personality, and potential, are unlikely to do justice to their capabilities. It appears that many of the stereotypes about women are not representative of women who hold or aspire to responsible positions in industry. The assumed differences give rise to all kinds of myths, prejudices, and biases. To counter these, women must be first seen as individuals, and not as representative of the entire female gender.

In fact, women have much in common with men, with more similarities than differences. Differences do exist, but mostly in ways that would serve to increase the probability of women functioning well as managers. It is recommended that organizations begin treating women as equal, but different. This is not because of moral obligations, statutory requirements, or pressures from outside interests groups to improve the gender ratio, but because they would more effectively utilize valuable human resources.

It is virtually impossible to legislate for social change, but if we want to truly accept women in industry, then we have to recognize the constraints imposed by their upbringings and education, and offer the kind of training and advancement that will help them achieve thrust, drive, and self-confidence.

The ultimate consequence of gender stereotypes is that they may become self-fulfilling. Unfortunately, too many capable women have given up or avoided career aspirations either to be consistent with a self-concept, or to adjust to a society shaped and influenced by men.

Stereotypes are so deeply enshrined in our belief system that attempts to change something so central to us will be met by resistance. But, it is vitally important that we continually question our own assumptions and become aware of them. It might then be possible to see someone not as a man or a woman, but rather as a person, a human being, a colleague.

Social and legal interventions will eventually bring a more equitable representation of women in management and industry. Industry has much to gain from the integration of women into its ranks. Inclusion makes sound economic sense and a virtue of necessity.

The corporate sector needs to shift gears from a reactive to a proactive approach to recruiting, developing, and retaining women by examining the stereotypes that hold women back. Often, the shelf life of that enhanced awareness is short. Given pressing, short-term concerns, women's issues are not on the front burner. Most importantly, what needs to be recognized is that talent comes in both genders, and superiors have to be more sensitive in recognizing female managerial talent among their employees, and must make concerted efforts to encourage and develop this talent.

After understanding the implications and consequences of stereotypes as external barriers, women need to overcome internal barriers to their own advancement. The next chapter examines whether such barriers are present and, if present, what can be done to overcome them.

## References

1. Wirth, Linda, *Breaking Through the Glass Ceiling: Women in Management*, Geneva: ILO, 2001.
2. ILO, *Women at Work: Trends 2016*, Geneva: ILO, 2016.
3. MHRD, *All India Survey on Higher Education (2012–13)*, New Delhi: Department of Higher Education, Ministry of Human Resource Development, 2015.
4. Heilman, M. E., 'Description and Prescription: How Gender Stereotypes Prevent Women's Ascent Up the Organizational Ladder', *Journal of Social Issues* 57, no. 4 (2001): 657–74.
5. Knowles, O. S. and B. A. Moore, 'Today's Woman Executive', *Business and Public Policy Administration Student Review*, Fall (1970): 72.
6. Decety, J. and P. L. Jackson, 'The Functional Architecture of Human Empathy', *Behavioral and Cognitive Neuroscience Reviews* 3, no. 2 (2004): 71–100.
7. Brackett, M. A., S. E. Rivers, S. Shiffman, N. Lerner, and P. Salovey, 'Relating Emotional Abilities to Social Functioning: A Comparison of Self-report and Performance Measures of Emotional Intelligence', *Journal of Personality and Social Psychology* 91, no. 4 (2006): 780–95.
8. Anastasi, A., *Differential Psychology*, 3rd edition, New York, NY: Macmillan Company, 1958.
9. Finders, A., P. D. Healy, and K. Zernike, 'President of Harvard Resigns, Ending Stormy 5-year Tenure', *New York Times*, February 22, 2006, www.nytimes.com/2006/02/22/education/22harvard.html
10. Mertz, Janet E., and Jonathan M. Kane, 'Debunking Myths About Gender and Mathematics Performance', *Journal Notices of the American mathematical Society*, 59, no. 1 (2012).
11. Carli, L. L., 'Gender Issues in Workplace Groups: Effects of Gender and Communication Style on Social Influence', in *Gender and Communication at Work*, edited by M. Barrett and M. J. Davidson, 69–83, Burlington, VT: Ashgate, 2006.
12. Kaufman, J. C., 'Self Estimates of General, Crystallized, and Fluid Influences in an Ethnically Diverse Population', *Learning and Individual Differences* 22 (2012): 118–22.

13. Karwowski, M., I. Lebuda, E. Wisniewska, and J. Gralewski, 'Big Five Personality Traits as the Predictors of Creative Self-efficacy and Creative Personal Identity: Does Gender Matter?' *Journal of Creative Behavior* 47, no. 3 (2013): 215–28.
14. Correll, S. J., S. Bernard, and I. Paik, 'Getting a Job: Is There a Motherhood Penalty?' *American Journal of Sociology* 112, no. 5 (2007): 1297–338.
15. Gohain, Manash, 'Girls as Good as Boys in Maths: NCERT Survey', *Times of India*, March 18, 2016.
16. Carli, L. L., 'Assertiveness', in *Encyclopedia of Women and Gender: Sex Similarities and Differences and the Impact of Society on Gender*, edited by J. Worell, 157–68, San Diego, CA: Academic Press, 2001.
17. Hollander, J., 'Sex Differences in Sources of Social Self Esteem', *Journal of Clinical and Consulting Psychology* 38 (1972): 343–47.
18. Anka, Carl, 'Men Feel Threatened by Intelligent Women: Study', New Delhi: *Times of India*, October 21, 2015.
19. Park, L. E., A. F. Young, and P. W. Eastwick, 'Distance Make the Heart Grow Fonder: Effects of Psychological Distance and Relative Intelligence on Men's Attraction to Women', in *Personality and Social Psychology Bulletin* (2015): 1–15, Society for Personality and Social Psychology, USA (accessed on August 25, 2015).
20. Costa Jr, P. T., A. Terracciano, and R. R. McrCae, 'Gender Differences in Personality Traits Across Cultures: Robust and Surprising Findings', *Journal of Personality and Social Psychology* 81 (2001): 322–31.
21. McKinsey and Company and LeanIn.org., 'In Corporate America Women Fall Behind Early and Continue to Lose Ground with Every Step', in *Women in the Workplace*, 2016.
22. Atwood, G., *Big Girls Do Cry but Not at Work*, Society of Women Engineers: Professional Development, 2006, www.swe.org/stellent/groupswebsite/@ public/documents/webdoc/swe_000423.pdf
23. Ely, Robin J., Pamela Stone, and Colleen Ammerman, 'Rethink What You Know About High-achieving Women', *Harvard Business Review* (December 2014): 101–09.
24. McKinsey, 'What's Stalling Progress for Women at Work?' December 2016, http://www.mckinsey.com/global-themes/women-matter/whats-stalling-progress-for-women at work (accessed on June 15, 2017).
25. Babcock, Linda and Sara Laschever, *Women Don't Ask: The High Cost of Avoiding Negotiations and Positive Strategies for Change*, New York, NY: Bantam, 2007.
26. Hewlett, S. A. and R. Rashid, *Winning the War for Talent in Emerging Markets*, Boston, USA: Harvard Business Review Press, 2011.
27. Singh, Namrata, 'Women Don't Want Soft Landing After a Break', New Delhi: *Times of India*, March 8, 2016.
28. Bridges, S. and K. Mumford, 'Absenteeism in the UK: A Comparison Across Genders', *Manchester School* 69 (2001): 276–84.
29. The World Bank, *Gender Equality and Development* (World Development Report), Washington, DC: The World Bank, 2011.

30. Singh, Namrata, 'India Inc sees Gender Parity in Promotions', New Delhi: *Times of India,* August 13, 2015.
31. Catalyst, *Fact Sheet: 'Passport to Opportunity: US Women in Global Business'*, Catalyst, 2000, www.catalystwomen.org
32. Stroh, L. K., A. Varma, and S. J. Valy-Durbin, 'Why are Women Left at Home: Are they unwilling to Go on International Assignments?' *Journal of World Business* 35, no. 3 (2000): 241–55.
33. Hewlett and Rashid, *Winning the War for Talent in Emerging Markets*, Boston, USA.
34. Schein, V. E., 'A Global Look at Psychological Barriers to Women's Progress in Management', *Journal of Social Issues* 57 (2001): 675–78.
35. Atwater, L. E., J. F. Brett, D. Waldman, L. Di Mare, and M. V. Hayden, 'Men and Women's Perception of Gender Typing of Managerial Sub Roles', *Sex Roles* 50 (2004): 191–99.
36. Rampell, Catherine, 'The Gender Wage Gap, Around the World', *New York Times*, March 9, 2010, http://economix.blogs.nytimes.com/2010/03/09/the-gender-wage-gap-around-the world/?_r=0
37. Crites, Stephanie N., Kevin E. Dickson, and Alicia Lorenz, 'Nurturing Gender Stereotypes in the Face of Experience: A Study of Leader, Gender, Leadership Style, and Satisfaction', *Journal of Organizational Culture, Communications and Conflict* 19, no. 1 (2015): 1–23.
38. *Economic Times*, 'Americans Have More Trust in Obama Than Clinton, McCain'**,** February 24, 2008, http://economictimes.indiatimes.com/americans-have-more-trust-in-obama-than-clinton-mccain/articleshow/2809177.cms (accessed on June 21, 2017).
39. Zenger, J. and J. Folkman, 'Are Women Better Leaders than Men?' *Harvard Business Review*, March 15, 2012, https://hbr.org/2012/03/a-study-in-leadership-women-do
40. Catalyst, *Women in US Corporate Leadership: Progress and Prospects*, New York, NY: Catalyst, 2003.
41. Hewlett, S. A. and R. Rashid, *Center for Work–Life Policy*.
42. Devillard, Sandrine, Sandra Sancier-Sultan, and Charlotte Werner, 'Why Gender Diversity at the Top Remains a Challenge', *McKinsey Global Survey*, 2013, http://www.mckinsey.com/business-functions/organization/our-insights/why-gender-diversity-at-the-top-remains-a-challengessed (accessed on October 18, 2016).
43. Lagerberg, F., 'Women in Business: The Path to Leadership', *The Grant Thornton International Report*, March 5, 2015, https://www.grantthornton.global/en/insights/articles/women-in-business-2015 (accessed on March 8, 2017).
44. Helfat, C., D. Harris, and P. Wolfson, 'The Pipeline to the Top: Women and Men in Top Executive Ranks of U.S. Corporations', *Academy of Management Perspectives* 20 (2007): 42–64.
45. Blau, F. D. and L. M. Kahn, 'The Gender Pay Gap: Have Women Gone as Far as They Can?' *Academy of Management Perspectives* 21 (2007): 7–23.

46. Kochan, T. A., 'Social Legitimacy of the HRM Profession: A US Perspective', in *The Oxford Book of HR Management*, edited by P. Boxall, J. Purcell, and P. Wright, 599–621, Oxford: Oxford University Press, 2007.
47. Welle, B. and M. E. Heilman, 'Formal and Informal Discrimination Against Women at Work: The Role of Gender Stereotypes', in *Research in Social Issues in Management*, edited by D. Steiner, S. W. Gilliland, and D. Starliki, 23–40, Westport, CT: Information Age Publishers, 2005.
48. Heilman, M. E., A. S. Wallen, D. Fuchs, and M. M. Tamkins, 'Penalties for Success: Reactions to Women Who Succeed at Male Gender-typed Tasks', *Journal of Applied Psychology* 89 (2004): 416–27.
49. Press Trust of India. 'Bias at Work: Men Preferred over Women in Hiring', June 27, 2017, http://economictimes.indiatimes.com/jobs/bias-still-at-work-men-preferred-over-women-in-hiring-survey/articleshow/59335538.cms (accessed on July 20, 2017).
50. Korn, Melissa, 'Choice of Work Partner Splits along Gender Lines', *Wall Street Journal*, June 2012, http://online.wsj.com/article/SB10001424052702303506 404577448652549105934.html
51. Wing, Jeannette (corporate vice-president, Microsoft Research), 'The Talent Pool of Women in IT is Fairly Small', New Delhi, *Economic Times*, February 9, 2016.
52. EY, *Worldwide Index of Women as Public Sector Leaders*, www.ey.com/government/womenleaders
53. Nash, Harvey, 'CIO's View of the IT Tasks Where Women in IT Have Most Positive Effects', *CIO Survey 2012*, http://media.harveynash.com/usa/mediacenter/2012_US_CIO_Survey.pdf
54. Times News Network, 'Hinduja Global Solutions', *Times of India*, March 16, 2016.
55. CII, *Understanding the Level of Women Empowerment in Workplace, CII Survey*, New Delhi: CII, 2005.
56. Pricewater House Coopers, *The Leaking Pipeline: Where are Our Female Leaders?* The report by Global Human Capital, Gender Advisory Council, Pricewater House Coopers, March 2008.
57. Dipboye, R. L., *The Survey of Business*, USA: The Centre of Business and Economic Research, College of Business Administration, University of Tennessee, 1975.
58. Catalyst, *Catalyst First Step India Overview Report 2013*, www.catalyst.org/system/files/india_firststep_final_1.pdf6 (accessed in December 2016).
59. Khambatta, P., *India's Economy: The Other Half*, Washington, DC, USA: Center for Strategic and International Studies.
60. Stone, P. and M. Lovejoy, 'Fast Track Women and the Choice to Stay Home', *Annals of the American Academy of Political and Social Science* 596 (2004): 62–83.
61. Heilman, M. E., 'Sex Stereotypes and Their Effects in the Workplace: What We Know and What We Don't Know', *Journal of Social Behavior and Personality* 10 (1995): 5–26.

62. Lyness, K. S. and D. E. Thompson, 'Above the Glass Ceiling? A Comparison of Matched Samples of Female and Male Executives', *Journal of Applied Psychology* 82, no. 3 (1997): 359–75.
63. ———, 'Climbing the Corporate Ladder: Do Female and Male Executives Follow the Same Route?' *Journal of Applied Psychology* 85, no. 1 (2000): 86–101.
64. Pomeroy, A., 'Peak Performance: Tough Choices, Mentors and Broad Experience are Critical for Women Who Hope to Climb the HR Executive Ranks', *HR Magazine* 52, no. 4 (2007): 1–2.
65. Lyness, K. S. and M. E. Heilman, 'When Fit is Fundamental: Performance Evaluations and Promotions of Upper-level Female and Male Managers', *Journal of Applied Psychology* 91, no. 4 (2006): 777–85.
66. Desvaux, G., S. Devillard, and S. S. Sultan, *Women Matter* series, Paris, France: McKinsey and Company, 2010.
67. Barsh, J., S. Devillard, and J. Wang, 'The Global Gender Agenda', available at: McKinsey and Company website, 2012, www.mckinseyquarterly.com/The_global_gender_agenda_3027
68. UNESCO, *World Science Report 1996*, Paris: UNESCO, 1996.
69. Sur, Abha, *Dispersed Radiance: Caste, Gender and Modern Science in India,* New Delhi: Navayana Publishing, 2011. Cited from *The Hindu*, October 18, 2011.
70. Nemilov, Anton (Russian scientist), quoted in 'Sacred Space', *Times of India*, April 25, 2005.
71. 'Women in the Workplace' 2016. http://www.mckinsey.com/business-functions/organization/our-insights/women-in-the-workplace-2016 (accessed on June 16, 2017).
72. *NES Global Talent Survey*. 'Attracting and Retaining Women in Oil and Gas: A Survey Examining the Gender Talent Gap', 2015, https://www.nesglobaltalent.com/sites/default/files/images/women-in-engineering-report-single_final.pdf (accessed on June 16, 2017).
73. Smith, R. A., 'Race, Gender and Authority in the Workplace: Theory and Research', *Annual Review of Sociology* no. 28 (2002): 509–42.
74. Waller, Nikki, 'How Men and Women See the Workplace Differently', September 2016, http://graphics.wsj.com/how-men-and-women-see-the-workplace-differently/
75. Nieva, V. F. and B. A. Gutek, 'Sex Effects on Evaluation'. *Academy of Management Reviews* 5 (1980): 267–76.
76. Gelfand, M. J., J. L. Raver, L. H. Nishii, and B. Schneider, 'Discrimination in Organizations: An Organizational Level System's Perspective', In *Discrimination at Work: The Psychological and Organizational Bases*, edited by R. L. Dipboye and A. Colelia, 89–116, Mahwah, NJ: Erlbaum, 2005.
77. Eagly, Alice H. and Linda L. Carly, *Through the Labyrinth: The Truth About How Women Became Leaders*, Boston, MA: HBS Press, 2007.
78. Elliot, J. R. and R. A. Smith, 'Race, Gender, and Workplace Power', *American Sociological Review* 69, no. 3 (2004): 365–86.

79. Kalev, A., F. Dobbin, and E. Kelly, 'Best Practices or Best Guesses? Assessing the Efficacy of Corporate Affirmative Action and Diversity Policies', *American Sociological Review* 71, no. 4 (2006): 589–617.
80. Corinne, A., Moss-Racusin, John F. Dovido, Victoria L. Brescott, Mark J. Graham, and Jo Handelsman, 'Science Faculty's Subtle Gender Biases Favor Male Students', *Proceedings of the National Academy of Sciences of the United States of America* 109, no. 41 (2012): 16474–79.
81. Stanley, Autumn, *Mothers and Daughters of Invention*, xx–xxi, New Brunswick, NJ: Rutgers University Press, 1995.
82. Frase-Blunt, Martha, 'Moving Past Mini-Me: Building a Diverse Succession Plan Means Looking Beyond Issues of Race and Gender', *HR Magazine* 48, no. 11 (2003), https://www.shrm.org/hr-today/news/hr-magazine/pages/1103blunt.aspx (accessed on June 16, 2017).
83. McKinsey and Company and LeanIn.org, 'Women in the Workplace', 2016, a study based on 'Women in the Workplace 2015 Report' and the seminar on 'Research conducted by McKinsey in 2015, http://www.mckinsey.com/business-functions/organization/our-insights/women-in-the-workplace-2016 (accessed on June 16, 2017).
84. Meyerson, D. E. and J. K. Fletcher, 'A Modest Manifesto for Shattering the Glass Ceiling', *Harvard Business Review* 78, no. 1 (2000): 129, https://hbr.org/2000/01/a-modest-manifesto-for-shattering-the-glass-ceiling (accessed on June 6, 2017).

# 3
# The Tyranny of Invisible Barriers

Do women executives harbor fears of holding positions of power and authority? I was provoked to contemplate this theme by one of the participants of a program on "Women in Leadership." The echoes of what she said were heard time and again in a wide-ranging series of interviews with women executives and freewheeling discussions during women's conventions. On the one hand, women agree that there is a need for them to take on stretch roles and assignments that will help them get noticed. On the other hand, women will over-analyze the challenge and shrink away from the work for fear of failure or the extra strain it will put on their home life; whereas men will put their hands up and be prepared to "learn by doing." Unless challenging opportunities are not sought to prove one's competence, how can you be entrusted with important clients and high-level roles?

This dichotomy made me wonder whether women managers—at least some of them—really want to succeed, as they often complain they cannot due to various organizational factors. Or do they, in fact, harbor the fear of holding power and authority deep within them, simply because it will challenge the current power structures in organizations. Some competent young women fear success because they believe it will cost them socially. Others claim that actually the major force holding women back from success and achievement is their wish to be taken care of.

While I was grappling with this strange observation, I happened to come across an article in *Fortune* (2003) that featured the 50 most powerful women in business. The writer of the article also wondered whether women really want power. "Many fast-track women are surprisingly ambivalent about what's next. Dozens of powerful women we interviewed tell us that they don't want to be Carly Fiorina... many don't want to run a huge company" [1].

I do not know whether this dilemma prompts them to choose "prevention" strategies—avoiding failure—rather than "promotion" strategies—actively driving success. "Prevention strategies derive from an internalized self of what one ought to do and focus on responsibilities, safety and security while promotion strategies derive from what one would ideally like to do and focus on aspirations, advancement and accomplishments" [2].

A need for power, which is associated with leadership, is equally strong in men and women. Research shows that men and women have different perceptions of power. Men think about power as more competitive and hierarchical, while women think of it as more cooperative and interdependent [3]. No wonder, women get placed in people-handling staff functions such as personnel where their emotional fine-tuning, according to the prevailing stereotype, is more appropriate that in decision-making functions. They also get excluded from the centers of power in management for the same reason. Powerlessness can also come from not being in the know or in the functions that are close to the problem-solving, change-creating actions that the organization is currently engaged in. However, women's perception of power as an instrument of public purpose rather than as a tool for personal ambition could produce radical changes in organizations that currently support a hierarchical notion of power over others.

New research suggests that women are not in leadership positions, among other things, because they do not want the jobs as much as men do. Shocking as it may seem, the paper published in the proceedings of the National Academy of Sciences incorporates nine studies conducted on various high-achieving groups. Combined, the research indicates and explains the phenomenon of women valuing power less than men. In one of the studies conducted on 650 recent MBA graduates, researchers had participants rank their current position in the industry, their ideal position, and the highest position they could realistically attain. Women had no doubt that they could realistically attain the same level of success as men, but they ranked their ideal position lower. Another study explains that finding by suggesting that women have more negative associations with power than men do According to Alison Wood Brooks, a co-author of the paper and assistant professor of business administration at Harvard, this is because women expect more stress, burdens, conflicts, and difficult trade-offs to go with high-level positions. Powerful positions stress women out because they have less time in which to attain a greater number of goals. In another of the nine studies, researchers asked about 800 working adults to rank their goals "defined as things that occupy your thoughts on a routine basis or things that motivate your behavior and decisions." The women participants of the study not only listed more number of goals but a smaller proportion of goals was related to achieving power. Clearly, women have more goals in life because they are balancing career and family simultaneously [4].

By and large, women in management fall into three categories. A small proportion of women are extremely career-focused. They are willing to make all adjustments to do well in their careers. At the other end of the spectrum, there is another small group of women that is family focused. But the vast majority that lies in between would like to combine career and family. It is this group which is ambivalent towards their career. It is this group that would like to have answers to their frequently asked questions, such as:

- Is it possible to be a woman and a manager without falling into a male stereotype?
- Is it possible to be competitive and ambitious without compromising with a woman's identity and self-image?
- Is it possible to move out of the female stereotype and be seen in a new light?

It becomes possible to risk such questioning during management development programs for women executives. These programs also provide the participants a chance to step aside from their day-to-day preoccupation and consider what they are doing from a different, perhaps more objective, position.

In fact, over the years, my experience has been that women-only programs, if well designed and executed, can provide many benefits. They may play a key role in building leadership skills and provide opportunities to learn from the experience of others who are qualified to provide support and validation. Just as women can benefit from single-identity programs [5] in the initial years of their career, they need to seek opportunities to be with their male counterparts in later years. Both are equally valuable for leadership development.

To that end, I always felt a need to present a balanced program, which avoids igniting a gender war. A program for women managers can potentially attract participants who have axes to grind. Unless handled carefully, the program can be utilized as an opportunity to further polarizing attitudes and risk antagonism towards men. For example, the assertiveness training could be interpreted as "how to assert yourself over men," and the session on networking could develop into "how to develop your anti–male wing." This is a scenario with little merit.

During one such program, I became aware that the internal barriers to women's equality and success are more inhibiting than the external ones.

In terms of career progression, women often talk about encountering "locked doors" or "the glass ceilings." But these locked doors exist as much inside oneself as outside. The external locked doors or the external barriers often get talked about and discussed, because, in this scenario, the responsibility rests with the other: the system or the social structure. In contrast, the internal barriers, the self-imposed barriers in terms of low self-esteem, erroneous assumptions, stereotypes about men and women, lack of confidence, realistic self-appraisal and assertiveness are more difficult to recognize and, therefore, more difficult to tackle. To make matters worse, many women also internalize these stereotypes and reinforce them, which creates a psychological (self-imposed) glass ceiling; this was true not only for women in lower positions with basic education but also for privileged, highly educated, and supposedly powerful women. Many a times, I have met competent and intelligent women managers who, unfortunately, do not *think* they are competent and intelligent. It is one of the oldest barriers in that it starts very early in life. It was as if the female potential was discounted, neglected, and restricted for so long that it stayed that way, even when the barriers were gone. Even cross-cultural studies have shown that no evidence of sex differences was found in achievement motivation, risk-taking, task-persistence, or other related skills. Then why do women managers find it difficult to value their own experience?

This viewpoint has been gradually crystallizing after my discussions with the participants of a number of programs I conducted on "Women in Leadership" over the past few years. I have been struck by what I found in these programs in response to the exercises I conducted. Many exercises examine stereotypes and assumptions about role-taking behavior.

For instance, given the opportunity to complete a sentence like "When Anita found out that she was selected as the head of the department, she…," a high proportion of women conclude with self-doubt, uncertainty about achievement, fear of isolation, rejection from peers, and negative endings of career interruptions. Few express surprise over success and being chosen as a head. "Will I be able to meet the expectations of my superiors?" is also an often-raised question. But underneath the surprise, there are self-doubts, confusion, and unarticulated tension. In one group, however, one young woman endorsed goals such as becoming an authority in one's field, obtaining recognition from colleagues, having administrative responsibilities, and being better off financially. Her response was met with raised eyebrows and rolling of eyes because she was departing from her stereotype.

During the group discussion that followed this exercise, one participant who was the head of the finance department of her company, addressed the problems of women combining career and family, yet never suggested that men could also play an equally important role at home. Indeed, she implied that she had been able to have a successful career because she *did not* have any children.

Another self-styled manager spelt out her recipe for success. She pointed out that, since there is this great heritage of male superiority and male dominance in industry and business, it would pay to keep the male bosses pleased in order to exist peacefully in that system. Because women are in a minority in senior management positions, particularly in large corporations, they need to lead in much the same way as their male counterparts. I was surprised to note how at the root of this unproductive thinking is the stereotypical mindset that man is superior in a corporate set up while a woman is his subordinate/inferior. God forbid if this becomes a corporate culture; then the organization can witness a high turnover of women, as was seen in case of a telecommunications company.

## Will She Fit in? Challenges of Fitting in the Organizational Culture

Three years ago, I was invited to meet a woman director of the telecommunications company. She expressed deep concern over the high attrition of women in the company. She told me that, being one of the only senior women on the board, she was entrusted with the task of finding a solution. She was not interested in exploring the issue from all angles and did not seem interested in any kind of a dialogue. Throughout the meeting she kept interrupting me. I thought that perhaps she was hard-pressed for time that day. An exploratory meeting was fixed with all the women employees the following week. The director had instructed a junior team member to coordinate the time and logistics, etc., with me.

Lo and behold! The junior team member exhibited the same kind of behavior as her boss—impatience, poor listening, and a closed mindset—telling me what to do, rather than asking what I would like to do. I wondered whether these women were exhibiting the control-command style of the company culture. The junior woman had perhaps learnt it from her female boss and the senior woman had learnt it from her male boss—the CEO—to whom she reported. My hunch was adequately tested in the large group meeting the following week. Two or three senior women dominated most of the meeting. Younger women were extremely hesitant to participate and speak. When I drew them out and they finally began to share their experiences, they were rudely interrupted by the senior women before they could even identify the problem. I could clearly see that the younger women were very uncomfortable. Exclusion, of course, can take many forms. It can also come from accepting boundaries without question.

Then, the seniormost woman said, "The HR is obviously not managing it well. The exit interviews show that women are leaving for personal or family reasons. The high rate of attrition can always be addressed by recruiting large number of women." That was her solution. So it was not the company or its the culture, it was the *women*. I was witnessing the traditional command-and-control model of leadership. The director did not get the complexity of the issue and had no time for exploration or explanation. No wonder, with this kind of a closed mindset, the women who worked for this company were either teetering on the edge (thinking about quitting, looking for a new job, trying to figure out whether there is less bias elsewhere) or actually exercising the only option they had: to leave.

It was then that I decided to confront her directly.

> Even if you recruit women in large numbers, the exodus may still continue if we do not look deep into the problem. What about the losses the company would incur in losing talented women? It would never get return on the investment made in recruiting and training women. Further, the invaluable company experience that developing executives acquire at every level as they move up through management ranks will be lost. It also takes an emotional toll on those who are left behind. The problem lies elsewhere and we must be open enough to look at it squarely.

That was the turning point.

It was also the beginning of understanding how women can sometimes be their own enemies without realizing it. In their efforts to fit into the prevailing culture, they were leading the younger women "to deny their authenticity." Women who work in highly macho "alpha male" environments lead by emulating the behaviors and values of their male colleagues in order to fit into the existing organizational culture and norms. But, in the process, they could do a disservice to their women colleagues by becoming more like men, by tuning off their empathy and interpersonal skills. Having said that, it is beyond doubt that women do face challenges when they initially break into male-dominated roles. They are in the minority, so they are forced into stereotypical categories defined by the dominant group, i.e., men. But, when successful, they can create a fair, level playing field for the women who follow in their footsteps. But before that they need to treat their career as progression and not as an accident.

## Career by Chance

The socialization and conditioning of our society still demands that, from early childhood, boys are brought up to be independent and expect to support themselves and their families. A girl is brought up with a hope that, in due course, someone will support her and look after her. She is, therefore, more likely to drift into a job and only become career-minded when at the age of 30–35 she realizes that she may have to work for the rest of her life. As a result of the attitude instilled in her by her traditional upbringing at home, school or university, a career is treated as "accidental" or even attributed to coincidence or luck. She sees her job as evolving step by step rather than as a career with a finite ultimate goal, whereas men visualize career as progression, a path leading upward to advancement, recognition, and reward. Consequently, women often don't make the grade. Although they are capable enough, they frequently lack self-confidence and drive. It would be a good idea, therefore, to set one's priorities right before any woman embarks on a career. She may find the going hard, harder than her male colleagues. She may well have to fight on several fronts: lack of self-confidence, male prejudice, and a highly competitive working environment. Unless she can face these and fight her way through, she will have little chance of success and each failure will only reinforce the stereotype.

There is a generational issue at play. The first generation of women who went to work did not have 'careers'. The last generation does. We now have a new cohort of women who need to be encouraged to talk more openly about their careers and use the toolkit of measures that are needed to cope with the work–life balance more effectively.

## Career as a series of stepping stones, *not* a linear trajectory

There's an implicit view that careers are still linear. Women wait until they are unhappy, look around for opportunities that seem better than their current job, apply for a few, cross their fingers, and take the best option that they can get. Then, they toil away until they are unhappy again, and the cycle is repeated. Most people end up with a career path of somewhat arbitrary events that, at best, is a gradually improving wandering path, and, at worst, just a series of unfulfilling jobs.

The solution to this dismal cycle? Let go of the idea that careers are linear. These days, they are much more like a field of stepping stones that extends in all directions. Each stone is a job or project that is available to you, and you can move in any direction that you like. The trick is simply to move to stones that take you closer and closer to what is meaningful to you. There is no single path, but, rather, an infinite number of options that lead to the sweet spot of fulfillment.

There has been a gradual transformation in this mindset in recent years. Many men have daughters and wives with talent and ambition who win their fathers' or husbands' support furthering their career aspirations. However, these shifts are being witnessed much more in the context of younger, educated urban women. However, as the social structure begins to change due to the increasing impact of economy, ecology, and technology, there will be changes in the roles of men and women which, in turn, will bring about changes in their psychology.

## Lack of proactive career management

Women—even high-performing women—still have miles to go in becoming intentional and specific in their efforts to manage their careers. They lack the critical experiences or skills required to take the next step, such as an international assignment, high-risk project, or major P&L responsibility. While many complex factors contribute to women hitting the glass ceiling, more proactive career management would help them identify and use the right tools to break through. Because women won't be handed the experience they need, they must speak up. Many women feel uncomfortable with the self-promotion of "asking for a job." Some find it easier to think of such conversations as expressing interest in or speaking up about new ways to be helpful. Regardless of the approach, women need to speak up. You don't want management to pass you over because they thought your silence meant satisfaction with the status quo. In a dual-career family, things become even more challenging, because marriage and parenthood place different demands on women than men. Considering that most women are caught up in day-to-day management of their lives due to dual responsibilities, they do not think about where they would be in five, 10, or 20 years. Of course, one has to answer more immediate questions about what one wants in the current job or the next, but perhaps it would be useful to do so in the context of longer, larger career goals.

However, there is hope that, as changes in the economy and post-industrial societies continue to erode traditional family roles, a new equilibrium may gradually emerge in which men and women will be very similar to one another in their approach and commitment to family and career.

For that to happen, women need to review and change old performance scripts and begin writing new ones. It is hard and time-consuming when a lifetime is devoted to performing a role based on a script written by someone else. I wonder whether it has anything to do with the process of socialization and conditioning women are subjected to in their childhood that almost trains them to deny issues of self-esteem and self-worth. Expectations based on gender also influence how women leaders think about themselves.

In one study, 98 percent of female executives chose from a long list of leadership qualities, the terms collaborative, flexible, inclusive, and participative to describe themselves. In contrast, only smaller percentages of these women also described themselves as assertive, decisive, and strong [6]. Why are women leaders expected to be collaborative and participative all the time? Because women carry the burden of negotiating two roles: a woman and a leader. So women leaders have to manage the delicate balance of retaining warmth and friendliness with the agentic qualities that people think leaders need to demonstrate in order to succeed. Most women carry a mental script written by early psychological conditioning that reads something like this:

> As a girl you must not be too ambitious, you must work hard and not make any waves (translated, it means "Do not take any risk."). You must not ask anything for yourself and fulfill others' expectations and cater to their needs. You must quickly come to terms with reality and adjust to it as soon as possible.

This brings us to the next question.

## Is "Ambition" a Bad Word?

Do women lack ambition? Does their socialization allow them to nurse and nurture ambition? Why is it that men are born with a fire in the belly (or so it seems), while women need something to get their lights lit? For men, ambition is considered a desirable part of grown-up life. In case of women, however, ambition is associated with egotism, self-promotion, manipulation or plain aggression. What are its implications for role-taking behavior? Is it socially sanctioned or condoned? Clearly, unless and until the needs of all the family members—husband, children, elderly parents, and others—are satisfied, the very right to have aspirations or ambitions would be questioned. Women still tend to shoulder the majority of domestic pressure. They run up against the reality of "the second shift" identified by Arlie Russell Hochschild [7]. When this is combined with the need to be able to travel, to work in different time zones, and to do what it takes to become successful, then women start to consider just what price they have to pay for their ambitions. Is it worth the effort?

No wonder, men and women express ambition differently. Women start out ambitious. Most young women, like young men, want to make it big. Those who reach senior levels retain that ambition [8]. But there are also those who turn down advancement opportunities for various reasons: reluctance to ask for positions that demand new skills or desire to continue with those that provide personal meaning. In fact, mothers with children desire more stability and a greater need to stay put.

I decided to take a two-year sabbatical after the birth of my son as I was unwilling to leave him with a nanny. At the same time, I could not see myself only dedicated to child-caring and -rearing, so I registered for the doctoral program and planned to catch up on my reading. Back in the office, it was interpreted that, despite excellent prospects and a chance of career progression, I was not ready to strive and was sidelining my work to raise a kid. To become a full-time mom for two whole years? What happened to her ambition, wondered my seniors and peers. But, being out in the world and doing well at work became less important to me at that point of time. Earlier, I used to worry about this assignment or that and whether it will succeed in leaving an impact on the organization. But, now I wanted to succeed at managing my family, raising and launching my children, helping my husband, and concentrating on my research. I was still ambitious but for the most enduring goals of my life, for which I was willing to put aside my near-term goals to ensure the long-term success of my lineage.

Are the roots of ambition in family, culture, gender or genes? Two of the biggest influences on your level of ambition are the family that produced you and the culture that produced your family. Men and women, therefore, differ in their appetite for competition.

But behavioral experts say that women are more selective about what they want, and at what cost. They are certainly not willing to engage in competition at any cost. If they do, they're competing for the most enduring stakes of all.

Look at the socialization that begins early for all the girls. It is no secret that girls receive less attention, less encouragement, and, therefore, less approval and recognition for their achievements than boys do, in families as well as at school. But, multiple areas of research have demonstrated that recognition is one of the motivational engines that drives the development of almost any type of skill. Mastery of any special skill and recognition by an appreciative audience go together. It is one of the most fundamental requirements for human growth and development. So girls crave recognition, yet shy away from it when given, so as not to ruffle any feathers. This double-bind can be confusing, stressful, and painful for most.

A rare longitudinal study by the renowned psychologist, Jerome Kagan, looked specifically at the relationship between mastery of skill and recognition, through acquisition of specific goals or behavior [9]. According to Kagan and Moss, "it may be impossible to measure the 'desire to improve a skill' independent of the individual's desire for recognition." Clearly then, ambitions are both the product of *and* the source of recognition. Ambition is an expensive impulse, one that requires an enormous investment of emotional capital. Like any investment, it can pay off in countless ways. The trick, as any good speculator will tell you, is recognizing the riches when they come your way.

There is no evidence that the desires to acquire skills or to receive affirmation for accomplishments are less present in women than men. Then, why is it that we find such dramatic differences between men and women in their attitudes toward ambition and how they realize it?

Women's innate modesty, this fear of success and achievement, and the early training in subordinating their needs to those of others—particularly men—is associated with societal ideals of femininity. It is so deeply rooted that it is largely unconscious and becomes tenacious part of the self. Research concludes that recognition, mastery, and ambition are interdependent, and are each critical to women's leadership development. So, women do not lack ambition, but rather, lack the resources necessary for success.

In this context, what can they expect from the social rewards? By and large, they are less frequent, more ambiguous, perhaps subtly discouraging and even less predictable! It gets worse. Often, the news of achievements is met with a response that is invariably designed to make them feel guilty. "All this achievement is very well. But what did you do with your six-year-old son when you were busy with that project or travelling?" These questions are never asked about men with families. This externally imposed guilt or self-doubt is detrimental to achieving a long-term goal. In order to master a skill, complete a course or finish a doctoral degree that requires prolonged effort, you must believe that you can succeed. However, because of the constant expectations of society to conform to the gender role and the routine underestimation of their own abilities by themselves, women tend to abandon their early ambitions. Even if they persist, they pursue them half-heartedly and often wonder whether the efforts justify the rewards. The corporate sector would do well do provide alternative ways for men and women to achieve and fulfill their ambitions.

## Living up to expectations

After floating along in an employment situation for several years, more for retaining the job than actively investing into a career, when women are about to reach a career goal which requires negotiation, trade-off, and redefining the scope of work, they hit another barrier.

The tacit expectation is that women in the workplace are not supposed to demand what they want and negotiate for what they deserve. Research has shown that both conscious and subconscious biases contribute to this problem. But this is also compounded by the fact that women often don't get what they want (the right kind of compensation, promotions, perks) because they don't ask for it or, rather, don't know how to ask for it. It seems the whole process of negotiation itself is endangered. Negotiation is especially tricky for women because some behaviors that work for men, like self-promotion and assertiveness, may backfire on women [10]. At every level of academic achievement, women's median earnings are less than men's median earnings. In some cases, the gender pay gap is larger at higher levels of education [11]. Even though a pay gap exists in nearly every occupational field, jobs traditionally associated with men tend to pay better than traditionally female-dominated jobs that require the same level of skill [12, 13].

This is because most women simply accept the employer's initial salary offer. Women do not realize that lack of willingness to negotiate, or the lack of ability to negotiate, can have a telling impact on the gender pay gap. In addition, the kinds of jobs pursued early in a career set the stage for an entire career of earnings. Since benefits and subsequent raises are generally based on initial wages, a lower starting salary could mean a lifetime of lower compensation and smaller retirement benefits. Observing this unequal treatment, women get disillusioned with their employers and languish or quit when a better offer comes along. They do not realize that this offer, in fact, can be used as a negotiating tool as men would do in the same organization.

Two of the biggest influences on one's level of competition or the ability to negotiate are the family environment and the larger cultural environment to which the family belongs. There are no hard and fast rules for the kinds of families that turn out to be the highest negotiators. Whether because of heredity or environment, there seems to be a dislike for hard bargaining or negotiation among women and a marked preference among men. Traditionally, it has been socially expected (and, therefore, accepted) for men to negotiate for raises, because negotiating conforms to the stereotype of men as assertive.

Similarly, the situations for which women would like to negotiate could be different from men in certain phases of their lives. It is entirely possible that mothers who appear to be unwilling to strive and are willing to quit the workplace altogether, may want to succeed in managing their family and in successfully launching their children into the world. They are ambitious all right, they might even want to negotiate hard, but perhaps in a different aspect of their lives.

It is, therefore, important that, as equal-opportunity employers, we confront this problem properly. At the individual level, seniors can instill confidence, encourage some risk-taking, be accepting of failure, and expand the areas in which they are likely to succeed. They can mentor the women they supervise, and advise them on the necessity of asking for resources they would need to do their jobs effectively and fulfill their professional goals. Seniors also need to ensure that young women understand how many aspects of their working lives can be negotiated. This can adequately compensate for women's limited access to many of the professional and social networks in which men learn these lessons.

There is an inherent difference between the way men and women ask for advantages and opportunities. For instance, men often ask for special assignments or openly talk about what they want to do. An equally qualified woman may be just as interested or motivated but may not openly ask for it. A good manager would want to pay attention to these personality differences.

Similarly, when a man asks for a raise and a woman doing a comparable job does not, a good senior should consider giving it to both or neither of them. That way he will prevent the woman from becoming disillusioned if she later discovers a pay difference. It is important to recognize that many women have a less assertive style than men—as assertiveness in women might be considered overbearing or pushy—and, therefore, they should not be left out because of it. By creating a workplace in which different responses are examined openly, sensitive seniors can open eyes to hidden barriers that block men and women from asking and receiving equally.

Similarly, women as young girls are never encouraged to inspect, scrutinize, question, and test external reality as it affects them; because this questioning or testing of reality stems from personal authority in which no investment is made in case of a girl child. On the other hand, testing reality, as Miller [14] points out, is the language of creativity. It is a more dangerous activity, but it is only in being agentic and creative that the individual—man or woman—discovers the self, or what can be called the "human identity" that goes beyond the bio-social confines of gender.

## The same old story

In the final analysis, therefore, the manifest issues of role stress, role conflict, exercising of authority actually hide the real issues of self-esteem and self-empowerment. Thus, the emergence of workshops on assertiveness training indicates how women could be resocialized to compete on an equal basis with men, than merely focus on women as victims.

While conducting one exercise called "Mentoring Sunil" and "Mentoring Sujata," that makes subtle, negative stereotypes and unproductive expectations apparent to the participants, the class is divided into two small work groups, and given the following scenario:

> Sujata, a 24-year-old college graduate and a person possessing a specific set of attributes, joins the company. One group is asked to describe how they would mentor her! The other group is given a similar story but the new entrant is Sunil. They are asked how they would mentor him.

After the discussion, the groups compare notes. Much to everybody's surprise, mentoring Sujata is different from mentoring Sunil.

The assumption is that Sunil is going to go further. He is told to go to the best business schools when possible, invest in his career in good time, and seek opportunities to get good, high-impact assignments. In the process, he is expected to speak assertively, compete for attention, initiate new activity, and influence others. Sujata may go into a staff position rather than a line-management position. She is expected not to draw attention to herself, support others, solve interpersonal problems, and try not to take credit for her accomplishments. Sujata is told: "Be prepared for a long marathon. It is going to be very demanding. Make sure you are well prepared. What about kids? Have you thought about them?" Sunil is advised to take risks, given postings where he is *visible*, while Sujata is asked to work hard and make efforts to adjust quickly to the work routine and the system in general. Sunil is asked to learn to play golf or whichever game is popular with the top management as a corporate game and to get to know the bosses well. Sujata is asked to fulfill superiors' expectations and learn not to be emotional while dealing with crisis at work. She is told that she would be watched all the time, as a result, even small mistakes would not be ignored. She will have to work hard to receive recognition for any individual achievement. To avoid these pressures, she might just want to become *invisible*. There are variations to these themes, but they are few and far between. While this mentoring may be helpful to certain women, it continues to place the responsibility for adaptation, change, and improvement on women alone, without questioning the values and cultural issues inherent in organizations.

It is interesting to note that, on the one hand, women managers complain about their lop-sided socialization and, on the other, they continue to socialize their juniors in the very same fashion, without even realizing what they are doing. Is it not astonishing? I have seen this happening in group after group at home, abroad, in groups from SAARC countries and in groups from developed nations with an international mix. Contrary to popular belief, lack of career planning and job discriminations in case of women are equally prevalent in Western countries despite the industrial progress.

There may be some culture-specific differences, but they are minor and peripheral. The similarities are striking and often disturbing. Women managers seem to be going around in a circle where the beginning and the end is one and the same. The point is, we need a break in the pattern and a new beginning or maybe several breaks followed by several new beginnings.

It is, therefore, important to recognize the implications of stereotypes to overcome them. The effects of below-the-surface, unconscious activation of gender stereotypes are far more difficult to deal with. Activation of gender stereotypes can be self-fulfilling by diminishing women's interest in leadership roles and even undermining their performance as competent managers.

## The Tightrope Circus

Having overcome *invisible* barriers with sheer grit and determination when women actually get down to starting a family and also scaling corporate ladders, they also hit *visible* institutional barriers. Why has the age-old business of having children become so difficult for high-achieving business women today?

This can only change if young men are taught to ask the same question young women do: "How can I combine career and family?" The backlash of feminism has been that we have convinced ourselves and others that "women can do what men can do. Give them a chance." Now, we have to once again convince ourselves and others that men can do what women can do. If we don't, then the double burden of working inside and outside the home—always a reality for poor, rural women and now for working middle class women too—will continue to be a problem shared by most women worldwide. This will have a long-term impact. Future generations would grow up seeing nurturing men and women as well as achieving women and men, and would no longer feel the need to describe human qualities as 'masculine' and 'feminine'.

Until then, the conventional benefit packages that the corporate sector offers need to be overhauled. By and large, they prove to be ridiculously insufficient. Women need reduced hour jobs, parenting leave, and career breaks, none of which is readily available yet. And, more than anything, they need to be able to avail of such benefits without suffering long-term damage to their careers. The corporate world has failed to develop holistic policies that would support working women. In addition to "benefits" questions, employers are now confronted with new questions of worker mobility. A working wife is less free to move in accordance with her husband's job needs; moreover she also needs to move to further her own career. Employers have so far not paid much attention to a spouse's relocation problem, and only recently have companies begun to offer married women promotion when changes in location are required. The prevailing assumption has been that women with families would not move. Yet, a woman's advance to a top corporate job often necessitates her moving which may conflict with her husband's career goals. As a result, too many career women either put their private lives on the back burner or too many qualified women decide to forego meaningful employment. However, as a large body of research demonstrates, the majority women are happier when they have both career and family. Therefore, it is unfair to expect a professional woman to sacrifice motherhood just as it is unfair to expect a professionally qualified woman not to start a family. Women are entitled to both career and family. Women, when they are old enough to have done with the business of being a woman, can feel very powerful.

It is, therefore, remarkable when a CEO recognizes this predicament and says sympathetically that

> There is always a time when people are prepared to go away from home and a time when they need to stay at home… Sometimes great people suddenly have marital problems, sometimes the only way to see their children is to stay in the country. They cannot be moved: if you try to pressure them to move, you can create a real crisis. You have to be flexible and pragmatic. [15]

Such CEOs are few and far between and they will go down in history.

Young women, therefore, seriously need to consider how they would expand their life choices. Despite the fact that young women are told that a serious person needs to commit to her career at least for the first 10 years of her job, they need to become highly intentional and focused if they want children. Often, by the time they contemplate having children, they are on the wrong side of 35, when infertility could become an issue. They also seriously need to choose a career that will give them the gift of time and, if possible, choose a company that helps them achieve work–life balance. Tough? Yes, of course. But worth the effort.

## How Can Dreams Be Realized?

After discussing internal barriers in the workshop, often the participant want to know how they can break them in order to realize their dreams. I throw the question back at them and ask, "If you were your own coach, what would you suggest?"

A good starting point for the analysis of realizing one's dreams and aspirations is the basic recognition that one can, in fact, have the freedom of making several choices. The common themes that have emerged over time are given below:

### Define personal goals

First and foremost, establish your personal goals and sort out your personal priorities and values. It is important that you see what is possible, ask questions, and avoid making assumptions about what you can and cannot do. Distinguish between short- and long-term goals and what is required to be done by you and what support you need from the organization in order to succeed.

If you must, take advice from those you respect, but don't let anyone decide on your behalf—whether father, brother, spouse or anyone else.

It is important that women carve out a life for themselves based on the values and priorities they believe in, with adequate satisfaction and meaning. It is equally important that women fulfill their own dreams. When women do not feel fulfilled in their lives it may be difficult for them to watch others fulfill theirs—whether spouse, children or colleagues. My assumption is that, when women feel fulfilled, purposeful, and aligned with their identity with integrity, they can balance the demands that multiple roles make on them with grace and dignity.

### Develop understanding of gender bias

Recognize gender biases and stereotypes and understand how they can act as barriers to success. Respond to stereotypes effectively when you see their behavioral impact on others and learn to effectively adapt to and interpret differences in gender styles and behavior. Invest in developing your own personal awareness and organizational awareness of gender differences and biases.

If gender stereotypes are pervasive, how can they be changed? Following are a few of the ways to challenge and change gender stereotypes:

*Make gender stereotypes visible.* Often stereotypes are unconscious and we are not aware of them. However, on a conscious level, we find them irrelevant. If we spell out gender stereotypes, this brings stereotypes to the conscious level. For instance, research has shown that women are quoted higher prices when negotiating for cars, even when they use the same bargaining strategies as men. Here, the stereotype that women are less effective in negotiations is served. If the stereotype is voiced, it becomes obvious and women react to it. This may happen because women want to make the extra effort to counteract the stereotype [16].

*Question assumptions.* Many of the assumptions we make do not hold up under scrutiny. For example, there is an assumption of gender difference regarding risk taking; some assume that women are less capable of managing risk-taking challenges. However, regular exposure to such assignments and relevant training and practice decreases the gender difference in risk-taking ability. Rather than focusing on elements in relation to gender we cannot change, it makes more sense to focus on assumptions we can actually change.

## Discard the ideal of a perfect homemaker and a professional

Given that women juggle roles, tasks, budgets, they need to keep track of children, adults and what they need. Women need to consciously plan and organize for household help as well as childcare help when required, which will set them free to discharge outside responsibilities.

More important is engaging everyone—spouse and children, parents or dependents—in running it. It is also important to recognize that there is no point adding to the stress by attempting to do everything by yourself. One can always hire domestic help, buy modern gadgets and equipment that can save time and labor, or appropriately outsource whatever service is available such as excellent childcare centers. Organizing reliable childcare option is key. Families need to feel secure that their children are in good hands.

## Never too late to fulfill a dream

It is expected that by the time we reach adulthood our goals are formed, our energies are channelized, and we are self-motivated. However, to a great extent, instances of recognition further reshape our ambitions and determine the efforts we need to make in realizing them. To sustain ambitions, women need to create avenues of recognition that are based on talent, skill, and competency or work assignments, rather than on subservience or mere appearance. This means identifying, critically evaluating, and purposefully developing those "domains," "disciplines," or hobbies that can provide recognition, appreciation, and endorsement. They need to make peace with the trade-offs they may have to make in life.

Different phases in life throw up different needs for connecting with mentors, opportunities for learning new skills, institutional recognition and changing cultural trends. It is never too late to get ambitious about something you really want to achieve, and certainly never too late to realize it. Seek and make effective use of coaches and mentors, and take help from someone who sees the bigger picture. There are times in the life of every working woman, when things can get too much to handle. It is during this time that you need to take help from someone who has a perspective. Some women find it harder to own up to needing help. It is not a sign of weakness. Reach out to people who can help you and seek continuous renewal.

Each of us has an inner compass, as Gloria Steinem [17] indicates, that helps us know what to do and where to go. Its signals are interest, excitement of being in a new territory, and perhaps a sense of growth. Listening to these internal signals and following them is itself the first step, the beginning of the journey. It remains to be seen whether women can find ways of bringing their whole selves into organizations, not only from the perspectives of women's identity, but from the organizational perspective as well. The result may be liberating for women and humanizing for organizations. Human resources are a synergy between men and women. Optimum utilization and development of the human potential will be fully realized when the female gender is seen as the untapped part of the total workforce.

In other words, there is no turning back from the fact that women are joining men in full partnership over issues at the forefront of the global agenda. As this partnership develops and strengthens, not only will women be empowered and strengthened, but men too will be released from the old polarities of gender that force them into limited and limiting roles. On the one hand, it is exciting to see the extent of human potential and, on the other it is disturbing to discover that so little of it is utilized. It is only by functioning together with unity and mutuality that men and women can actualize their maximum potential and learn to discover their inner resource, complementarity, and creativity.

One of the ways to discover one's potential is also through joining and participating in networks. I discovered this accidentally. Networks can provide emotional support, advice on work-related problems, and information about a wide range of employment related issues. Let's explore that in the next chapter.

## References

1. Mero, J. and P. Sellers, 'Power: Do Women Really Want It?' *Fortune*, October 13, 2003: 80–100.
2. Ely, R. J. and D. L. Rhode, 'Women and Leadership: Defining the Challenges', in *Handbook of Leadership Theory and Practice*, edited by N. Nohria and R. Khurana, 377–410, Boston, MA: Harvard Business Publishing, 2010.
3. Schwartz, S. H. and T. Rubel, 'Sex Differences in Value Priorities: Cross-cultural and Multimethod Studies', *Journal of Personality and Social Psychology* 89, no. 6 (2005): 1010–28.
4. Brooks, Alison Wood, 'Explained: Why Few Women at the Top', New Delhi: Bloomberg/Times of India, September 26, 2015, www.timesofindia.

indiatimes.com/home/science/...few-women-at-the-top/.../49111410.cms (accessed on June 17, 2017).
5. Corporate Executive Board, 'Fostering Women's Leadership', *Women in Leadership*: 7, http://www.diversityresources.stlrbc.org/wp-content/uploads/2013/10/HRLC-Fostering_Womens_Leadership.pdf (accessed on June 17, 2016).
6. Gardener W. L. and S. Gabriel, 'Gender Differences in Relational and Collective Interdependence: Implications for Self-views, Social Behavior and Subjective Well-being', in *The Psychology of Gender*, 2nd edition, edited by A. H. Eagly, A. E. Beall, and R. J. Sternberg, 169–91, New York, NY: Guilford Press, 2004.
7. Hochschild, Arlie Russell with Anne Machung, *The Second Shift: Working Parents and the Revolution at Home*, New York, NY: Viking Penguin, 1989.
8. Barsh, Joanna and Yee Lareina, 'Changing Companies' Minds about Women', *McKinsey Quarterly*, September 2011, www.mckinsey.com/business-functions/.../changing-companies-minds-about-women (accessed on June 17, 2017).
9. Fels, A., 'Do Women Lack Ambition?' *Harvard Business Review*, April 2004. ttps://hbr.org/2004/04/do-women-lack-ambition, (accessed on June 17, 2017).
10. Carter, N. M. and C. Silva, 'The Myth of the Ideal Worker: Does Doing All the Right Things Really Get Women Ahead?' *Catalyst Report*, 2011, www.catalyst.org/system/files/The_Myth_of_the_Ideal_Worker_Does_Doing_All_the_Right_Things_Really_ Get_Women_Ahead.pdf
11. Bowles, H. R. and L. Babcock, 'How Can Women Escape the Compensation Negotiation Dilemma? Relational Accounts are One Answer', *Psychology of Women Quarterly* 37, no. 1 (2013): 80–96.
12. American Association of University Women, *The Simple Truth About the Gender Pay Gap* (Report), Washington, DC: American Association of University Women, Spring 2016, https://www.aauw.org/files/2016/02/SimpleTruth_Spring2016.pdf (accessed on June 17, 2017).
13. Hegewisch, A. and H. Hartmann, *Occupational Segregation and the Gender Wage Gap: A Job Half Done*, Washington, DC: Institute for Women's Policy Research, 2014.
14. Miller, Eric J., *Work and Creativity*, London: The Tavistock Institute of Human Relations, 1983.
15. Browne, Lord, 'The Strategic Logic of Diversity', talk delivered at the Group Chief Executive of BP, Berlin, June 19, 2002.
16. Kelan, Elisabeth, 'Bound by Stereotypes', *Business Strategy Review* 19, no. 1 (Spring 2008): 4–7.
17. Steinem, Gloria, *Revolution From Within*, Boston: Little Brown Company, 1992.

# 4
# Networks as Catalysts for Change

"There are years that ask questions and
years that answer them"

—Zora Neale Hurston

After questioning and observing insensitive organizational patterns and practices prevailing in our organizations over the years, I realized that most of us—women executives—were undergoing transitions that were, in some sense, the result of vast and somewhat invisible social changes. Whenever we had an opportunity to get together in the course of a convention or women leadership programs, what became clear through our chance interactions and dialogue was that there were some underlying patterns that were true for us all. There were both subtle, internal kinds of changes as well as the need to respond to the external changes that were happening all around us.

After tiring of the endless discussions about all that was "breaking down," I was finally eager to find out what was "breaking through." More specifically, I wanted to know what I could do to help "the breakthrough" happen! Personally, I have never had the option of restricting my choices on the basis of gender or measuring my worth on the basis of minority. My professional training at the Tata Institute of Social Sciences had taught me not to remain content with only raising questions, but to identify the exact problem and to be part of the solutions, if possible. I was eager and willing to do my part—if I could only figure out what that was. There seemed to be something waiting and wanting to emerge but no one was quite sure what it was. Until one day, when it emerged on its own accord quite unexpectedly.

In October 1989, the Nehru Centenary Celebrations Committee in collaboration with the Bureau of Public Enterprises and the Standing Conference of Public Enterprises (SCOPE), organized a convention on "Women in Public Sector," among many events that the Committee had planned during that year. For the first time, the Convention brought 500 women executives from all the public sector enterprises in India together at New Delhi. After the formal presentations were over, we spoke about our burning concerns, shared our experience, and came to an agreement in the Open House Session that certain things needed to be changed in personal or organizational situations to further women's growth and development. We unanimously endorsed a collectively felt need for creating a National Network which would provide a platform for pooling creativity and competencies in harnessing the full potential of women. As an employer organization, SCOPE emerged as a natural choice to provide that platform.

What struck me most in that convention was that instead of demanding that the organizations do something about women's concerns and their resulting predicament, there was a critical mass of women who wanted to act and influence the corporate world around them. The excitement was contagious. The collective energy and enthusiasm in the FICCI auditorium at New Delhi was palpable. One concern persistently came up: How long should we continue to hold "others" (management/family members) responsible for our development? When do we accept responsibility for our own growth in a manner that enables us to give our best to our organizations?

This became the main driver behind setting up the Forum whose newly enrolling members had already decided by an unspoken agreement to create an Answering Forum and not merely a Questioning one. By mutual consent, they had decided to move towards what could potentially become "the answering years."

Until then, there had never been a significant number of women who with some authority in the corporate world saw their situation as clearly as they saw it simultaneously. Never before did women who had education and positions of privilege also see themselves as members of a community with common concerns, vulnerabilities, and experiences. The sharing of these life experiences with each other in the Forum, and with other women professionals, suddenly assumed special significance in order to move forward and to energize one another towards one common goal. There was an implicit recognition that women carry the burden of grappling with a deficit of social capital and relative exclusion and continue to feel isolated in their organizations, and simply want to belong to a community of women with whom they can share experiences about similar workplace challenges.

With the able guidance of the then SCOPE Chairman, the Forum was launched as a follow-up to the National Convention, under the aegis of SCOPE in 1990. It had a central apex body with the positions of president, secretary and treasurer at New Delhi, and four regional chapters in Chennai, Mumbai, Kolkata and New Delhi, on the lines of the organizational structure of its parent body, SCOPE. Each region had the freedom to nominate its president, vice-president, secretary, joint secretary and treasurer. All the women executives who were present in that first SCOPE meeting, whose enterprises were located in the four geographical regions and who volunteered to take the work forward, became the co-founding office bearers.

One thing was common to all of us. We were all very high on excitement, commitment and hard work, but very low on organizing funds. We primarily worked out of our offices for a very long time as the Forum did not have any resource to set up a central office, nor did it have any corpus funding. In fact, we even willingly put aside a small contribution to take care of administrative exigencies. It felt like a privilege to be able to work on the workplace issues that affected so many of us.

In the initial months, I remember working tirelessly in a group in the small committee room of the SCOPE office, day after day, sometimes after office hours, sometimes on holidays, developing memorandums of association and objectives, drafting information brochures, developing action agenda, etc. In short, doing everything that was needed to be done to set up the new body, which we had decided to call the Forum of Women in Public Sector (WIPS). As an employer organization, SCOPE had 250 public sector enterprises as its corporate members. It acted as a springboard to launch this Forum within the network of its member companies with the following objectives:

- To promote the growth and development of women in the public sector.
- To assist the public sector undertakings in harnessing the full potential of women employees.
- To play a catalytic role in improving the status of women in and around public sector undertakings.

During our early discussions, we were clear about the role the Forum would play with the managements of public sector enterprises. It would not act as a pressure group or as a union or association for taking up issues of "supposedly" discriminatory matters. In fact, we believed that we could save our fire for more important battles, rather than fight those of individual grievances. The important battles were, and still are being fought, for getting decent jobs and bringing about real equity in the workplace. It was decided that the Forum would dedicate itself to creating awareness about good governance, embodying concepts of inclusiveness, openness, and fairness to all women. Crucially then, such governance in public sector enterprises would incorporate a gender perspective in order to take into account women's and men's differing roles, responsibilities, needs, opportunities, and access to resources, and increasing women's decision-making power. The Forum would, therefore, act as a catalyst and a change agent in the initial years for:

- Creating awareness about women's issues at workplaces.
- Sensitizing public sector managements to the complex needs of women employees and the special needs and abilities of women professionals.

- Developing a database of women employees in public sector enterprises.
- Focusing the spotlight on enterprises that undertake best practices and do commendable work for the development of women on a national platform.

The Forum offered corporate membership to public sector enterprises and kept the individual membership fees to a bare minimum. This resulted in many women executives and employees enrolling themselves as members. We organized the first national meet in New Delhi in 1991, which was attended by a 300-member delegation. It provided an opportunity to all the members to come together and share their experiences on a common platform. The meet was such a runaway success that we began hosting regular national meets as annual networking events, with invited speakers and panel discussions, where high-ranking women from the public sector as well as those from unconventional professions such as the army, navy, railways and the Foreign Service, would speak about their career, leadership and work/family challenges.

I noticed time and again that this sharing and interaction had a healing as well as an inspiring quality. When high-performing women share the critical issues that matter to them, they bring their own particular point of view and their own stories borne from experience. As a result, those who felt helpless and isolated in their respective organizations, realized they were not alone. More and more professional women saw each other as allies, not competitors. Many understood the need to nurture strong relationships with their co-workers and spoke of their commitment to fostering other women's careers. Networking relationships provided social support, role modeling and information about overcoming discriminatory obstacles. By sharing experiences and strategies with women in similar situations, networking members learnt how to manage their own career trajectories.

In the words of a woman manager of a Fortune 500 company:

> I found it extremely useful to network with my counterparts in other organizations. I learnt one or two things about dealing

with difficult situations. It facilitated in terms of finding role models and sharing advice about advancing in the presence of barriers that still exist in organizations. Considering that we (women) are in a minority in our organization, we have to make special efforts to keep connected. Promoting change can benefit the organizations as well as the men and women in it. This insight can motivate one to work on one's own or in collaboration with others.

## Reflections on Formative Years of Women's Network

However, it was not entirely easy to work on the issues related to the Forum in the initial years. Some of the seniors in our organizations reacted to the news of the setting up of the new Forum with skepticism and ridicule. Some dismissed it as a waste of time. Others gave strict instructions against using any of the official resources—time, infrastructure, etc.—for the Forum's activities. As a result, for some of the enthusiastic office bearers, attending monthly meetings became a difficult proposition.

The initial National Meets were held at New Delhi. But in order to give wider exposure and to encourage participation of women from different regions, it was decided that the National Meets would be held at the four regions located at the four metro or II-tier cities by rotation. There were at least two occasions when two of our committed office bearers did not get permission to officially attend the National Meets at other locations. Such was their commitment that they willingly took personal leave and spent their own money on travel and accommodation.

Today, when I look back on the first formative 10 or 12 years of the Forum, enrolling 70 corporate members, 5,000 individual members and organizing successful National Meet after Meet in four metro cities without any corpus funding, I am struck by a sense of wonder at the way we stuck together, gathered momentum and persisted. Although the Forum never had sufficient funds of its own, paradoxically, getting funds through the sponsorship of the National Meets—which were attended by up to 700–800 delegates in the peak years—from public enterprises was never a problem. Admittedly, too much time and effort was spent in seeking relatively small amounts. All said and done, it was a great collective effort. It also reflected a new mindset, brimming with a heady sense of possibilities that everyone shared. It seemed as if the hour had finally arrived for us to live up to our potential, realize our dreams, and surpass our goals.

The Forum gradually developed as a safe community where women in the public sector could compare notes, give voice to their dilemmas, and emotionally support one another without worrying that others would misunderstand or misjudge them. In the process, we also learnt that networking is vital for gathering and sharing valuable information about workplace practices, learning about opportunities to enhance work effectiveness, or even potential pitfalls, increasing professional and social visibility, and building credibility, influence, and reputation. The bonding through networks both within and beyond organizations resulted in long-term relationships.

Research has shown that women with dense networks of female colleagues have a competitive advantage in breaking through the "glass ceiling" into the senior ranks. Such women can better look out for one other's interests—speaking up for one another in the other's absence, and informing one another of developing opportunities.[1]

## Fundamental Interventions That Made an Impact
### Creation of systematic database

There was no systematic database on women in public sector. The number of women in management earlier was so insignificant in public sector enterprises in India—which is considered the largest, gender-neutral employer of women—that data on women was clubbed with special category minority/statutory groups such as ex-servicemen, physically handicapped people, etc.

Clearly, gender equality requires a bias for action. This bias may not have been purposeful, but it had certainly gone unexamined and was preventing the systems from focusing a spotlight on women's issues. The data system needed to be gender disaggregated for better planning and policy formulation. Developing methodologies for collecting data on women's employment in the public sector was important. Once corrected, it paved a way for creating a systematic database on women in the public sector.

The only systematic database in public sector enterprises (PSEs) on women was then created by the WIPS in 1998–99. Although, out of the 240 public sector enterprises then, only 58 forwarded data in response to the questionnaires sent to them, the data reflected significant trends and highlights, as given below:

- Women employees constituted a small portion of 6.7 percent of total employees engaged in PSEs, totaling 28,589 women employees [2].
- A large percentage of women employees were at a lower hierarchical level and largely in non-critical functions.
- Only 10 (0.03 percent) women executives were of the rank of General Manager or above.
- Maximum women employees (64 percent) were in the age group 31–45 years and only 13 percent were in the 20–30 age group. This indicated an alarming drop in recruitment in the last 8–10 years as compared to 10–20 years.

Other than recruitment data, there was no qualitative data available in the PSEs about working women with regard to turnover rates, absenteeism, occurrence and return from maternity leave, individual expectations vis-à-vis career opportunities attained in one's tenure, and performance in relation to factors such as age, marital status, family size, and age of children. The striking revelation was that women filled up only a minority of management positions and, in most cases, remained invisible in senior positions. If women's work was considered unproductive and, therefore, unvalued, it was because it was not recorded; and because it was not recorded it remained unaided. This has been a vicious circle.

## Creation of best enterprise award

To recognize and promote best practices on women's development, WIPS also constituted two national awards: the Best Enterprise Award and the Best Bank Award, in 1992 and 1995, respectively. The membership was made open to public sector banks in the same year. This was in recognition of the finest efforts made by an enterprise or a bank in promoting the growth and development of women. The criteria for Best Enterprise Award included focus on formation of WIPS cells, membership drive, good practices in recruitment, promotion and training, and CSR activities in the period under review.

## Sensitization on burning issues through constructive debates

On two specific occasions, we also utilized the platform of National Meets to conduct a constructive debate on the burning issues of the time. The objective was to build greater awareness on important issues in order to learn to appreciate different perspectives.

For instance, in the Fifth National Meet held in Calcutta in 1995, a national debate was held on "Equal Opportunity to be Made More Equal to Women" and on how "Stereotyping in Jobs," holds women back. In that session, two white papers were presented as thought inputs, and further enriched by invited addresses of speakers from a variety of professions. It was gratifying to note that the predominant view that emerged in the Q&A session was also seconded by a record number of 800 delegates who attended the Meet that year. The consensus was that women should be assessed on their merit on equal terms.

## Opinion poll on reservation at entry level

The Sixth National Meet in New Delhi was held in 1996 against the backdrop of an ongoing debate on reservation for women in the Indian Parliament. It was attended by 700 delegates. Considering that in previous Meets there had been several panel discussions that focused on the need to introduce reservation at the entry level for qualified women as a target for employers, we decided to feel the pulse of women delegates on the matter on the second day of the Meet.

The delegates were handed out slips with the following text:

> As per data available with Department of Public Enterprises, women constitute approximately 6–8 percent of total workforce in public sector enterprises. To encourage their intake at the entry point certain state governments have announced reservation of jobs in their respective state run organizations. Please indicate your opinion on the matter by ticking your option whether you support reservation for women at the entry level in public sector, whether you support reservation for women at the time of promotions and if so indicate the desired percentage.

**Poll at WIPS Meet 1996 on Reservation for Women**

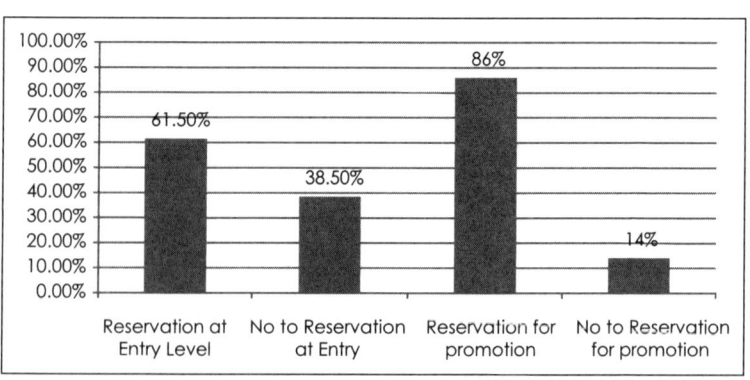

1. Percentage of poll respondents willing (yes) is 61.5 percent or not willing (no) is 38.5 percent for reservation of women at entry level.

2. Percentage of poll respondents willing (yes) is 86 percent or not willing (no) is 14 percent for reservation of women for promotions.
3. Desired percentage by poll respondents is 30 percent in both the categories.

On the second day, the Meet was attended by 400 delegates of which 276 responded to the survey. Of these 61.5 percent preferred reservation at entry point and 38.5 percent categorically refused a need for such a provision. Of the 236 delegates who responded to the second question, 86 percent supported reservation at promotional level and 14 percent replied in the negative. The delegates, after much debate, also passed a resolution for 30 percent reservation. It was felt that this provision would be able to deal with the attitudinal barriers at the entry level. A similar resolution was also passed in the National Meet held in 2013.

As is widely known, the glass ceiling is a reality and it underscores the continued need for many, novel initiatives. Those who said no to reservation at the promotional level felt that it would alienate them from their male colleagues, and breed complacency. Instead, they felt the organization should introduce women friendly, fair policies. In the absence of rigorous proof, even if we take the response to this poll as merely an indication, we need to acknowledge the fact that the reservation issue will lose all its meaning if it is treated as a dogma or if its use compromises on competence.

In fact, any proposal that solely benefits women and divides the members of the workforce into "us" and "them" may generate a few short-term concessions when the costs to men are not too high, but they cannot serve as the basis for the kinds of sustained reforms needed to transform corporate India. On the other hand, universal strategies that help all members of the workforce and uphold the ideals of equity and effectiveness can serve as a foundation, even if such strategies help women more than men.

## The ripple effect

Learning, adaptation, and flexibility is a two-way street. The question is, just as women employees need to learn how to fit into the organization, what is the organization willing to learn from its women employees?

There are many ways to effect change. Although many recognize that the glass ceiling will not shatter without internal change, one accomplishment of the Forum during the mid-1990s, can be termed as having a ripple effect.

During every National Meet, the Forum devoted a session to developing an action plan for the coming year, and to review the progress on planned targets in the previous year. This was in order to develop a package of recommendations to be implemented at the enterprise level. These recommendations were then regularly sent by the apex president to the concerned ministries as required, such as the Department of Public Enterprises for creating a database at the national level, the Department of Women for setting up support services such as daycare centers and crèches, and the Department of Personnel for introducing adoption leave, or the Ministry of Labor for amendment to provisions of the Factories Act, and so on.

More than anything else, the Forum proved to be an excellent laboratory for developing skills like leadership, team building, garnering corporate funding, and communication. And, obviously, when we demonstrated collective responsibility for a common cause, we added to our reservoir of goodwill from governments, public sector managements, and the general public.

## Collaboration with Other Agencies

During that time, the Forum also collaborated with many women's organizations with a similar agenda, committed to helping women employees gain their full potential and integrating women into mainstream activities. These included the Springboard Women's Development Program, supported by the British Council at New Delhi, and delivered through an accredited trainer from the UK, the

National Commission for Women, the Women's Cell at CII, several ILO initiatives, etc. This turned out to be an effective strategy to keep alive the notion that working towards women's development was an important thing to do and women belonging to different groups cared about it.

In several of these joint meetings with professional associations, there was a consensus among the participating agencies for a comprehensive plan of action for gender mainstreaming through various strategies that would bring a gender perspective to public policies. These included special measures to address current imbalances, allocating adequate resources, and establishing or strengthening mechanisms to implement the plan.

Gradually, we could reap from what we had sown earlier. A review was done after 10 years. As a result of our effort, it could be seen that

- A database on women employees was created in PSEs and presented in annual reports.
- There was a 20 percent annual increase in the number of women employees receiving training of different types.
- There was 10 percent of growth in the development of support services by enterprises like crèches, daycare centers, and counseling centers for women employees.
- There was formation of Women or WIPS Cells in all enterprises in at least 50 percent of the PSEs that became members of the Forum.
- There was a significant rise in the number of women entering newer, non-traditional areas such as industrial relations, vigilance, sales, aviation, inspection, engineering, and international trade.

The reasons and motivation for this change of attitude could be many. Some companies wanted to be seen favorably by their employees, customers, and other stakeholders. Some companies wanted to move women to higher positions as role models for many young recruits or even to attract young talented women to the company. Some companies simply wanted to capture the competitive advantage in an era where talent would be in short supply Whatever may be the reason, it was clear that it was increasingly beginning to dawn on corporate leaders that superior organizations are built by superior people and that the success of their company also depends on their attitude towards men and women of caliber and competence.

## The fight for amendment to the Factories Act

This new mindset was repeatedly reflected through many young women engineers expressing the long-felt need for making amendment to the Factories Act of 1948 to provide flexibility in their employment during night hours. This issue came up time and again during the "Open House Sessions" of the National Meets—right from the first meet itself—year after year. The Act did not permit women to work in any factory or industrial establishment except between 0600hrs and 1900hrs. Getting shop floor assignments, for all-round work exposure and for career progression, are considered critical for any technical/professional executive, especially engineers. But women were not considered fit for these assignments due to the prohibitive Factories Act. This created a roadblock to their career path.

The Forum took up the matter with the Ministry of Labor on behalf of SCOPE as the employers' organization. This was also discussed at the apex level meeting of the Forum. Many were pessimistic that no amendment would ever be made to the Act in the near future or even in our lifetime. Therefore, the consensus was that it was not worth spending time or energy on this project.

I was not convinced. It made me wonder about a dilemma we face from time to time. Must we always work on the issues that give us immediate returns and ignore those that are long term? Admittedly, we may not see results on the long-term issues in our time, but these efforts can create a holding environment, a pathway for enabling change to take place in the future. The second option is, of course, an arduous path with no milestones, no points of destination in sight. It requires firm faith, lots of patience, commitment, and conviction that the end justifies the means.

The more I thought about it, the more I wanted to take it up on behalf of the Forum. Moreover, my personal background contributed towards the decision. Throughout my childhood my parents emphasized the importance of doings things for others and for the larger good. Dinner table discussions often centered around such heroes. My parents took part in the freedom struggle of India as mere teenagers and, like many others of their generation, were prepared to dedicate their lives for the freedom movement. As a political prisoner, my father was jailed for three years with late Vinobha Bhave, a close associate of Mahatma Gandhi. During that time, many freedom fighters thought that India would never get independence in their own lifetime. However, they wanted to make it somewhat easier for future generations, even though their goal looked unattainable at the time. But Mahatma Gandhi, as a true, visionary leader, had created an irresistible image of independent India that was something to fight for, something to give one's life for. Imagine the joy of those freedom fighters who never thought that the dream would become a reality in their own lifetime! Evidence tells us that progress owes itself to the demands of the unreasonable men and women, who don't even pause to worry whether they would be around to taste the fruit of their labors.

So, emboldened by this legacy, I persuaded the apex committee members and we decided to take up the cause anyway. As the wider debate around this issue began to unfold, two positions were immediately taken. While the central employers' organizations favored the idea, the central trade unions were totally opposed to the idea of employing women during night shifts, mainly on the grounds of the possibility of sexual harassment of women workers. Interestingly, this apprehensive mindset was also endorsed by many working women and their families.

I often wondered why is it that shop floors, factories, or industry establishments are singled out as "unsafe" places for women. How come there is no objection to women working night shifts at hospitals or in the aviation industry?

The Ministry of Commerce, in the meantime, took up this issue of amendment on the grounds of productivity. It sent a proposal to the Ministry of Labor in the year 2000, recommending that female workers should be allowed to work in the third shift in the Export Processing Zones to stimulate India's exports. These zones were set up as enclaves separated from the domestic tariff area by fiscal barriers, to provide an internationally competitive duty-free environment for export production at low cost. By allowing women workers to work in the third shift, it would not only help to utilize the installed capacity but would also be cost effective in the competitive international market. This would also lead to increased employment opportunities for women. Finally, the Ministry of Commerce was also of the view that productivity as well as the turnover of women was much higher than that of men in the field of electronics. Something needed to be done about it, and that was the light at the end of the tunnel.

So when I received the notification from SCOPE to attend a meeting to be convened by the Ministry of Labor as president of the Forum, I was overjoyed. Naively, I thought, here is my chance to represent the voice of women who want to change the old ways of doing things and develop new mental models.

But when I walked into the dimly lit conference room full of people, on 10 January 2000, for some reason my heart sank, as if intuiting a negative outcome. The agenda was circulated in advance. One by one, the representatives of the trade unions began strongly opposing the idea of employment of women during night shifts on the grounds of exposing women to potential sexual harassment. I began to feel more and more depressed. Finally, someone noticed me and said that there is only one woman here who is surely going to support us, because women from good families would never give consent to such strange arrangements!

For a moment, there was a deafening silence. For some unfathomable reason, I got tongue-tied. I just did not know what to do. Should I collude with the stereotype and reaffirm that women value extrinsic/comfortable conditions, therefore, no night duty should be prescribed for them? Should I drop the cause as a hot coal because there was no support whatsoever?

The blinding moment passed, and, with a flash, I realized how women struggle to deal with what men think a woman must be and do. This realization, for some strange reason, gave me the courage to stick to my guns. I suppose the fetters fall the moment you resolve you will no longer be under any domination.

I cleared my throat, found my voice, and put forward an argument that women's safety is undoubtedly a major area of concern in India today. However, that must be balanced against the need to empower women to be treated as equals in the workplace. This means not placing constraints on women by prohibiting them from doing night shifts. In any case, the state must protect all citizens, including women, at any time of the day or night. To assume that this duty will not be fulfilled and hence to keep women indoors at night is the wrong approach. It is not a favor to them but a disservice. Many professionally trained women would not like discrimination of any kind provided there are proper arrangements of safety, security, and adequate transport facilities.

Someone from the group reiterated that women from good families would not like to do night duty and get themselves exposed to all kinds of unsocial elements.

"How come good families do not mind sending the women doctors to hospitals for night duty? Or, for that matter, any essential services duty?" I persisted.

"That is different!" I was told.

"How so?" I asked. There was no answer.

The meeting was adjourned, since no consensus could be reached that day.

So I could not quite forecast then how many meetings it would take) and how much convincing it would need to get that amendment endorsed.

On my way back from that meeting, I could not help thinking about the particularly slow progress of women in the 20th century. For, up until the 1960s, women were best known for their roles as wives, mothers, sisters, nurses, and secretaries. As women's liberation movements asserted that women were also entitled to human rights, the international community responded with a series of conferences that have contributed to putting women's concerns high on the global agenda. Yet, most women who managed to claim the positions they deserved in the world, did so at the expense of the feminine principle—the qualities attributed to the gentle side of personality, like care, respect, patience, empathy, mercy, etc.—and achieved their positions only by developing an iron-fisted control over others. Both men and women possess this feminine principle, but throughout history, it has often been equated with emotion, weakness and vulnerability. In fact, as a result of this association, the feminine principle has been unfortunately flushed out from the mainstream of human development to a backwater labeled as "woman's issue" in the social, political, and economic arena. If the suppression and control of the principle has given rise to any problems, then they are to be corrected in an enduring way through a change of consciousness that has nothing to do with gender because it is not biological and everything to do with the ideology of realizing the human potential.

I also wondered on that day, just as I have often wondered thereafter, why women's movements, despite all the efforts, commitment, and investments, have not attracted the larger number of women they should have or retained all they have attracted. Is it because they see no other alternative, or is it because of the oppositional paradigm that we have inherited from patriarchy itself, which assumes a champion and a challenger, a victorious and a vanquished? Clearly, women feel themselves to be too profoundly connected with men in a variety of roles to even suggest or sustain a campaign of this kind for any period of time.

I could not, therefore, believe my eyes when after five years on one fine day in March 2005, I read the news item that the government had decided to allow women to work in night shifts and amended section 66 of the Factories Act, 1948, in a major first move towards a liberalized labor law regime. What's more, provisions for adequate safeguards with regard to female workers, occupational safety and health, protection of their dignity and honor, and the transportation from the workplace to the nearest point of their residence was to be provided in a notification soon after the amendment bill became law. Though the Factories Act is a central piece of legislation, the responsibility for its administration rests with the state governments. As a result of this legislation, selected states such as Haryana, Rajasthan, Punjab, Madhya Pradesh, Tamil Nadu [3], and Andhra Pradesh [4] allowed women to work in night shifts or are in the process of doing so. In 2015, Maharashtra also joined the league [5].

Aha! Contrary to popular belief, things can change in your lifetime after all!

## The Struggle for Sustainability

During my tenure as president of the Forum, I realized that the coming together of so many women to make a beginning was not that difficult. Working together, maintaining commitment, and making progress was also relatively easy. But sustaining this progress year after year was certainly a challenge. In the initial years, there was a lot of enthusiasm, a lot of energy, although little agency. Other than the agenda of creating awareness and sensitizing corporate management on women's issues, there was no specific demand for seeking change.

So what were the key challenges in maintaining sustainability?

### Organizational issues

Considering that it was a network, with loosely knit systems and structure, we needed to take extra care to set up good systems and management practices, and to lay down a code of conduct for the office bearers. The bylaws were made at the time of inception, when the Forum was young and there was much faith and camaraderie among the founding office bearers. Except for minor amendments, they were never reviewed as the Forum got stabilized. As a result, rules regarding disciplinary action, role competencies of office bearers, or matters related to exit or dissolution that any mature organization would need, were not even considered or discussed for incorporation in the bylaws.

We should have developed a strong leadership pipeline considering that, for most office bearers, the Forum's work came after their own jobs and family demands. Often, we would think about a successor to head various regions, only when vacancies arose or it became absolutely urgent due to the earlier incumbent's transfer or resignation. Therefore, succession planning as well as training for the role was missing.

I think that succession becomes an even more important when a system or a network does not have a formal structure of authority or hierarchy. It may have something to do with the fact that we met only biannually over specific events, or meetings. The rest of the year we kept in touch over phone or through correspondence. As a result, we did not get enough opportunities to establish and reinforce adequate systems, processes, operating mechanisms, and cultural values that could guide the actions and decisions of the organization. We moved from issue to issue, from year to year, which, on reflection, was a big lacuna.

## Fund-raising issues

We raised money year after year through the contribution of the enterprises and by bringing out souvenirs with advertisements sponsored by PSEs. Admittedly, it was getting increasingly tough every year to raise funds for the Annual Meet's expenses. The real question was, how long could we expect the PSEs to go on contributing? At the same time, we did not want to give a wrong signal or to dilute the credibility of the Forum by putting up stalls (as was suggested by one of the regionals presidents) that would make it look like a bazaar or a vanity fair. So, although it was not a popular decision, a few of us decided against it in the apex committee meeting. It had its own backlash.

Clearly, leadership is not a popularity contest. A leader has to wake up the organization to the need for continuity in the midst of change, and also deal with stiff resistance in the process. A leader, therefore, cannot be faint hearted or overly concerned about popularity. It may well be that one of the requirements of becoming a leader involves learning to grapple with very hard trade-offs and an almost reckless testing of one's limits.

## Selection of office bearers

There was another issue about suitable nomination or selection of office bearers and appointments to the leadership of regional chapters instead of taking volunteers. In view of the formative and evolving status of the Forum, interested candidates were generally nominated to various posts on the apex body or regional chapters by nomination and general consensus, rather than through elections. To bring transparency to this process, eligibility criteria and a proper application format was developed after five years, so that the right members could be given the responsibility after ensuring support from the management of the enterprise they represented. It was recognized that, apart from enthusiasm and ambition, which is undoubtedly welcome, newer office bearers must also bring in relevant experience, aptitude, capability, and demonstrate respect for the Forum's objectives. They must also be associated with the Forum for a certain number of years. Above all, this process of nomination was created in order to be seen by all members as fair and reasonable. But the new office bearers did not want to wait to fulfill these conditions. Some even seemed to be there for short-term and quick gains and not entirely for their commitment to the cause. I often used to wonder then if the Forum had slipped its moorings and started to drift. The drift had been so slow that it had scarcely been noticed, but it had carried the Forum a dangerous distance from the relatively placid waters of developing the talent and potential of women.

## Vision development

Success is never final. After 10 years of successful existence, it was important to develop a clear vision of the future. The business environment around us was rapidly changing so it was but natural that the roles, responsibilities, and rights of women would also undergo change. I often wondered how many of our members seriously felt a need to develop competencies and multiple skills required not only for individual transformation but also for the transformation of their enterprises, which worked towards creating better value and at lower cost than their competitors.

Realizing that the future cannot be co-authored if there is no frank and honest conversation about it, an entire session was slotted to develop a shared vision for the Forum in the National Meet of 2002.

Developing a vision can be a difficult process. It is not always possible to show people the future. You might not even be able to envision it yourself. There was a group within the Forum's office bearers that wanted it to be independent from SCOPE, and to be registered as a society and to go ahead on its own steam. Another group preferred the status quo. Many felt the need to wait till the Forum was mature enough to tackle a whole spectrum of challenges that the independent status would unleash. We needed to solve our differences quickly, stay focused on the shared goals, and realize that this networking was tied to a larger purpose. But in our effort to take everyone on board and because of our unwillingness to take casualties, people got mixed signals. Every social movement has to deal with dissension within its ranks because it is impossible to build consensus on every position and every solution.

Clearly, the Forum was facing an "adaptive challenge" it had not faced earlier [6]. As a result, the differences of opinion could not sustain the mutual relationship that had bound us all together until then. I could see the limits of my own interpersonal influence, and painfully learnt that no matter how much you try to salvage a situation, every situation cannot be turned around.

The Forum at that time required massive restructuring and infusion of fresh blood, but its DNA as an informal networking organization perhaps held it back from the rigors of transformation. So I do not know whether it was the DNA factor or the abilities of the senior office bearers to steer the Forum through the period of transition as each one of us had to accept responsibility for our contribution to the situation, or the vested interests of certain members, or all of the above which was responsible for rubbing off the glue that had held its office bearers together until that time.

One of my biggest realizations during that time was that empowerment does not mean freedom from discipline or responsibility, or the absence of a system. It only means a system that has not been imposed upon by someone, but which is instead self-imposed. Empowerment is not merely doing what you like but also not doing what you like. While empowering people with rights, it is also important to enhance their understanding of complex issues and tolerance for multiple perspectives. This, of course, is a slow and long-term process. It is one that must be supported by all and in which ethical attitudes and conduct must be nurtured and reinforced at all levels. Unless that has been done, nomination or selection for holding public offices should not be done. As Abraham Lincoln tells us, "what is morally wrong can never be politically right."

But I am glad that, although the Forum faltered during that period, it survived the existential crisis. Slowly but steadily, it got back on track. Till now, 26 Annual National Meets have been organized under its banner, no small feat.

In the final analysis, therefore, I want to acknowledge the support of the hundreds of enthusiastic women that facilitated the setting up of the Forum, and the tireless efforts of many founding officer bearers that held it together in the initial years and beyond. Nor do I want to discount the role played by SCOPE in legitimizing the Forum in its formative years and continued support thereafter. Legitimacy is important, because it provides good returns to developing social capital [7]. Finally, I want to acknowledge the right climate of affirmative action created by women's movements worldwide that made the initial inroads into the corporate sector possible. The challenge to the Forum now is to remain relevant in rapidly changing times.

All these efforts were like effective tree shakers. Now it is time for jam makers to pick up the fruit and make the jam. I am not sure whether it's possible to play both roles effectively at the same time. For me, the jam maker's role has just begun.

## The Power of Intercorporate Network for Change

Considering I belonged to petroleum sector, it was only natural that I carried forward the agenda there. Towards that end, as a Director of the National Petroleum Management Program (NPMP), I offered a roundtable on "Women in Petroleum Industry: Emerging Issues" in 1996, in a bid to help highlight what the industry could be doing to attract and retain female employees. NPMP was specially set up- as a learning network of oil and gas companies in India, to deal with specific industry needs emerging from the economic reforms process initiated by the Government of India in 1991. Among other things, NPMP organized international conferences, seminars, and workshops on critical themes, and also instituted 10 awards for excellence covering various facets of management.

The roundtable was intended to stimulate an industry-wide conversation about the policies, measures, and practices needed to promote and develop the female talent in the petroleum sector. By inviting policy makers from the administrative ministry as well as directors of human resources and senior HRD practitioners from the hydrocarbon industry, we had hoped to garner their collective wisdom. The inaugural session of the roundtable was addressed by the then secretary of the Ministry of Petroleum and Natural Gas, Government of India.

Prior to the roundtable, I conducted a survey in the petroleum industry in 1995, seeking very basic information on women in oil and gas enterprises such as number, grades, age, qualifications, assignments, posting, leave records, training, and support systems (crèche counseling, etc.), to basically identify and examine any problem if it existed. We had planned to develop the inventory of recommendations for the directors of HR, so that they could be built on the prior initiatives already taken by the enterprises. This would then form an input to policy formulation with regard to women in the petroleum industry.

The survey discovered that women constituted only 5.4 percent of the human resource in the oil industry. Despite all things being equal, intake of women in the first three years of the 1990s was negligible, as can be seen below:

| Year | 1992 | 1993 | 1994 |
|---|---|---|---|
| Men | 1,900 | 1,575 | 1,511 |
| Women | 132 | 123 | 128 |

*Source:* NPMP Survey, 1995.

*Note:* There were 12 oil and gas companies in India (before smaller companies were merged into big companies) during the period the survey was conducted. Instead of presenting company specific data for the three years, aggregate data has been presented for both decades.

### Recruitment of Men and Women in the Petroleum Industry 1995

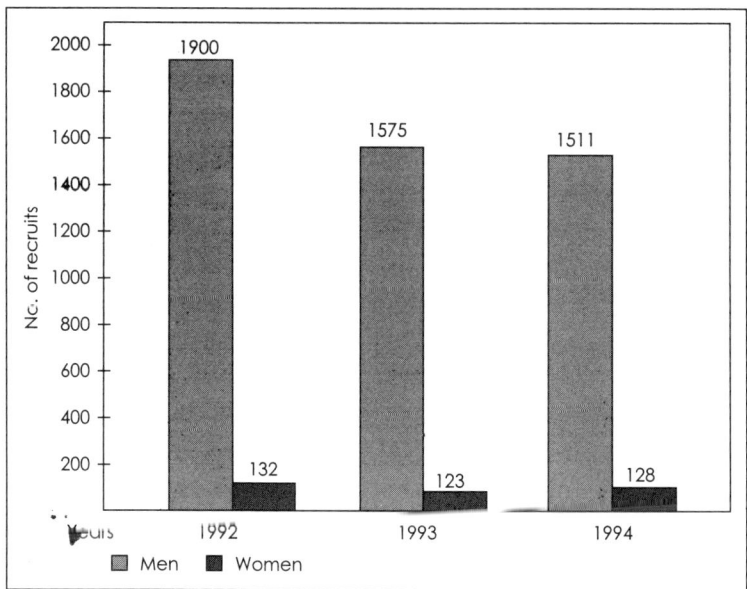

*Source:* NPMP Survey, 1995.

To track progress and find out whether the picture has changed after ten years I repeated the survey once again. There has not been much progress.

| Year | 2002 | 2003 | 2004 |
|---|---|---|---|
| Men | 1,208 | 1,307 | 815 |
| Women | 99 | 126 | 117 |

*Source:* NPMP *Survey,* 2005.

**Recruitment of Men and Women in the Petroleum Industry 2005**

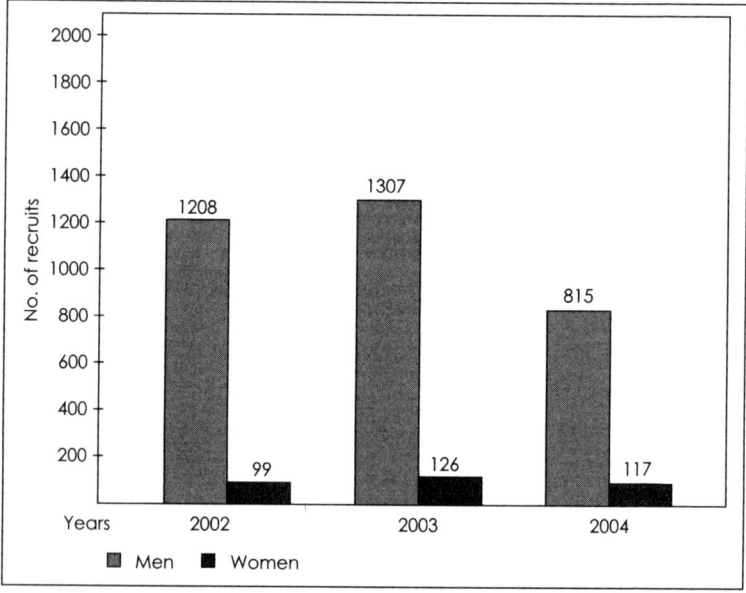

*Source:* NPMP *Survey,* 2005.

It is common knowledge that historically the oil and gas industry has been predominantly male and women have been underrepresented. The industry is based on science, engineering, and technology, and comparatively few women have pursued careers in those areas. Then, there are certain physically demanding disciplines such as drilling and production which are ideally suited to men. Attrition is not a major problem in the petroleum sector because PSEs in the petroleum sector offer life-long employment. But considering that demand for talent and expertise is far outstripping supply and half the experienced workforce is set to retire in the next decade, the sector is facing a crippling skills shortage. In order to power future energy projects, the oil and gas industry must act in time to fully tap into this enormous potential. (The total percentage of women employed across the public sector in India is 19 percent, the lowest among G20 countries) [8].

The key findings of the survey were presented during the petroleum sector roundtable given as follows:

- Women employees constitute only 5.4 percent of the total manpower. When this is compared with the number of women in all the PSEs it was corresponding to 5.9 percent. Despite all things being equal, the new entrants' ratio between men to women for the three preceding years of the survey was very negligible. In 1992, it was 14 women to 86 men; in 1993, it was 13 women to 87 men; and, in 1994, it was 12 women to 88 men. There were relatively few women in the more senior grades namely deputy general managers and general managers.
- Women were totally absent from the boardrooms.
- The age profile of the women was in the following range:
  58 percent in the age group 25–35 years
  30 percent in the age group 36–45 years
  12 percent in the age group 46 years and above

That meant, as many as 3,811 women employees (58 percent) needed flexible work procedures and childcare facilities during the first five years of their married life to be able to effectively combine career and family and to be active, responsible parents.

## Formation of intercorporate committee

It became clear to many that all was not well with regard to women in the industry. As a follow-up to the roundtable, an intercorporate committee was formed to make concrete recommendations to the

Ministry of Petroleum and Natural Gas (MoPNG), so that it could be adopted on an industry basis [9]. The members of the intercorporate committee acted as champions of this agenda in their respective companies. As internal change agents, they knew what would work in their culture and what would not. They focused on surveying the attitudes and comprehension of their broad employee base, and then facilitating implementation of practices.

The set of recommendations which emerged from the roundtable and developed by the intercorporate committee were as follows:

- To provide equal opportunities for advancement with female role models.
- Selection panels to comprise of at least one female member when applicants are women.
- Flexible working hours and more support to women with children by extending maternity leave from three to six months and shared parenthood leave for fathers.
- Provision of two-years' leave for childcare in the entire career, but not less than a minimum spell of six months.

These were first forwarded to the then secretary, MoPNG and, after proper scrutiny, the secretary sent it back to the CEOs of oil and gas enterprises for serious consideration and effective implementation. Some of these recommendations seem far ahead of their times, given that the extension of maternity leave of six months was approved only recently.

In addition, the roundtable succeeded in recommending the constitution of two awards, one for Best Enterprise for Women's Development and the other for Best Woman Executive, to be included in the NPMP scheme of Awards for Excellence. The main objective was to continue to focus attention on best practices and to further sustain women's development in the industry.

The main argument for promoting this case was that, if resource optimization was of utmost importance, then women who form an important segment of this resource could not be neglected. If companies seek maximum return on investment in human resource, then they must find best ways to retain them. Similarly, if reforms in social, economic, and political structures were being considered to give women a greater role in decision-making, then this must be reflected through industry practices.

No change, however, takes place without effective follow up. To ensure effective follow up, the agenda on "women's issues" was regularly placed in the bi-annual meet of personnel chiefs of the petroleum sector for several years.

Initially, there was some enthusiasm for this agenda. However, a few debates on the agenda flopped in subsequent meets, disintegrating into a painful mixture of skepticism and ridicule. Some people dismissed the discussion as a waste of time as they did not see it as their problem. This reaction was more from the senior male executives in the age group of 45–55 years, whose spouses were perhaps not working women. The younger male executives were much more receptive, understandably so, because in most cases their spouses were working. But all said and done one could say that, over time, such discussions created a climate for what was always seen as a "taboo" or "non-important issue" by breaking the collective silence, and converted a critical mass of senior leaders and industry HR practitioners to undertake/implement organizational changes wherever possible. The essential catalyst that continues to nurture the change remains leadership by example. Without it, nothing is possible. One of the many reasons that made it possible for women to be on the boards of oil and gas companies today is the climate created by such efforts.

## Lessons from the Intercorporate Initiative

So what have we learnt from this initiative in the petroleum sector?

### Ensure top commitment, cascading down to all management levels

It is important to keep senior management in the front and center. To overcome the resistance of senior people and to send a clear message to all concerned, the secretary, MoPNG, Government of

India, actively endorsed the women's initiative and set up two awards for women's development under the aegis of NPMP.

## Make the initiative very visible

By appointing an intercorporate task force to develop recommendations and by forwarding them to the administrative ministry, that in turn sent them back to the enterprises for implementation, the message was quickly flashed to the whole industry that this was an important agenda. That helped save the roundtable from being just another "program of the year" that led nowhere or "only the HR thing."

## Begin with dialogue and discussion as the platform for change

We invited the significant stakeholders in the industry to attend the intensive roundtable to first identify and then examine gender-based assumptions in mentoring and giving important assignments in the open discussion.

The members of the intercorporate task force each had a goal to "invite conversation" in their respective organizations. If that resulted in an uncomfortable initial conversation, then they were prepared to help people through the rough spots and get to a more enlightened open space for everyone.

## Make an airtight business case for cultural change

The most important strategy is to convince employers that gender equality is a best business practice. This requires documentation. Document the business imperative for change before you can justify the investment and effort that the initiative would require. No organization functions in a sociocultural vacuum; therefore, the employers must integrate it in the social fabric to bring about a multiplier effect.

## Develop a flexible system of accountability

We first asked the intercorporate committee members to measure the already existing initiatives in the enterprises. By making a presentation to the directors (HR), we worked with them to select their focus areas for change under the initiative.

## Periodic assessment and follow up

The conversation on the important issue was followed up with concrete operational steps. The effectiveness of gender-diversity programs, to be well implemented in the companies or industry, need clear follow-up processes in place. They have to be assessed on a regular basis, and their effectiveness has to be evaluated at various levels of the organization.

## Ensure equality proofing while developing policies

One has to ensure that while developing "new, women-friendly policies," there must not remain any gaps, as it can create a backlash in a manner that pushes organizations into developing anti-women agendas. Further, it is also going to require explicit initiatives to advance women's interests, initiatives informed by the analysis of numbers that are hard to come by due to lack of adequate database and grounded in the argument that advancing the interests of women benefits everyone. We realized that narrowing the gaps in policy, in opportunities at work and at decision-making levels would require reworking conventional assumptions. The worst aspects of these hidden assumptions are that they can be self-fulfilling.

## Give discretion to implement what is appropriate

Depending on the culture, history, and size of the organization or an entire industry, a different and sensitive approach is needed to transform the climate of the organization positively for both men and women. Just as each organization, each industry, is unique, its expression of inequity is unique too. The companies had the freedom to implement what best suited their culture. The cost of these changes, when weighed against the benefit, would be small. Many of the policy changes cost nothing but they are worth much. It is not only an investment in women, but also in their families and societies in the long run. It is a way to get onto a path of equitable, sustainable development.

Networking, as I have discussed in this chapter, proves beneficial as it serves in cost-effective ways. It also provides a great learning opportunity. Just as joining networks develops social capital, successful women leaders develop intellectual capital by cultivating a skill set in order to deal with the challenges and complexities they face at the workplace. This is explored in detail in the next chapter. The recommendation of cultivating a skill set is illustrative and of a not-one-size-fits-all kind. It is an aid for effectively coping at the workplace.

## References

1. Brass, Daniel J., 'Men's and Women's Networks: A Study of Interaction Patterns and Influence in an Organization', *Academy of Management Journal* 28: 327–43.
2. Department of Public Enterprises, *Public Enterprises Survey 2015–2016: Vol. I*, Department of Public Enterprises.
3. Narasimham, T. E., *Women on Night Shift: A Lesson from Tamil Nadu*, Associated Press, August 12, 2014.
4. 'AP Government Allows Women to Work in Factories in Night Shifts', *Press Trust of India*, April 4, 2015.
5. Mahamulkar, Sujit, 'An Equal Music: Maharashtra Nods for Women in Night Shifts', *Times of India*, May 21, 2015.
6. Heifetz, R., *Leadership Without Easy Answers*, Cambridge, MA: Harvard University Press, 1994.
7. Burt, Ronald, 'The Gender of Social Capital', Selected Paper No. 80, Chicago, IL: The University of Chicago Graduate School of Business, 1999.
8. EY, 'Worldwide Index of Women as Public Sector Leaders: Opening Doors for Women Working in Government', 2013, www.ey.com/government/womenleaders.
9. Hazarika, A., 'Leading and Executing Change Through a Learning Network', *Vikalpa* 33, no. 3 (2008).

# 5
# The Skills for All Seasons

Once a caterpillar asked a butterfly,
"How does one become a butterfly?"
"You must want to fly so much, you must enjoy flying so much that you just stop being a caterpillar," said the butterfly.

A strong, burning desire, together with the willingness and capacity to undergo fundamental change, is required to do anything new and different. When a caterpillar is transformed into a butterfly, its DNA may remain the same, but it undergoes a dramatic alteration. A butterfly is not a caterpillar with wings strapped to its back, and flying is not simply another form of crawling. It is an entirely different behavior, one that cannot be performed by a caterpillar, no matter what! Transformation, then, is all about making multiple, discontinuous behavioral changes and taking new initiatives for growth.

What are the requirements for a successful transformation? What is required for a successful corporate career? Obviously, there is no clear roadmap for being a successful woman executive/leader. The signposts on the road to success display considerable ambiguity which can keep capable women from bringing their talents to fully bear on organizational challenges. The positive side is that it allows multiple paths to effectiveness, numerous competencies to succeed. What really matters is one's willingness to take an inventory of the skills one has, constantly honing and refining them, and simultaneously cultivating the skills required for the new role. The implicit assumption is that women are operating from an initial base of competence and need to continuously build on it.

Although no one skill or even a skill set can guarantee flourishing careers to women, awareness of individual competencies, acceptance of their incremental contributions, and sensitivity to organizational culture can certainly be determinants to success.

It is important not to confuse performance with potential, and potential with readiness to handle the next job. For instance, the traits that make an individual successful in one role, such as attention to detail, can be detrimental in a more senior role where too much focus on detail or micro-managing can come in the way of looking at the big picture and hinder performance.

Some people are born with innate abilities: confidence, competence, drive, ambition, etc. Some develop the abilities instinctively as they grow up. But there are many skills that can be learned as one goes along. It may necessitate stock-taking, benchmarking, and changing and modifying one's personality and behavior.

By and large, most executive women I have come across in various settings mentioned specifically that they are still very much struggling with how they need to present themselves. They are learning to adapt by trial and error to various situations and different work environments as they encounter them. They recognize that it is possible to change one's views, habits, and responses by modifying one's thoughts and actions. Flexibility is critical to learning as well as to success. At the same time, one wonders whether traditional methods of development designed for men would adequately address the needs of women executives. For one, they have to overcome obstacles due to unfair practices and, second, they have to focus on successful methods by drawing on the skills and attitudes they develop from their experience as they go along.

Organizational culture is the single biggest determinant of behavior in the work setting and its impact is visible in all areas. To initiate appropriate changes that will lessen inequitable barriers to senior leadership positions, it is essential to address fundamental questions about the norms of behavior commonly found in work settings. These include policies and practices that favor the behavior of men, who are usually in the majority. Some of these are quite apparent, but others are subtle and may come across as gender neutral. But, as we know, there can be "unintended consequences" of supposedly gender neutral policies. Without making an effort to understand the complex issue, a majority of women tend to underscore the need to work hard and do their jobs well. They keep thinking that if they just work hard enough, well enough, and long enough, promotions will be guaranteed. It is true that women may have to work harder and smarter than men to be perceived as equals. Most women believe that, while they concentrate on doing good work, their organizations or bosses must take care of their needs for advancement, career development, etc. This is a common expectation. While doing good work is a "necessary" condition, it is not a "sufficient" condition. Rising to the higher levels in business settings generally requires obtaining a line-management role with responsibility for operations that generate profits and losses. But, because women may not be offered tough assignments or line-management opportunities, they have to actively seek experiences that can qualify them for promotions. Yet, actively seeking gets complicated by the commonly shared cultural expectation that women must use their knowledge and skills to benefit others in the organization. So, grabbing on to the best assignments can seem unwomanly and selfish.

## Is the "Cream" Being Pushed to the Top?

A general assumption in many companies is that the "cream will rise to the top." This unexamined assumption can tend to keep women from climbing the corporate ladder. In most companies what passes for cream "rising" to the top is actually cream being "pushed" to the top by an informal system of mentoring and advocacy. As far as women are concerned, it is usually difficult to secure a promotion above a certain level without a personal advocate or a sponsor.

Senior executives who only sponsor people like themselves—mostly men—don't do much to contribute to the cause of getting the best from every employee.

Survey after survey dispels the "pipeline myth," which assumes that, once women reach professional positions, a number of them will automatically rise to senior leadership positions. The pipeline no longer seems to be the primary issue. The main problem appears to be top leadership's failure to ensure that women get the profit-and-loss experience that would qualify them for the most senior positions [1].

Performance appraisal is another system where unexamined practices and patterns can have disastrous effects. For example, there are companies where official performance appraisals differ substantially from what is "said" informally, with the result that employees get their most accurate performance feedback through the grapevine. And if the grapevine is closed to women, they are left at a severe disadvantage.

Many studies indicate that women get limited exposure to the mix of assignments and diverse opportunities that can give them multi-dimensional exposure. This may work against women, who need to develop and demonstrate skills, and strengthen technical efficiency, because women often get sidetracked into non-technical or support jobs. Even if they are high performers, they move forward only inch by inch in middle management. Once in middle management, perhaps their careers can take off. However, in the case of men, high performers are fast tracked early in their careers. This difference in the career trajectories of men and women executives suggests that most companies implicitly have two different pathways for access to the top jobs.

Of course, all this wisdom dawns only in retrospect. One does not have either the hindsight or the maturity to reflect on this issue while in the thick of things. Many people tend to think about such issues as "taboo" topics. Women's issues are not something you discuss openly. The general perception is that, if you need to discuss it, then it must be a problem! But, once the hesitation is overcome, a considerate, sensitive senior might get more conscious about giving opportunities to women executives, such as attending important meetings, recommending critical, high-level decisions, etc. My experience tells me that women tend to advance further when their seniors understand or acknowledge the fact that "gender" can be a potential hazard. Then they can begin to help them deal effectively with some of the hazards.

It is during this period—the early phase of a career—that women need to focus on strengthening skills and competencies by taking in-house as well as external courses and seminars, by staying well-informed about organizational objectives and the macro environment, and reading relevant professional journals.

## The Strategies for Success

Although the meaning and definition of success is unique to each individual, and the organization one works for, when it comes to corporate success, it is a combination of one's own characteristics, political savvy, and a good deal of organizational support. It is for this reason that most successful women display similarity in certain attributes/skills, despite the diversity of industry (banking, insurance, petroleum, manufacturing retail, FMCG, etc.) in which they work.

A woman has to first establish a level of competence needed to convince everyone that she is equal to men. Women can demonstrate this competence by mastering job-related knowledge and being exceptionally well prepared for meetings. It may not be fair, but women need to perform beyond expectations and deliver more than their seniors expect, over and over again.

But, clearly, skill building or development involves real work one has not done before. It requires getting out of the comfort zone to do something that is different and, therefore, potentially stressful. Some are perfectly satisfied with their current work profile, even if that limits their career options. As has been famously said, "Not everyone has a flame that can be lit."

However, there are many who would not only like to light their flame but also see it burning bright. For them, some strategies are identified below. These are not a set of one-size-fits-all strategies, because such strategies seldom reflect the complexity of women's lives. It would be more effective for women to consider the general principles and how to apply them in their own situations. These seemed to have worked well for many successful women. They are not prescriptive but illustrative and, most importantly, can be learned. They are as appropriate for a new recruit as for an industry veteran.

## Understanding the culture and politics of the organization

Successful people—men and women alike—are sensitive to the cultural environment they work in, and are aware of organizational politics. Culture has been defined as the invisible glue that holds the organization together. It derives from the shared values, beliefs, practices, and norms that are held by the members of the organization. Before joining an organization, it is important find out as much as possible about its culture and value system, because organizational culture may dictate employee behavior. Understanding and personally aligning to the organization's direction and priorities can also facilitate effective influencing.

> Maria was overjoyed when she bagged a new role as Director, Customer Service at a five-star hotel. She excelled at customer service and problem solving with focus on achieving results. But, soon she realized that the new workplace had a deeply ingrained culture of "face time." The more hours you put in the better. The 24/7 service, 365 days a year, was grueling. She began working 50–55 hours a week and, when she added a commute of one hour every day, it became a 12-hour day. On top of that, her manager expected her to be at work before him and leave after him. After adjusting to that incompatible routine for days on end, Maria noticed that "she was increasingly becoming the person she did not want to be." She longed for life outside her work as earlier. After eight months, Maria realized that she could not continue this way for long. At the first available opportunity, she switched to another role that was not as high profile or high paying but offered a more predictable routine.

It is, therefore, important to "know thyself" and your business-related priorities and values. The cultural fit is very important. Failing to fit will increase your chances of either lack of engagement or even separation.

Many women dislike and reject organization politics intensely and view themselves as apolitical. They confuse being political with being scheming or untrustworthy. But it is impossible to avoid politics in organizations even if most women prefer to be left alone to do their jobs. Like it or not, organizational politics are an integral part of daily working life. They can help or hinder you in achieving objectives. Women need to learn to map the power dynamics in their organization and how to ethically use them to support their strategy implementation. They also need to learn ways to identify and counter people who are acting overtly or covertly to obstruct their strategy implementation.

Organizations are a complex maze of constituencies populated by turf watchers, those who sit on the fence, and those who seek power. Those who are politically savvy accept this as a reality and deal with it. They are sensitive to the impact on others of what they say or do and realize that going about it in the wrong way can cause avoidable conflicts and misunderstanding. But, just as the hierarchical organization has to change in order to give and demand fairness to women, women have to develop organizational sensibilities to be able to contribute effectively in changing times. Just like the feminist adage, "the personal is political," I would say, "the organizational is political." In fact, the understanding of organizational politics will aid in getting things done, and to identify and influence the actual decision makers.

## Seeking mentors and role models in the organization

Executives, men and women alike, need different kinds of developmental relationships at different points in their careers. We need both technical as well as emotional support, coaching, and advice from someone who is knowledgeable, wise, and experienced.

Technical support is required in terms of how to do certain things and emotional support in terms of sharing the experience, the thrill of doing it. This is particularly relevant in early careers when one is not certain about implementing a technical instruction or an advice, or one is not certain about assuming certain work behaviors; for instance, an aggressive style of marketing. Through his or her knowledge or experience, the mentor can answer questions, provide evaluation and analysis of situations, and offer suggestions for career development. Also, a mentor can provide a wealth of information about the company that may not be readily available or may require years of personal experience, e.g., how do the formal and informal networks in the organization work. It takes time to build confidence, credibility, and competence in a new role. For women in senior positions, it is a lonely journey. In any case, at the higher level women are greatly outnumbered by men. Many feel they have no one to discuss career issues with or seek advice from. These feelings of isolation and the lack of role models creates the need for a mentor. The importance of a mentoring relationship is increasingly being recognized. It is not confined to learning how to do a job, but extends to coping with the political processes that operate in organizations and personal relationships. The mentor may give feedback on performance and because he/she is usually outside the direct reporting line, such feedback can be constructive but without the evaluative overtones that exist in similar discussions with one's boss. Mentors can also offer support, encouragement, and coaching that would not only be critical for job satisfaction but also career commitment. In fact, one can seek advice from different mentors at different times for different types of career issues.

A mentor therefore has a personal relationship with the person or the protégé. It is, therefore, difficult to have several mentors at the same time. A close mentoring relationship is formed when both parties see parts of themselves in the other person. The young executive sees someone whom she wants to be like in the future. The mentor sees someone who reminds him/her of himself/herself years ago.

If this is true for all executives, then what would be the inherent difficulties of mentoring across gender?

For one, mentors and role models could be hard to find. Considering very few women are in senior positions it can be difficult to find a woman who has experience and is accessible.

In many cases, the mentor can be a man and this can pose some problem to women. Cross-gender relationships being rare in most organizations, tend to be more noticeable. The possibility of such public scrutiny can discourage people from participating in such relationships. It is, therefore, important to identify mentors who:

- Have a reputation for developing others and who are going to stretch you.
- Know a lot about the organization, how it works, where it is going.
- Who have a wide range of skills to pass on and are known to be good at what they do.
- Whom you respect and who have time for you.
- Who can connect you to the world outside of work through a wide network of contacts.

Women in senior positions need to look out for younger women they can mentor. There is surely some virtue in making sure that others are empowered as we go along.

Many surveys reveal that, while a huge majority (95 percent) view mentors as important for career advancement, a large proportion (42 percent) of the participants said they were neither a mentor nor a mentee. In order to help women progress to senior positions in all sectors of the industry and become the role models of tomorrow, this needs to change [2].

The importance of a mentoring relationship cannot be denied in any field, whether it be industry, academia, or science. Mentorships have been reported to be most helpful in three areas: career planning, coaching and guidance; protection and career risk management; and increasing aspiration levels and providing a role model [3].

The US National Research Council (NRC), the National Academy of Sciences committee in charge of a Gender Differences report determined that women who had a mentor did better than women without one. They reached this conclusion by analyzing the results of two national surveys, of tenure-track and tenured faculty in six disciplines (biology, chemistry, mathematics, civil engineering, electrical engineering, and physics) at 89 institutions. They found that, in chemistry, for example, female assistant professors with mentors had a 95 percent probability of having grant funding versus 77 percent for women without mentors. Across the six fields surveyed, female assistant professors with no mentors had 68 percent probability of having grant funding versus 93 percent of women with mentors [4].

Like anything else, mentoring relationships come to an end or fade out in case they serve no purpose or are ineffective. This is because mentoring needs change. I have had the privilege of having three mentors in three different phases of my career, and have benefitted tremendously from their and guidance.

I, therefore, strongly recommend new officers to actively seek out mentors, both formally and informally. Organizations can create an enabling environment for success by formalizing the mentoring process. As a prerequisite to this system, organizations need to identify potential mentors, train them, and ensure that they are paired with high-potential, promising women executives. This will ensure all junior executives have equal access to a mentor with a focus on a specified time frame.

## Being open to constructive feedback

One difficulty often talked about by men is how to give developmental feedback to women as their peers or subordinates in a work environment. It can be an extremely uncomfortable situation for both parties, but particularly for men. Usually, when a man wants to give feedback to another man it is given straight without any frills or fuss. This is because both the appraiser and appraisee have had similar socialization.

But a man may experience some hesitation in giving feedback to a woman, especially if it involves a certain amount of constructive criticism. He might unconsciously hold a stereotype about women which may lead him to interpret that women are more emotional, and, therefore, might get upset with his observations. In fact, emotional displays can suggest a temperamental weakness in work environments which are predominantly masculine. It may also reinforce the negative stereotype of women that they are more emotional and less professional. As a result, women may lose the opportunity to learn from a valuable insight. Dealing with criticism can be painful. But, by extracting valid points from it, one can learn, improve, overcome hurdles, and press on towards one's goal.

As we all know, feedback and/or evaluation is important for all, but more so for women as they advance in their careers. Women need to identify areas where they need improvement and areas where they excel. However, women frequently do not have the opportunity to discuss specific areas in which they may receive effective feedback. When I look back on my own career, I realize how true this has been for me too. Of the five or six significant bosses I worked with and learnt from, only one or two bothered to take time out to give me specific feedback about my performance that required behavior change. At another time, one of them specifically asked me to give a developmental feedback to a woman executive because he did not want to take that "risk" as he put it.

Feedback is never easy to take, even when you know it's essential to your development and you trust the person delivering it.

So what can be done?

## Depersonalize the feedback

Most women tend to take things too personally whether it is good humored teasing or criticism. Women tend to dwell on the comments for weeks while a man who teased her in the first place will forget all about it. It is, therefore, equally important not to take things too personally or too seriously. Learn to laugh at yourself occasionally and you will be gaining an incredibly valuable skill. The question to ask is: "Do they treat me any differently from anyone else?" Perhaps not! It is, therefore, important to depersonalize issues and externalize feelings by first identifying them and then expressing them appropriately. Getting better at receiving feedback starts with understanding and managing those feelings.

Be open to feedback. Don't be resentful when you get it. Learn from it and extract value from it even when it is poorly delivered. With practice, one can learn to do it effortlessly.

## Separate the message from the messenger

> Bella, a team leader at a pharmaceutical company, received glowing comments from her peers and superiors during her 360-degree review, but was surprised by the negative feedback she got from her direct reports. She immediately concluded that the problem was at their end: "I am a perfectionist, and some of them can't handle that," she thought. In this way, she changed the focus from her management style to her subordinates' competence, preventing her from learning something important about the impact she had on others.
>
> A couple of days later, when her targets started sliding down, she realized that she was responsible for the team performance. She was accountable for both—her style as well as their performance. That's when she decided to talk to her team and ask, "What can we do together to improve the situation?" It led to a rich conversation beneficial to all. In order to get full benefit of the feedback one has to separate the message from the messenger and then consider both.

This is not to say that women's ability to express emotion must be seen only as a weakness and not a strength. In fact, women's ability to express appropriate feelings and emotions, or vulnerability for that matter, may actually add a humanizing dimension to an otherwise cold and cutthroat work environment. This humanizing dimension could have a very positive effect on the quality of life in organizations.

Women are also accused of being too involved in their work, too attached to their assignments, departments or functions. It is seen as a deficit. Any feedback about such assignments is difficult to digest. Just as tapping into one's personal experiences, as well as making personal connections, is important for learning, the timely letting go of negative experiences and dysfunctional attachments is part of further development.

Otherwise, our personal experiences of success or failure, rewards or punishment can act as a screen for future decisions. One unknowingly continues to take perceptional shortcuts or overlook details or emerging patterns. Therefore, holding on to personal or professional grievances, negative criticism beyond a point may not serve any purpose. Making a conscious effort to depersonalize from such experiences will pave the way for ongoing growth.

## Developing ability to take initiatives

Young girls are brought up and socialized with a different set of assumptions, beliefs, influences, and assessments from young boys. The stories that are told to young girls are different from those told to the boys at an early age. These stories reinforce stereotypes and traditional behaviors. The themes of the stories told to young girls are: "Do not fight the system," "Try and adjust to the environment," "Do as you are told," "Don't tell others what to do," "Don't challenge, quickly fall in line, after all you are a girl." These stories tranquilize them into passivity, into rejecting leadership roles, into being recipients of favors and welfare given by others. These stories do not expand into wonderful possibilities and do not actively shape them as agents of change. The themes of these stories are beginning to change here and there, but they have not changed dramatically enough to make any significant difference.

Is it any wonder then that women lack experience in taking initiatives and in taking smart risks in adult life, despite the fact that an increasing number of women have access to professional training, education, and experience?

It seems that this "baggage" of socialization is difficult to discard. One has to make great, and conscious, efforts to overcome it. The ability to take charge of one's life, to take decisions concerning self and work, to be assertive when required, are all qualities conventionally associated with masculine behavior.

Women demonstrating the very same qualities are often perceived as excessively aggressive or unladylike. How does one then develop agency or the very useful ability to take initiatives?

In my workshops, whenever I have asked women what is it that may be holding them back from doing something they always wanted to do, many of them say that it is the feeling that they cannot do it, the feeling that they are not smart, talented or experienced enough. It is the fear of making the first move, which is also an aspect of risk taking. This feeling gets transferred into work situations. We need to learn from Marissa Mayer, CEO of Yahoo, who says, "I always did something I was a little not ready to do. I think that's how you grow. When there is that moment of 'Wow, I am not really sure I can do this' and you push through those moments, that's when you have a breakthrough" [5].

Another barrier for women is waiting to be asked. Many women feel that people will ask them to interview for a position, if they are qualified, but often that's not true. People don't always know what you want to do, if you don't tell them. You can't be afraid to ask. It is surprising how often you can get what you want when you just ask for it. However, one powerful assumption that can act as a barrier for some women is relying on the organization rather that doing it on their own whenever possible. They need to define a career path for themselves.

For instance, if you are approached to take on a new project or assignment, you should seriously think about taking it instead of wondering about your capabilities. If other people did not think you were qualified, they would not have offered you the project. Challenging assignments that push people to do something new or different are very important for leadership development. It is also important to have broad-based knowledge and competitive skills in a complex business environment. Women must ensure that they are "seen" exercising their knowledge, skills and abilities. Women will not be able to capitalize on "expert power" if they are not perceived as experts. They need to clearly signal their sources of power. It might mean taking risks and initiative in using skills rather than waiting to be consulted.

Sometimes, women have difficulty in stepping outside the given frame of reference when it comes to their job descriptions. Women often self-select out of opportunities because of their own comfort levels. They may feel that if someone else is already doing a particular assignment, it becomes out-of-bound for them. They hesitate to deal with it. However, in the era of developing overall employability and multiple skills and functions, it is important to be flexible, adaptable, and to be able to cross over boundaries to other functions. The implication for developing agency also requires taking full ownership, responsibility, and accountability for one's own development. To create a life of your own definitions, you need to find out what makes you grow, and then move on to the interesting possibilities primarily focusing on being responsible for one's development and moving out of one's comfort zone for new roles.

Increasingly, people need to be more accountable for their own work, take responsibility for their own performance. Organizations will recruit and invest in people who are self-motivated, self-driven, self-tutored, and who are willing to use a variety of methods to understand what's required in a new situation and facilitate the development of new capacities.

I know of a few senior corporate women who intentionally moved out of their comfort zone to try on "unfamiliar behaviors" that go with the new role requirement. It could be as a member of a cross-functional task force or dealing with senior-level assignments. The new role may even require entertaining important clients or business delegations after working hours, something that cannot be delegated at times. One has to learn to put up with such requirements even if it means going against the grain.

## Building resiliency and change readiness

Organizations are constantly undergoing change in today's business environment. They redefine their mission, restructure systems, acquire new companies or merge with global counterparts in business, set up operations in emerging markets, or simply close non-core loss-making units. Similarly, a change could mean a change in role, job content, level of responsibility, a change in location or employer. Managing and adapting to change, and mastering it, are emerging as key traits for successful executives.

How does one cope or be comfortable with all-pervasive change? The first reaction is to resist as it throws one out of the comfort zone. But, the ability to recover from it and use it to one's advantage is absolutely necessary to thrive in times of change.

During times of transition and specially during times of change, women need to create that space and time to cope effectively with the emotional wear and tear of daily living, mainly because they risk being less effective or productive in their career and personal life. Often, they are the fulcrum around which the family rotates and, at the same time, they are also expected to perform effectively at work.

> Nikita felt settled in her life in Mumbai these past five years. She loved her job as a divisional marketing manager in a consumer durables company. She had a supportive husband and two children who were studying in a reputed school in the neighborhood. She travelled frequently for work so the children were used to her absence from home.
> 
> But then she heard some news that disturbed her peace and tranquility. Her company was looking for someone to head the expanding Bangkok office. It is the kind of opportunity she had always wanted. Her boss felt she could be right for the role. But the timing? It was utterly wrong. Maybe this explained her migraine attacks that were getting more frequent lately. She was confronted with multiple uncertainties. Can she manage it? What impact would it have on the family? These questions kept her awake at night.

> Her first reaction was to refuse it. It was too frightening. But then she realized that it would mean stunted growth. So she decided to speak to her boss who felt she should accept the role that would be career defining. Then she discussed family implications with her husband exploring all the dynamics reflecting on all the priorities, options and trade-offs. It meant the children had to stay in Mumbai for the rest of the school year till they moved to Bangkok. After talking to everyone, she felt that everyone could handle the separation for a period of time. She also reached out to her network of friends and family for their support and advice. Her mother offered to come and stay with the children. These conversations helped her in gaining great clarity and confidence.
>
> Nikita finally took the plunge. The first few months were indeed difficult. She felt torn between missing home and her familiar work environment and getting to know the unfamiliar one. But things gradually settled down and the transition went smoothly. She now looked forward to rejoining her family in summer. Her family valued her resiliency in dealing with the times of transition.

Resiliency is an ability to first accept and then recover quickly from change, that is, from viewing change as negatively stressful to positively challenging—the ability to see the glass as half full. It requires adaptability, persistence, optimistic outlook, and active coping to be able to bounce back from adversity. Women demonstrate flexibility, durability, and adaptability while juggling multiple tasks and responsibilities. However, change is so pervasive that, despite good intentions, we end up resisting it. Yet, resiliency can be developed to deal with the pressures and uncertainties of personal as well as organizational life. Resiliency is a gender-neutral quality. It will increase the ability to handle the unexpected that change brings as an opportunity for development. By becoming resilient one can learn from the lessons change can bring.

The good news is that it can be developed. In interviews with 250 high-ranking women executives, McKinsey researchers found that they attributed their own success to resilience and grit. Perseverance through challenging circumstances can shape a woman's ability to lead [6].

## Honing influencing skills

Just as a good golfer carries different clubs in his golf bag to hit the ball on the fairway—a driver to tee off, a wedge to take it out of a hazard, and a putter to gently roll it in the hole during a round of golf—a manager today relies on learning a variety of influencing styles to get his work done. This is because success today hinges on the cooperation of several people across your organization over whom you may have no formal authority: peers and superiors from other divisions, customers, vendors, virtual teams, outsourcing partners. Influence, in short, is utilizing the power of persuasion to gain the support of others. Research [7] has identified five distinct styles: rationalizing, asserting, negotiating, inspiring, and bridging, of which asserting and negotiating are extremely relevant to women leaders. Men tend to use the assertive style, while women tend to use the negotiating style more. However, ironically, they use it for others and not for themselves.

The interpersonal orientation that draws women to work with people also makes them vulnerable to be emotionally affected by certain encounters. They may be provoked by some, drained by others, or feel nurtured by some. It is difficult for most women to be impersonal. This can work both ways, as an asset as well as a liability. It is, therefore, important not to be drawn off-center by what another person does or says, stay calm, and communicate and act effectively in the midst of emotional turbulence or difficult situations.

Assertiveness is a skill that every woman needs to acquire as an important tool for effective communication, because the socialization of women does not naturally prepare or arm them with it. Often, women are ridiculed for lacking aggressive, competitive business instincts, but, on the contrary, they are also scorned for being too aggressive. This double bind needs to be finessed to some extent by combining assertive behavior with gentleness.

Often there is confusion about what is assertive, and what is termed as aggressive. As we know, an aggressive person accuses or attacks others. As a result, people often end up feeling defensive, hurt, and upset. An aggressive person tends to disregard others' rights or feelings, threatens or questions them, and wants to win at all costs. On the other hand, an assertive person speaks clearly, honestly, sharing her views and feelings so that her position is heard. She takes up responsibility for herself, lets people know exactly where she stands, and challenges ideas or inputs with which she disagrees. Assertiveness means taking charge of oneself, being aware of one's rights, setting goals, making choices. It does not mean winning at any cost, or at the expense of others. It also means respecting oneself as much as one is expected to respect others.

Many women think that they will not be liked or appreciated for their assertive behavior. In fact, my experience suggests people will take you far more seriously when you exhibit consistently assertive behavior. Such perception often hinders assertiveness behavior from reaching its full potential.

As one senior bank manager remarked,

> Even though I was in a very high position in the bank, I had to initiate my own contacts and did not see others coming to me. So I had to take the lead, I had to take the initiative all the time.

Despite others' reluctance to reach out to her, her assertive strategy allowed her to develop valuable relationships. Mastering the art of influence through assertiveness and persuasion are essential skills for anyone on a leadership path.

## Why negotiate?

As you take on different roles in the organization, you need to influence your peers to endorse your agenda or to commit to your desired goals, and your superiors, whose sponsorship and resource allocation you need to achieve your departmental strategy. At times, you need to negotiate to claim value for the work you already do. So one needs to give and take in order to reach an outcome that satisfies the greater interest.

Often women managers wrongly view negotiation as a tool for manipulation. If conducted with an eye towards mutual benefit, it can vastly enhance one's influence. But women are often not comfortable with negotiation. The roots may lie in early socialization, in their discomfort with confrontation, or even in some degree of self-promotion. Whatever the reason, negotiation or bargaining is difficult for women in the workplace because it is a "power" and "influence" issue more than anything else. At another level, it is also an issue of "self-esteem." Glassdoor's 2016 survey reveals that 68 percent of women accepted the salary they were offered and did not negotiate their salary in their current/most recent job; a 16-percentage point difference when compared to men [(52 percent) 8].

Evidence also suggests that women who initiate salary negotiations are seen as more demanding and less likable than women who accept the salaries they are offered [9]. There is an assumed penalty for entering negotiation, as one has to say good things about oneself. To avoid the pitfalls of negotiation, women need to be well informed about typical salaries and benefit packages, and compare themselves to equally qualified men. They also need to rely on their own merit, track record, and achievements. Then, they must overcome any inhibition in initiating negotiation.

Paradoxically, women can act as powerful negotiators on behalf of their organizations (as countless examples will prove), but feel shy of asking for themselves and, consequently, collude with and further reinforce the stereotype that good women should not ask for themselves.

Knowing what your skills are worth, making clear what you bring to the table, emphasizing common goals, and maintaining a positive attitude are some negotiation tactics that have been shown to be effective for women [10].

Then, they have to take a look at their styles of negotiation. Women generally sport a style that is less aggressive than men. They have to take care to make the right impression at the beginning by acting twice as tough and unyielding. Men approach negotiation rather differently. By and large, they want to "win at all cost," while women approach it with a "win-win" strategy. By itself, this strategy is not bad if women learn to ask for what they want and, in case not provided, they must refuse to back down, or be willing to make trade-offs in order to get things accomplished.

It is important to consider cultural context. Asian cultures demand women to have modesty, respect toward seniors, and deference for collective decision making. Negotiation which involves elements of self-marketing can prove to be very uncomfortable and challenging. Evidence suggests that people do not appreciate women who initiate salary negotiations compared to women who meekly accept the salaries they are offered [11]. Women are penalized for self-promotion and negotiations require some degree of self-promotion.

Sometimes, it is helpful to have someone senior who can present the woman manager's case in a negotiation. Research [12] shows there are two benefits associated with having an advocate when a woman is being considered for an important assignment or a promotion. The woman is perceived as more prestigious if someone is advocating for her. That is the authority principle into action. For instance, if an advocate for a candidate makes demands based on the candidate's merits, it does not harm the candidate. But, if a woman has to play broker for herself, she often appears self-aggrandizing and it rubs people the wrong way. It also harms the prospects of the candidate. Research shows that women who are anything but modest about their accomplishments are harmed interpersonally. Men can also do themselves damage by being boastful, but people expect them to be aggressive and boastful so it hurts them far less. This demonstrates the power of the double bind in operation as far as women are concerned. Even then, it is important to keep updating one's skills as may be necessary in a continuously changing work scenario.

## Dealing with the challenge of being yourself

Empowerment, by its very nature, implies a shift in the balance of power. It means a change from the top-down ways of centralized governance to a more participatory system of decision making. It means a greater responsiveness on the part of the political system to the needs of its diverse workforce. It means transparency in dealings, openness to scrutiny, and an unequivocal right to information. Empowerment stands on the foundation of authenticity, and it's a tough challenge.

Authenticity is at a premium among leaders today. We are told to bring our full selves to the office and to tell our personal stories to establish trusting relationships. Authenticity begins with self-awareness: knowing who you are, your values, emotions, and competencies, and how you are perceived by others. It is also acting upon those values while transparently interacting with others.

In order to succeed in a corporate environment, can women afford to be themselves? Perhaps not yet. Women who transparently reveal their values, place themselves at risk if those values are not shared by their male colleagues. For instance, a female vice-president of a company said, "My reluctance to promote myself and advertise my accomplishments gets penalized by my senior colleagues. They underestimate my value. I have a hard time dealing with this cutthroat competition and obsessive self-promotion at the top." Understanding the organizational or cultural context is very important before any self-disclosure. Despite its potential benefits, self-disclosure can backfire if it is ill-timed or inconsistent with the organizational ethos.

> Rita, a highly competent and intelligent manager of public relations, was asked to make a presentation to a group of media people. Exhausted after a sleepless night with a sick baby and making slides for the presentation, to add spice, she decided to share that experience on the spur of the moment, much to the discomfort of the audience. In the process, she lost her credibility as a professional. She could have saved that story to share over a cup of coffee with her women colleagues.

Self-disclosures, however genuine, must further the task at hand, to help people get a better understanding of one's thinking and rationale. Instead of seizing the opportunity to enhance her credentials through the presentation, the ill-timed disclosure diminished Rita's status and worried the team leader about its impact on the guests. Getting self-disclosures right takes a deft touch, for leaders at any stage of their career.

The challenge is how to create more acceptance of one's behavior and values without violating one's sense of authenticity. The most helpful cultures are those in which there is recognition and appreciation of the non-work aspects of life—where all employees are able to bring their authentic selves to the workplace and to seek support for work–life challenges. Often, the top management is seen as enthusiastic about bringing in and promoting women to higher levels of responsibility and to realize the goals of equal opportunity. But, sometimes, they are clueless about how to define it as an organizational problem. Even more prevalent is their inability to figure out how to provide leadership on the issue. The actual decisions about who is ready to move up the corporate ladder are generally left to middle-level managers. In most organizations, middle management is made up primarily of men who may feel threatened by the interest and enthusiasm of the top management in developing women who are different from them. Also, the middle-management cadre could also represent a microcosm of society with certain values, and prejudices, about women. Dealing with women as peers or colleagues challenges their entrenched belief systems. They need to be sensitized to create the conditions under which all individuals have equal opportunity to succeed according to their ability.

Women have to be sensitive to the fact that they challenge the status quo of power equations by their presence, actions, and decisions. This can result in articulated or unarticulated tensions or oversensitivity to certain issues. Without screaming or thrashing about it, they need to take it in their stride at least in the initial years until they have proven their worth. Many women leave in frustration as they do not feel valued or respected. The most common reasons given by women for leaving are: poor relationships with their superiors, unchallenging, demeaning assignment, no growth opportunities, no recognition for achievements, unfair compensation for delivering the same results or, in some cases, better results than their male colleagues.

However, the burden of adaptation does not have to be borne by women alone. More and more employees, including men, are coming to the workplace inclined to celebrate their difference and less willing to adapt blindly and give up one's own uniqueness. Just as the corporations have a right to demand good performance, they also have to recognize their obligation to share the responsibility of adapting. Women, therefore, need not wait to seek opportunities or leadership until a level playing field is created. There will be initial challenges in breaking into male bastions, but if dealt successfully can create organizational change for the women coming after them.

## Defining "work–life balance" for yourself

Work–life balance is an issue for many women all over the world to varying degrees depending on the domestic support, country, and culture. Work-life integration is a tightrope walk, as most senior executives will tell you. However, by making deliberate choices about which opportunities to pursue and which to decline, rather than getting pressure prompted or simply reacting to emergencies, women executives can engage meaningfully with work, family, and community.

In my coaching practice, I have frequently seen that executives tend to ignore work–life balance until something goes wrong. Work priorities go for a toss due to a personal crisis: hypertension at the age of 30, a heart attack or a death in the family, relocation due to international postings at a time when family responsibilities are particularly critical. This kind of disregard is neither wise nor healthy, because one loses one's freedom to choose between multiple priorities. The trick is not to let anyone else or any situation define your work–life balance. One needs to own one's choices and trade-offs.

The challenge of balancing family, work, and community affects a large number of people, but it mostly affects working women with dependent children or elder care. For example, it is a common observation by many women that their senior tends to reward those who stay beyond working hours or are readily available to work on weekends, while her spouse or children want her home for several reasons. The problem stems from an outdated idea that time spend on the job equals an employee's value to the organization.

How can a super-performer—one who is seen as an energetic, high-achieving, dedicated individual willing to give the company unlimited time—shift gears after becoming a parent without damaging her professional image? How can a person demonstrate seriousness and commitment, and still leave the office on time, or avoid late meetings and business dinners? The demand for long hours affects women differently from men. Owing to the anticipated conflict of such work with childcare responsibilities, some women in high status careers tend to remain single or forgo or delay childbearing.

These competing demands can make the woman executive feel completely torn or stressed or guilty if she gives priority to one set of demands over the other.

Even in dual-career families men have less demands because wives accept most domestic responsibilities. Women still take most of the responsibility for home and family. Women's paid employment has led to the expansion of women's roles rather than redefinition of gender roles for both men and women. This reflects higher expectations from "mothering" as compared with "fathering."

Various surveys have indicated that people devote far less time to leisure than earlier, despite advances in technology that promised to make modern life easier and free from drudgery. In women's concern for their spouse, their children, and all the other important people in their lives, as well as concern for their work, they sometimes forget about themselves. They must find time for themselves and their own friends and pastimes. It is important to reevaluate from time to time what is important and meaningful, what one wants out of life.

In fact, senior women executives find it difficult to take advantage of family-friendly policies even if the organizations provide them due to the nature of the job, their own critical role, and the expectations from them. In the event a difficult situation arises when one has to accord the highest priority to the family, it may be a good idea to discuss it with your boss, so that alternative arrangements can be made in advance; for example, rearranging your work schedule to come in earlier, work later, or work from home for some time. It is now increasingly possible because, in a technology-based workplace, work is something you do, not a place you go. Flexible work arrangements and flexible schedules should increasingly be made part of organizational culture. These family-friendly policies will bring down the high turnover rate. Second, this dilemma will not arise if the goal is equity and not equality. This means everyone's life outside of work must be treated with respect but not necessarily in the same way or identically. Third, those senior managers who feel they cannot lend enthusiastic support to family-friendly policies as they will be perceived as favoring one group of employees (such as women) over the other (such as men), need to remember that flexibility is no longer considered a "woman's" issue but a "family" issue. Today's children are tomorrow's labor force. When parents raise their children well, society at large will reap enormous benefits.

However, developing personal effectiveness in managing multiple roles over time is of paramount importance. Personal effectiveness often depends on being able to take control of things which seem out of control, such as time and stress. In any case, there are two ways of looking at balancing family and career and the multiple role-taking they generate. If not well managed, the multiple roles can create stress, strain, and anxiety. On the flip side, having multiple roles can enhance health and well-being, because each new role creates opportunities for learning, and building social support and skills not known earlier. Having multiple roles expands an individual's capacities, because a problem in one role can be buffeted by success in other roles. Skills and resources acquired in one role can be effectively used in another. For example, time management skills acquired at work can be useful not only at home but also for community work.

In fact, parenting is a job like any other. The more time you devote to it, the better you get at it. Women can be good managers, not in spite of having children, but because of them. Consider some of the lessons that being a parent teaches: the importance of self-discipline, the benefits of a long-term view, the ability to set limits, the training in subsuming one's needs for the sake of collective needs. All these skills and values can surely be transferred to work-related management

Try out some of the practical solutions given below:

## Managing multiple roles and emerging role stress

Most senior executives today feel that they cannot achieve "balance" through constant juggling, which prevents them from engaging meaningfully either at work or at home. It is, therefore, important to define what "balance" means to you. For a travelling marketing executive, it could mean being home at least three times in a week, for another, it is connecting with the children over the weekend or focusing on their education, or having a family holiday together. It is during this family time that one has to decide when, where, and how much to be accessible for work by managing communications technology (emails, text messages, voice mails, etc.). Women rarely see themselves as working for the family as men do, but they have to deal with the emotional guilt of not spending enough time with the children, the guilt of being absent when needed at home, the guilt of missing out. I have felt these tensions myself, and have to deal with them all the time. Sometimes, I could handle them well, sometimes not. But I always wanted my children to know that work is important to me and a big part of my identity. Working has not only augmented my motherly life but has also expanded my whole being for my children. Therefore, this tension has to be weighed and balanced against the growth and fulfillment of working.

## Review and reduce the number of roles

If you are always running late, tend to work with a backlog, feel guilty about not having enough time for family and home, then take a look at your various roles and the demands they make on your time. You may perhaps practice withholding commitment, to enable you to do something outside your normal work-related tasks: school events, professional conferences, club events, garden festivals, and so forth.

Many women have a tendency to accept a project or additional responsibility immediately, as they find it difficult to say no, and then have second thoughts about it. Remember, you only have 24 hours in a day. If you are already feeling stretched, then this additional commitment will stretch you further and you will end up resenting it.

Each of the roles an individual takes on in life is an expression of a different aspect of him or her. No one role can express all of who we are. However, there is still the all too common pitfall of losing oneself in one role. By recognizing one's distinct roles, one is less vulnerable to the pains of exercising leadership whether at home, work, or in society [13].

## Time management

Demands for long hours present another challenge that women need to negotiate. Expecting constant availability from employees can produce stress and can actually reduce organizational productivity. Requiring long hours all the time can also reflect lack of planning, task orientation, and inability to delegate. Women executives are often quite accessible and find it difficult to resist interruptions. Having an open-door policy is useful but it has its own costs. It will leave you less time to handle other tasks. Communicate with superiors and colleagues and generally plan for the future. It is important to stop others from spending your time by being too accessible. It is not which part of your life is more important, but what is more important right now.

It is also important to identify what is important, what is the key goal, and keep track of how you use your time in achieving it. It is time to make changes in case you are not meeting that goal. Time is money. It needs to be spent like any other resource. It must get you the maximum return.

To maximize the benefits of time management, it is important to set priorities and organize the day in a manner that people at work know when you are available to them just as people at home do. At work, you need to set deadlines for meetings and conversations and, most importantly, stick to them. This effective utilization of time will help you take on, rather than shirk, responsibilities, as well as take initiatives in doing new or different things.

## Building support networks

During demanding times, it is family, friends or colleagues who help us out of the jam. It is important to stay connected to those people who are close and take a personal interest in our lives. Managing a family and professional life requires a strong network of supporters. On one end is a spouse or partner, followed by friends and paid help, with support from extended family on the other.

The relationship with partners is very important. The facility of turning to partners for emotional support or for a fresh perspective on a problem which cannot be discussed with others is absolutely invaluable. Sometimes, partners urge you to take business risks or pursue job opportunities that may not look immediately attractive, but can lead to long-term satisfaction. In short, partners can help you make deliberate choices about work, travel, household management, community participation, leisure activities, and so on.

Many women keep their networks separate for fear of harming their image. Some never mention their families at work for fear of appearing unprofessional. For instance, one woman had been coached not to mention daycare pick-up or other family responsibilities, lest she incur a "motherhood penalty."

Network at work matters too. Trusted colleagues or friends from other functions serve as valuable sounding boards. Networking is important to stay more current with what friends and colleagues do outside of work. Women never seem to find enough time for it, but professional networking is extremely important in producing recognition of high-quality work. To that end, actively building your profile and networking as a routine and priority activity is important.

## Keeping relationships professional

While managing various roles and role-related relationships, it is extremely important to keep the professional relationships professional. Even though it is best to remain professional at all times, you don't have to stop being yourself. The need for integrating various life roles is a main driver in case of high-achieving women. It also contributes to psychological well-being.

As far as organizations are concerned, they can take heart from new research that demonstrates a positive relationship between multiple roles and managerial performance. As commitment to a non-work role increases, so does the effectiveness in the managerial role [14]. Although people can experience stress from multiple roles at times, it is clear that life associated with work and family responsibilities provides mental and physical well-being. There are several reasons for this benefit. Multiple roles expand the capacities of the individual. Success and skills acquired in one role can be transferred to another role. Similarly, problems in one role can be dodged by success in other role. Multiple roles add more color to life [15].

Breakthrough women in organizational settings need to carefully monitor whether their natural disposition—warmth and friendliness—undermines or enhances their effectiveness. Women can remind themselves of their worth and unique identity, assertively seek demanding assignments, expect rewards for good work, and learn to negotiate well when required. They can seek support from male and female mentors and develop multiple networks. It is important to remember that balancing work and family can provide long-term health and happiness.

It is not enough to be blessed with talents, abilities, skills, or opportunities. What matters is what you do with these assets. Do you bury them in the ground or invest them wisely so that they grow and multiply year on year? Finally, each one of us has to reflect upon our education, training, and experience to see which choices led us to where we are today; and what choices we should make that will fuel our future.

Complementary to this theme of development is executive coaching as a technique to provoke greater performance and unlock deeper potential in business leaders. In the next chapter, therefore, I deal with certain themes that I repeatedly see in coaching women leaders that can be effectively addressed for further advancement.

## References

1. McKinsey and Company and LeanIn.org, 'Women in the Workplace', 2016, a study based on 'Women in the Workplace 2015 Report' and the seminar on 'Research conducted by McKinsey in 2015, http://www.mckinsey.com/business-functions/organization/our-insights/women-in-the-workplace-2016 (accessed on June 16, 2017).
2. NES Global Talent, 'Attracting and Retaining Women in Oil and Gas Engineering: A Survey Examining the Gender Talent Gap', 2015. https://www.nesglobaltalent.com/sites/default/files/images/women-in-engineering-report-single_final.pdf
3. Dworkin, T. M., V. Maurer, and C. A. Schipani, 'Career Mentoring for Women: New Horizons/Expanded Methods', *Business Horizons* 55, no. 4 (2012): 363–72.
4. Bonetta, Laura, 'Reaching Gender Equity in Science: The Importance of Role Models and Mentors', *Science* 327, no. 5967 (2010), https://www.sciencemag.org/careers/features/2010/02/reaching-gender-equity-science-importance-role-models-and-mentors
5. Businessinsider.in, 'Nine Entrepreneurs Share Their Best Business Advice', New Delhi: *Economic Times*, January 18, 2017.
6. Yee, Lariena, 'Fostering Women Leaders: A Fitness Test for Your Top Leaders', *McKinsey Quarterly*, January 2015, http://www.mckinsey.com/business-functions/organization/our-insights/fostering-women-leaders-a-fitness-test-for-your-top-team (accessed on June 16, 2017).

7. Chriss, Musselwhite, and Tammie Plouffe, 'What's Your Influencing Style?' *Harvard Business Review*, January 13, 2012, https://hbr.org/2012/01/whats-your-influencing-style (accessed on June 17, 2017).
8. Glassdoor team, '3 in 5 Employees Did Not Negotiate Salary', Survey, May 2016, www.glassdoor.com/blog/3-5-u-s-employees-negotiate-salary/
9. Babcock, L., M. Gelfand, D. Small, and H. Stayn, 'Gender Differences in the Propensity to Initiate Negotiations: A New Look at Gender Variation in Negotiation Behavior', in *Social Psychology and Economics*, edited by D. De Cremer, M. Zeelenberg, and J. K. Murnighan, Mahwah, NJ: Erlbaum, 2006: 239–59.
10. Babcock, L. and S. Laschever, *Ask For It: How Women Can Use the Power of Negotiation to Get What They Really Want*, New York: Bantam Dell, 2008.
11. Bowles, H. R., L. Babcock, and L. Lai, 'Social Incentives for Gender Differences in the Propensity to Initiate Negotiations: Sometimes it Does Hurt to Ask', *Organizational Behavior and Human Decision Processes* 103, no. 1 (2007): 84–103.
12. Cialdini, Robert B., The Uses and Abuses of Influence, *Harvard Business Review*, July–August 2013, https://hbr.org/2013/07/the-uses-and-abuses-of-influence (accessed on June 17, 2017).
13. Hazarika, Anjali, 'The New Road to the Top', *Economic Times*, March 8, 2007: 16.
14. Ruderman, M. N., P. J. Ohlott, K. Panzer, and S. N. King, 'Benefits of Multiple Roles for Managerial Women', *Academy of Management Journal* 45, no. 2 (2002): 369–86.
15. Greenhaus, J. H. and G. N. Powell, 'When Work and Family are Allies: A Theory of Work-Family Enrichment', *Academy of Management Review* 31, no. 1 (2006): 72–92.

# 6
# Coaching in the Rush Hour of Life

A successful CEO once told me that when he was in business school, he considered the quantitative "hard" subjects, such as finance and operations management to be the most important topics he studied. He had little respect for the "soft" subjects, such as organizational behavior and human resource management. Eighteen years later, sitting across the table, he recognized that it is his people management skills—working with and developing people—that are the key to both his personal success and that of his organization. So, it is not just the executives who benefit from one-on-one coaching; their employees can gain immensely too.

Many people make the observation that it is challenging to run a fast-growing company or a technology startup. They are right. But the hardest part is not scaling up the technology or the business model. It is growing up your own capabilities, as many leaders would suggest. Becoming a good leader demands tremendous self-awareness. It requires an understanding of how others perceive you, experience you, or respond to you. Being an effective mentor is also an essential part of that success. It is an intensive journey. One way of getting ready for this journey is to have an executive coach who can help you along.

Coaching has come a long way from the days when organizations engaged coaches to address a derailing behavior of a top executive, and get him or her back on track. Today, it is about developing the capabilities of high-potential performers or in facilitating transition. It is an effective technique in developing both male and female leaders, and is particularly helpful in the case of executives who believe in continuous learning and development. The saying, "It is what you learn after you know it all," resonates here.

However, just as the demographics of any leadership program mirror the corporate reality, so does the miniscule number of coaching engagements for women. The average attendance in any leadership program the world over is only about 20 percent women. The percentage of women who are nominated by their organizations to receive executive coaching is not be more than 6–8 percent, approximately. That broadly corresponds with the number of women at the senior level in most organizations.

According to a recent survey in the US, women continue to lag behind men in the amount of coaching they receive. In a survey of about 3,000 human resource professionals, 19.9 percent of the respondents reported that women do not receive the same amount of coaching as their male counterparts [1].

It is a pity because coaching has been shown to increase productivity in just the first year. In one study, 75 percent of women engaging in executive coaching were promoted within six months, and 90 percent reported being excited about their jobs and enjoying improved quality of professional life [2].

The challenges associated with transition and change are both the cause and, if addressed correctly, the solution. Failure at this time is often a disaster for both the person and the organization. During career transitions, women, as much as men, need support from within the organization. However, many high-potential women have a difficult time asking for help, because they do not want to appear stupid. Being unsure or unclear about how to proceed can be experienced by anyone. Asking for information is not a sign of lack of competence or confidence, but often a step in moving forward. But a lot of women I coach try to figure out everything on their own, before they finally decide to come for a coaching engagement.

They do not want to ask for inputs. Many think asking questions or seeking guidance suggests lack of knowledge. They do not want to be seen as someone lacking the competence for a certain position or as someone not meeting the expectations of a given role. It may have something to do with the prevailing stereotype, which suggests that women are unsuitable for senior management; or it may have something to do with the early socialization women are subjected to, which directs them not to be demanding or seek redressal for their developmental needs.

Among life's most vital transitions are those concerning family and career. Transitions are often hard to deal with, whether you want to move from one department to another in your own company, or join a different company in a different sector, or go on a long leave prompted by pregnancy or medical emergencies. A lot goes through your head at that point.

These are times when anyone undergoing a transition needs to talk to a trusted friend, mentor, guide, or coach. This is what coaching in the rush hour of life is all about, when the pressures of work coincide with the demands of family life [3].

## Leadership Transitions

Then, there are the transitions at three basic leadership levels. Let's look at them briefly:

1. First-line leaders (independent executives or individual contributors): At the first level, it is about self-management and working with others as a team member. For them, any of the competencies from self-management (including emotions) to time management, and from presentation skills to operating skills, such as timely decision making or priority setting, can become important for success at work.
2. Middle-level leaders (promoted from being independent executives or individual contributors to managing people or teams; leaders who are managing other managers or leaders): At a

middle level, leadership is about leading and motivating people to get work done, involving others in critical initiatives, leading change, or even making tough calls on hiring or firing. The middle level, with 5 to 8 years of work experience, is the time to launch one's career. For young women it is also the time to launch a family. It is during this period that providing support to mothers, to-be mothers or the mothers returning to work after maternity is critical. It is about ensuring smooth transition support from one maternity phase to another. For instance, during maternity, it is about maintaining communication and keeping abreast of the developments in the organization, and during post-maternity, it is about preparing for a confident return and successful reintegration. In some cases, it can be also about reskilling and considering second career options.

It is, therefore, important to understand a coachee's environment, in particular the organizational issues he or she faces. In the case of young women executives (mothers-to-be or returning from maternity), it means understanding that even the most progressive, modern organizations have been created by men for men. They tend to have systems, policies, norms, and structures that further male lifestyles. So life cycles associated with women are either non-existent or not recognized. On top of that, parameters of success are measured in masculine terms. Different standards of behavior are applicable in case of male and female managers as we have seen in the chapter on stereotypes (Chapter 2). It is, therefore, important for the woman manager to understand, with the help of her coach, how she may be perceived in her specific organizational context and to determine how to manage those perceptions.

Senior-level leaders (those with the higher responsibility of managing a function or managing an entire business): It is all about making complex decisions, understanding the business, and developing organizational/political savvy, having a strategic perspective, and being skilled in delegation. It can also be about behavior change. Your domain knowledge and technical and functional skills get you to the senior level. But then on it is more about the influence and impact of your behavior on those around you and refined people skills. One's blind spots are less obvious when things are going well. But they can be devastating when the role requires a different performance. For instance, the warmth and friendliness that won you popularity in the earlier role can come in the way of confronting a direct report who is affecting your unit's performance. The hard work, diligence, and drive that fetched you promotion after promotion can come in the way of delegating at the higher level. As is well known, no one who wants to do it all by herself can become a great leader.

These three transitions—entry level, middle level, and the top level—broadly correspond with three grief points in a woman's career. Women are poorly represented throughout the talent pipeline. Women who want to enter the corporate world encounter two major barriers at these levels. They are unable to enter the corporate world due to pre-pipeline problems (low graduation rates of women in industry feeder programs such as engineering, computer science, etc.) and poor health of recruiting pipelines. Once they enter, they fail to advance into middle-management positions due to biased promotional practices. As a result, they get stuck in the middle. After that, they continue to struggle to get promoted to top-level positions [4]. As can be seen, women's priorities and concerns change with age, stage of life, and career goals. So one solution does not fit all. In fact, women's changing needs require a "whole person" solution even when working on professional issues.

At a minimum, transitioning to a new role requires different ways of thinking and, in making that mental shift, the support of a senior is necessary, and which is often missing. What is fortifying is the fact that your good performance in the earlier role got you the new role. That strength, however, is soon going to be a weakness if you do not hurry and understand what's required for the new role. It is definitely not going to be more of the same thing. As Marshall Goldsmith famously said, "What got you here won't get you there."

Successful career transitions rarely happen without learning new skills and shedding outdated competencies. Like snakes shed their skin in the process of renewal, the new role demands developing new competencies. Rarely will there be time to acquire the new skills. It is important to take some of your free time and devote it to your self-development. Engage in the learning process and look at the time as an investment in your future. This is an extremely important step for women who often spend much of their "free time" taking care of others. You need to clearly explain to your loved ones that this is a temporary but essential step for improving your collective future.

Once, a senior woman manager told me,

> "It is not that I am allergic to constructive feedback. But sometimes it is difficult to develop clarity in a male-dominated organization with just a few of us women in the minority. Such an environment makes it hard for me to get an accurate picture of how others see me. For example, whenever I receive negative feedback, I have to examine whether that feedback is an honest reflection of my behavior or performance, or is it colored by the feedback giver's issues, assumptions, or biases regarding women."

In the next section are certain common themes or developmental needs that repeatedly emerge in coaching conversations with women executives. Not every female coachee has "women's issues." There are, of course, variations to these themes and, sometimes, it is amazing to see that variations among women coachees are greater than the differences among the genders. In that sense, each coaching engagement is unique.

## Five Signature Themes in Live Action
### Managing emotions

Monalisa works as a financial advisor for a prominent, financial services institution. She is directly responsible for big corporate as well as high net-worth clients, managing a team of seven individuals.

She is 40, has sound business acumen, and good domain knowledge. She is methodical, dependable, hardworking, and self-driven. She has been identified as a high-potential manager. She has been nominated for coaching by her organization for the purpose of accelerating performance and taking her skills and competencies to the next level.

Today, she is in a state of shock over the feedback she has received.

"I am surprised that on my face my team tells me I am doing fine but, in my feedback, my direct reports have issues on all accounts. I am driving them hard; I am not sensitive to signs of over work; I don't understand their problems; I get rattled and lose my temper; I am not motivating enough. In other words, I am a terrible boss."

In order to get an accurate picture of how she is perceived, we got a 360-degree feedback assessment filled by her boss, peers, and direct reports. The reports confirmed both her excellent abilities and the fact that she was abrasive with her colleagues. She was stung by the feedback and needed courage and compassionate support to confront herself. I realized that it was time to establish the context of the feedback.

I said, "The feedback is to be seen as a 'personal snapshot' at one point in time. It does not capture everything about who you are. We can together make sense of the data if you like."

Almost on cue, she said in a raised voice, "I don't want to see any more reports. I know I have an issue of losing my temper." "I have accepted it," she added, but her tone suggested she was rejecting the feedback and didn't want to deal with it.

"I can feel real tension here, I can feel your distress, your anger," I said, helping her to see what she didn't want to see.

"Do you want to talk about a situation? What triggers this emotion?" I gently asked her.

"When there are too many things to do at the same time, or when plans are delayed, or when deals fall through, I get very anxious and I lose my temper."

"So, it is actually about handling pressure, keeping cool, and maintaining composure, right?"

She nodded.

"Anger is a powerful emotion. It can be constructive as well as destructive. But right now it is also giving you some information. What is it?" I asked her.

"What information? I fear that my boss will scream at me if I don't get the results; I will get a bad appraisal. In my industry, attrition is so high. It makes me so insecure about my job."

"So underneath that anger is actually the fear of losing your job, right?

"Right," she said.

"Monalisa, you have a choice between feeling an emotion and acting on the emotion. Can you stay aware, watch the fear, and not allow it to hijack the present moment? Can you name that emotion and see what happens?"

"I am feeling scared that if I don't get the results I will lose my job. Something I value is at risk. The work that I value, the job that I value is at stake."

After that statement there was a pause. She fell silent. After a couple of moments, there was a big sigh. In that moment something shifted. I almost felt as if the cloud of that dark emotion hanging over her head had begun to drift away.

"I can see that the job is very important to you. What does it mean to you?" I asked her.

"Oh! It is everything. It is my identity, it's prestige, it's financial security, and the work relationships. In fact, it is actually who I am as a professional."

"If it means so much to you, what do you *do* or *don't do* to save it? What do you do when you get scared?"

"I work hard. I drive myself hard and work long hours on weekdays and over the weekend too. No breaks, no exercise. I haven't even read a book in the last two years. In fact, I have developed high BP lately. Thank, god, it is now under control."

"Maybe you need to start the exercise regime. You need to work on releasing work stress through regular exercise."

"Yes, I have been planning it for weeks."

"You know there are lots of things that do not go well at times and can derail schedules, but do you think losing one's cool can be helpful in saving your job or building your career? If you drive yourself hard like this, how do you see yourself after 10 years?"

She looked down. There was a long pause. When she looked up, her eyes were moist. "I can see that I am not only driving myself hard, but I am also driving my team hard."

"Have they ever told you that?"

"No. But I can see that they are overworked. Because even I am overworked."

"What do you do then?" I asked her.

"I act as if I have not seen those signs. I drive them harder."

"How do you think they would view the situation? If you put yourself in their situation, how would you feel?" I asked her.

"Oh, I would hate it. I know they must be cribbing like hell," she said with a touch of remorse in her voice.

"Would you like to do something about it? Would you like to find out about it?"

She nodded.

"Shall we then take a look at your reports and see what your team is saying?" I gently asked.

By then, the resistance was gone. The door opened and the feedback was finally invited in. Thereafter, we spent two productive hours in developing an action plan. I asked her to keep a journal, noting each time she lost her cool, along with the person involved, the provocation, her responses, and the outcome. It was about practicing impulse control and identifying trigger points. Responding directly with "I" statements, rather than "You" statements. It was also about leading the team, listening to them, informing them about future changes that would impact them, consulting them before implementing changes, and helping them learn from their mistakes. She then proceeded to set up goals with timelines and accountability, simultaneously ensuring periodic check-ins. We also discussed what she needed to do in order to delegate work that would free her time and how she could check herself and others from working too hard.

Follow-up sessions revealed that she was on the right track. She had not only learnt to accept but also to deal with pressure that triggered distressing emotions. She had realized the risk of not accessing or attending to her challenging emotions. She had also acquired a precious new skill: the ability to monitor her behavior consciously, and modify it as needed.

Distressing emotions like anger, fear, or shame are triggered when we feel threatened, attacked, or get caught in wrongdoing. They serve us well when accessed and connected.

Often, anger is a sign of engagement with life. If used constructively, it can destroy inertia and move people to action. People who are angry are touched deeply by the events of their lives. As an emotion, it has its limitations and it certainly has very bad press. It becomes a problem when people become wedded to it as a way of life.

Anger, in fact, is a demand for change, a passionate wish for things to be different. It can be a way to re-establish important boundaries and assert personal dignity and integrity. If we bring mindfulness to it, then it will help us welcome anger and use it constructively. It will be our path to awakening like these beautiful and poignant lines of Rumi convey:

> This being human is a guest house.
>   Every morning a new arrival.
>   A joy, a depression, a meanness
>   Some momentary awareness comes
>   As an unexpected visitor.
>   Be grateful for whatever comes
>   Because each has been sent as a guide from beyond. [5]

## Standing up to be counted

Seema is one of those people who make their jobs look easy. She is competent, collaborative, relationship-oriented, a good listener, empathic, and reasonable. She has been with her company for eight years. As a manager of her business unit, she is responsible for keeping her unit running smoothly and providing best-in-the-class customer service.

During our coaching conversation she clearly looked upset and restless. She narrated an incident in office, where she felt ignored and unappreciated. In her words:

> "Our CEO took an important meeting to discuss budget proposals for approving extraordinary expenditure. I had put up a proposal for a new application of digital technology that would greatly improve customer service. So I prepared well for the meeting and did a lot of home work—as I always do—so that I could defend it."

During the meeting, I made an observation and a suggestion around a particular topic under discussion which he did not respond to. Not long after I spoke, my colleague (who happened to be a man) suggested a different idea and the others followed up with questions to him. After a problem arose with his suggestion, another colleague of mine who is also a man picked up my suggestion. The CEO said, "Great idea! I will go with your judgement. I need to rush for another meeting right now but we need to explore this idea more. Let's schedule a meeting next Friday."

"I was aghast. He was not even aware of what he had just done. I wanted to say, but that's what I had proposed. But somehow I did not manage to. This happens to me all the time. I hesitate to interrupt. The tendency not to assert myself holds me back," she said sadly.

"Nobody realizes how hard I work, how many problems on a daily basis I deal with," she continued. "Customers want the best service, low price, instant troubleshooting…I handle all these problems without passing the buck upwards. Most of my colleagues think I have it easy. They wonder whether my seniors have set the bar lower in my case only because I do not make a fuss. In contrast, my peers make such a noise about what they do, how they surmount obstacles, meet the targets, etc. I just don't do that."

"Do you want to be valued for your contributions?" I asked her. "Then you need to let people know what *you* yourself value about your work. You may not be recognized for your contributions, if you do not promote yourself appropriately. As a result, your name may not figure in the shortlist of promising assignments as well as promotions. Your CEO may simply be unaware of your skills, your merits, and your efforts. On top of that, his own unconscious bias would also be at play as you have seen in the meeting. Even well-meaning people can be unaware of how their unconscious biases shape their behavior. Sometimes, in situations like this, those of us who are different (or in the minority), need to remind people to treat us appropriately."

"I am so focused on completing the job at hand that I never have the time to canvass or position myself for promotion," she said.

"What about important meetings such as the one you just described? Do you present your point of view? Do you ask for clarifications?

By doing so, one creates an impression that one is actually interested in learning more as well as in the outcome. How else will the seniors know? Just as your talent remains unutilized, your organization misses out on important information about customers or competition, new solutions or opportunities," I offered. "Yes, I completely agree. I am guilty on all counts. I am hesitant to share my views for fear that I will call undue attention to myself," she said.

She was deliberately downplaying her 'difference' from the mainstream. She wanted to blend into the majority group of male colleagues which was homogenous. Fear of being different was stifling her talent.

This was confirmed by her 360-degree feedback reports in which her boss as well as peers did not view her as the talented leader she thought herself to be. In her case, her own ratings were not an inflated view of herself, but a realistic assessment. However, my hunch was that the reason for this disparity was that no one knew her accomplishments. Her raters simply did not know the extent of her contribution or the quality of her work.

After a brief pause, she said, "I think it all boils down to confidence. What holds me back is not competence but confidence. In meeting after meeting, I see under-qualified, under-prepared men leap forward while over-prepared 'me' hides in the shadows, holding myself to an impossible standard of perfection no one even cares about."

"Okay. So what do you really want to achieve? How will you go about achieving it?" I asked her.

"Starting from next Friday, Mission Visibility will be undertaken. My homework is nearly done. But I will still conduct due diligence in order to mitigate certain potential risks related to my proposal. This will enable me to field all possible questions. But, most importantly, I will set the tone early on. I will speak up and speak early. I will state my departmental needs and refuse to back down."

"Speak early and loudly enough so that everyone hears what you have to say and do not save your questions for the end," I said.

"I will find some meaningful comment to add at the beginning of the meeting so people will acknowledge my presence. I will ask all the 'inconvenient' questions, if any, early in the meeting so that others will sit up and take notice of my contribution and the value I bring to the table. I think this is critical when the rest of my colleagues tend to operate like a clique. What I learnt from my last meeting is that it becomes much harder to 'break in' towards the end. I must move in early if I have a point."

"Not only that, you must keep repeating yourself until you are heard. Eventually, the message will sink in and people will take notice of you, and accept the new, improved you. What else would you like to do differently? One Friday meeting, perhaps, is not good enough for people to know what you are doing," I said.

"Are you then suggesting I do self-promotion on a daily basis?" She asked.

"What would be the right thing to do in your company environment?" I asked.

"Perhaps I may have to drill the message home every time I get a chance."

"Yes. You can't always rely on others, such as your boss, to increase your visibility for you. Instead, you need to figure out how to maximize your exposure so that you'll be 'in the running' for opportunities when they arise."

"You may have to do it three ways: up, down, and laterally. Stepping out of your comfort zone to talk about your work may feel strange at first, but doing so will build your confidence. Look at it this way: every manager or leader has to play a dual role when it comes to promotion. The managerial role demands that not only do you have a responsibility to promote yourself but also the work of your team. The team members will feel let down by a boss who does not talk about their accomplishments or does not actively promote them to the senior management." I could see that this line of argument had convinced her.

She enthusiastically said,

"For that to happen, I need to understand my audience. Like a true marketer, I need to understand my customer's needs at the three levels of the organizational hierarchy. Long before I have a shot at a promotion, I have to increase my work with a variety of people and build credibility and visibility."

"Take agency over your own promotion. Consistent and appropriate self-promotion will make you known in the organization. If your reputation is in line with realistic achievements, then the visibility will carry over to the other departments. The other options are to join professional associations, to take up speaking engagements, or to write articles for your company newsletter. This will help you to become visible and get on the radar of your company. So, this is a long-term process, to be done day after day after day."

Research has shown that in meetings and conferences men gain the floor and often keep the floor for longer periods of time. They are more likely to interrupt women speakers than men speakers. Because men are perceived to have higher status or leadership, they get more opportunities to express opinions and direct interaction. Such behavior then further increases men's status or leadership [6].

The visibility created by participating in meetings or speaking up when necessary, has benefits not only for the individual but also for the organization. Further career progression often depends upon taking risks and advocating for oneself, something women are discouraged from exhibiting. This may explain why women's career progression suffers all the way from the entry point to top leadership positions. Their academic achievements remain just that: *academic* achievements. They do not get translated into high-leadership positions.

"Great minds think alike," is still the reflective mindset of many leaders and organizations, primarily because of the male-dominant work model that exists even today. It has its own benefits in certain situations, for it ensures speed in decision making and problem solving. However, it downplays unique subjective differences and experiences that can facilitate flights of creativity.

Women often don't get what they want and deserve because they don't ask for it. Speaking up in meetings, advocating for oneself, and creating the right kind of visibility are all important elements of managing a successful career. Why should women be penalized for doing that?

## Ability to deal with trouble

Rita has been a successful executive in a tech industry and, eight months ago, she was promoted to head a division with the responsibility of managing a large team. She is warm, friendly, caring and supportive, and very popular with employees from her as well as other departments. She knew that the key to successful team-building lies in identifying an objective for her team and then establishing a common cause for achieving that objective. In consultation with her team members, she developed a game plan to execute an important project and then assigned roles and tasks to each one of them, with clear timelines for delivery.

During this process, which unfolded over a week, she noticed that one team member was particularly resistant in the meetings. In the follow-up meetings, he also missed his deadlines by three-four days. She was not very comfortable about giving negative feedback. So, she hoped this problem would go away since the delivery schedule was known to all. But the problem persisted. She found it difficult to have a conversation with a direct report who did not understand the impact of his behavior on the team. Despite her reluctance to give the feedback, she tentatively tried once and failed miserably. He pushed back and gave excuses.

Being a caring and supportive leader has its advantages. A related pitfall is that sometimes this considerate style is not in the best interest of the teams or, for that matter, of the organization. Conflict management is critical in a leader's role. Just about everything that gets to the leader's desk has an element of pleasing someone and making someone unhappy at the same time. When a leader avoids conflict or dealing with trouble of any kind, it can destroy the performance of a unit or an organization. If decisions are not made, problems fester, creating a cascading effect of unproductive behavior. A leader can constructively manage and channelize conflict by getting to the root of issues. She can apply rigor to the team's thinking and can ultimately drive the best outcomes. So, cultivating this skill can be a powerful tool to help the entire organization.

In my conversation with her, Rita said,

"I go to the second or third mile to support my team and address their needs personally and professionally. I give a long rope before I pull them up. I often find myself too lenient because I want them to do well. I do not want to be harsh. But I can see that he is becoming a problem employee."

"The question is, will you be able to take a quick decision when the going gets tough? Will you let him go if he shows no signs of improvement?" I asked her.

She kept quiet. I could see that concerns about her lack of ability to handle the situation were now mixed with worries about "Am I too weak to be an effective leader at a high level?" and "Am I not being tough enough?"

"I know it is tough to give negative feedback. But let's consider the consequences. Suppose you do not give him this feedback, how will you give him a chance to improve?" I asked her.

"If he is any good, he should know what to do," she said.

"If that was the case, things would have been sorted out by now, right? Obviously he has not improved and that's why this conversation. Have you thought about how his performance will affect the team performance? What message is going out to those who are working hard in your team? That you are probably shielding him and playing favorites?"

"No. No!" She reacted sharply, "That's far from it."

"Then have you thought about how you will defend your actions to others? To your seniors?"

She realized that the problem was at her end too. Performance management is all about setting performance standards, monitoring employee performance, providing feedback and support for performance improvement, and exiting employees who cannot meet standards. Failing to take timely action would hurt her team as well as her own career prospects.

I talked to her about the possibility of using "difficult conversation" as a tool. Difficult conversation is a powerful, practical tool to navigate turbulent interpersonal waters. While these conversations can be uncomfortable, they can also lead to new ways of working. Therefore, it really helps to prepare for a difficult conversation. Talking about one's feelings and points of view paves the way for greater understanding. In our session, she practiced having a difficult conversation through the medium of role play, in dealing with pushback, in staying firm, and in delivering an "'improve or go' message if need be."

Back in the office, her task was cut out for her. She decided to put the employee on a performance improvement plan. She outlined three key result areas and performance indicators with a realistic timeframe for him. In their meeting together, she clearly communicated her expectations, took questions, and scheduled regular checkpoints to monitor the performance improvement plan.

The results of the meeting were not very encouraging. So she fixed a meeting with the vice-president, HR, to apprise him about the problem employee and the possibility of letting him go if he did not show any improvement. In that meeting, she learnt that his previous manager had faced the same difficulty with him. He, probably, did not confront him as well. That's the time she came to terms with the fact that she might have to let him go. She apprised all concerned senior managers and took necessary clearances in case required.

The outcome of the performance improvement plan was not good. It was with heavy trepidation that Rita scheduled a meeting with the problem employee. We extensively worked on this meeting: how to keep the communication to the facts, and focus on the problem and not on the person. She took pains to explain that he was not a good fit for the role and the skills required. She told him that he might fare better in other roles and in other organizations.

A fortnight later she called me up.

"I finally let the employee go after six months. Earlier, I would have kept him for at least one year only because I could not deal with the situation. I consider this a major milestone for me. I have learnt to deal with things firmly and in a timely manner. It is a key to my team's performance. More importantly, I have come to recognize the equal importance of accomplishing the task as well as being concerned about relationships. It is a key to my own performance."

## The pitfalls of overcommitment

Margaret Bradley, a British national, is the chief of the procurement and purchasing division of a multinational automobile company. At 45, she has achieved a leadership position due to her passion for seeking excellence, ability to address one exciting challenge after another, and a track record for taking balanced decisions for the benefit of the company. With an innovative orientation, she has the ability to see many possibilities. She is enthusiastic, competent, and draws intellectual stimulation by challenging and discussing new ideas. She likes to test her limits, those of her team members, as well as the system.

As someone who is adventurous and entrepreneurial, she likes seeding ideas and developing new project proposals, but has a tendency to ignore the follow through on existing ones. While she gets excited about future possibilities and new projects, she has difficulty in picking up those with greatest potential due to lack of time required for due diligence and analysis. Her company was dedicated to teamwork but she was often "too busy" to develop her direct reports.

Lately, she has encountered serious issues of time management. She complained about not being able to make sufficient time to manage all the work activities, some of them with conflicting priorities.

Totally committed to her work, she had the tendency to take on too much responsibility. As a result, she was stretching herself all the time. Working long hours and staying in office for up to 11–12 hours had become the norm. This grueling schedule had left her with no free time. What she regretted most was not having enough time for horse riding, a favorite pastime. Moreover, for days on end, she didn't get to see her partner, who worked for an English pub at night and got back home only after she had left for work. In her own way, she had challenged the traditional female scripts that call for a given behavior at a given time. It became clear that she was overcommitting herself.

"My career has taken such a center stage in my life that everything else has become secondary," she said.

"How did this work in the past? And why is it not working now?" I asked her.

"Earlier, my responsibility was considerably less. I could manage it well. But now I am managing a function with a much larger team. They all want my time for solving problems, issues about cost, quality, supply chain, and people management. I have to manage my function with optimal resources. There are challenges in every area. Everyday. Day after day. It leaves me with no time for my own work. Every 10 minutes there is someone knocking on my door."

"Is it possible to structure your time? And let the team know when you will be available on normal days?"

"Yes," she agreed. And we went about developing a plan for organizing her time and setting priorities.

"It will be very difficult though," she murmured.

"What would happen if you did nothing right now?" I challenged her.

There was a long pause.

"The cost will be high. I might not be able to meet the targets," she said.

"You say you cannot do that. What would it look like if you could?"

"Couple of things," she said.

"Firstly, I have to stop people coming to me for decisions they can take at their level. Secondly, I have to learn to delegate some important aspects of the project which I tend to do myself. Thirdly, there are some good people in my team. I have to start sharing both responsibility and accountability with them."

"So why are you not delegating? What is holding you back?" I asked her.

"Ironically, my involvement, my high sense of responsibility, and my commitment to my role. Once in a while my direct reports do tell me that they are exhausted from pursuing one project to another."

In our conversation together we had explored many situations where the impact of her decisions was different from the intent of her actions.

"Are there any real costs in pursuing new projects?" I asked.

"Unfortunately, yes. New projects have to be managed over and above the existing ones and the routine work. As a result, my team constantly gets stretched. With my hectic schedule, I sometimes overlook the pragmatic consideration and constraints, departmental resources, and the requirements of my team members. As a result, a realistic assessment of facts gets compromised. I see limitations as challenges to be overcome. They are gateways to new innovations. My team wants facts, details, resources, and right answers all the time. It just occurred to me that I could do better if I select my team carefully with complementary skills."

"What is the cost of not changing and continuing in the same way?" I asked her.

There was a pause.

"I will reach a burnout. I am overextending myself already. I am overspending my energy without any break, rest, or renewal. I get so exhausted. I will reach a burnout soon." With that, she let out a big sigh.

I let the realization sink in deeply so she could reflect on that insight. After a long pause, I asked her, "So what will you do differently?"

"I need to pause, slow down and learn to relax. I have to create free time for myself to recharge my batteries. I need to go home in time so that I can catch up with my partner and try and go horse riding at least three times a week, if not more."

Clearly, she was doing several things right or she could not have been successful. The problem was that she wanted to do *many* more things right. That was the reason for her overcommitment.

I did not want her to tackle too many changes at the same time. So, I asked her, "What is the one vital thing that needs fixing? What is that one thing which will have a cascading effect on all other things?"

"Delegation," she said, "Delegation may improve the speed and quality of my decisions, reduce my overload, enrich the subordinate's job, increase their intrinsic motivation, and provide opportunities for development of their leadership skills." She said it all in one breath. "So delegation it is," I agreed.

That was the breakthrough. She focused on two areas for improvement: mentoring direct reports and time management. Thereafter, we went about setting goals with clear accountability and a timeline. I facilitated her in identifying potential obstacles that could come in the way of achieving her goals, so that she could deal with them.

Similarly, I helped her identify and create a support system that could accelerate her progress towards her goals.

One of the traits of high performers is a commitment to self-improvement. These people have a hunger for learning and growth. Commitment is a conscious choice to align ourselves with genuine values and a sense of purpose. It can lead to greater freedom, and more options and choices, whereas overcommitment leads to greater degrees of bondage.

## Developing a strategic mindset

Neena is a vice-president in a global role in a leading software company. She is one of the seniormost women in the company. She has had years of glowing reviews that led to promotions in her earlier roles. To outside observers, Neena, an IT professional by training with an eye for detail, appeared to be a perfect candidate for the job. However, she was unable to make a leap from her earlier role to the current role because the same qualities which had been a virtue for her in previous roles proved to be a hindrance in her new position. Added to that was the fact that Neena liked to keep to herself and social interaction was not a prime motivator for her. But a desk can be a dangerous place from which to have a worldview.

Neena could not free herself from day-to-day operations enough to take on the strategic role of a team leader. She persisted in focusing on what she felt most competent doing, instead of dealing with what the new position demanded: a subtle but fundamental shift in responsibility from tactical to strategic and from operations to a global perspective. In the current role, she had outperformed on every measure she could think of except one: big-picture thinking. A recent performance review with her manager had disturbed her a lot. In the written comments, he had noted: "Neena needs to understand the big picture of her division and how it contributes to the company's overall vision. She needs to network with her peers from other functions, seek their inputs."

In our session, she said defensively, "I am not sure whether this data is valid. He has been here only for the past six months. Often, I just get about 10 minutes with my boss. How can he possibly judge me in that short time? I am so bogged down with my work that I do not even get time to meet my peers. What do they know about me to say this?"

When I looked at her reports, the line which jumped at me was exactly this: "Neena does not seek any feedback." I noted that there was a big gap between her own assessment (which was good) and that of her raters: boss, peers, direct reports (which was not good). Assessing her strengths and weaknesses was the first step towards enhancing her self awareness.

It was to Neena's credit that she quickly realized that over-focusing on the present was creating an imbalance, as she had ignored other important aspects of her role. These were the business drivers such as the impact of globalization on business, the larger business context of which her company was a part, anticipating future trends that would impact the technological expertise needed to increase productivity. She needed to be analytical and systematic, and learn and develop abstract models. It was like exercising only the right arm and ignoring the left arm when you needed to be "ambidextrous."

I advised her to focus on just two critical priorities, strategic thinking and networking, which were somehow interconnected.

Neena then developed a learning agenda for herself over the next six months. Every week, she would find seniors and peers from other functions to learn from their perspectives on organizational trends. She developed a focused set of questions to guide her inquiry, such as: How can I push my project to the next level? What are the biggest challenges our company is facing or will face in the near future? What are the most promising unexploited opportunities for growth? What do we need to change to exploit these opportunities? What do I need to focus on? How do I go about achieving the results?

I also advised her to study two business competitors who had pulled off brilliant strategies in the recent past.

In a short period of time, the results were there for everyone to see. She successfully adapted and practiced the new behavior of stepping out of her office and her comfort zone and meeting people. Although initially difficult, it became easier day by day. It built great self-confidence and created a momentum over time.

Executives perform many balancing acts, but one of the trickiest is figuring out how much time to spend on the nuts and bolts of the business and how much to devote to the big picture. Each has its dangers. Too great a focus on details can render executives clueless about trends and business drivers, but too little can result in a lack of vital information.

It also made me wonder whether women executives are generally perceived to be less strategic compared to their male counterparts. Top leaders always score significantly higher in this competency since most top leaders are men. In this rapidly changing world, the capacity to make and execute strategy is a competitive advantage. If women get an exposure to strategic perspective, their relative scores will be the same as we saw in Neena's case. This is also confirmed by research [7].

As can be seen from the examples above, women in most leadership roles face complexities not encountered by men because of continuing uncertainties about their ability to lead. The next chapter looks at the ambivalence people have about women's leadership and whether people resist women's leadership more than men's.

## References

1. Laff, Michael, 'Women Receive Less Coaching', *Training and Development*, 61, no. 1 (January 2007): 18.
2. Woods, Michael and Welyne Thomas, 'Personal Leadership Development Study', thesis, 2002.
3. Frissen, V. A. J., 'ICTs in the Rush Hour of Life', *The Information Society*, no. 16 (2000): 65–76.
4. Krivkovich, Alexis, Eric Kutcher, and Lareina Yee, 'Breaking Down the Gender Challenge', *McKinsey Quarterly*, March 2016, http://www.mckinsey.com/business-functions/organization/our-insights/breaking-down-the-gender-challenge (accessed on June 15, 2017).
5. Barks, Coleman and John Moyne, *The Essential Rumi*, San Francisco: Harper, 1997[1995].
6. James, D. and J. Drakich, 'Understanding Gender Differences in Amount of Talk: A Critical Review of Research', in *Gender and Conversational Interaction*, 281–312, edited by D. Tannen, New York, NY: Oxford University Press, 1993.
7. Zenger Folkman Inc., 'A Study in Leadership: Women Do It Better Than Men', Boston: Zenger Folkman Inc., 2011.

# 7
# When the Boss Is a Woman

During a media interview, I was once asked, "What's more difficult than having a woman boss?" The answer for me was simple: "Being one." The reason: I have never had a woman boss.

For years, women have been bossed, but women can also prove to be good bosses. And being a boss is any day better than being bossed. From my own experience of being a boss, I can tell you that is true. Moreover, I do not think having a woman as a boss is a difficult proposition. Except that, as a woman boss, you have to be careful not to let others define you because they may, too often, define you in negative terms. What you do with that definition is up to you. As Toni Morrison reminds us, the "definition belongs to the definers—not the defined" [1].

There are all kinds of expectations from a woman boss. If you are soft-spoken and polite, you should be confrontational; if you are task-oriented, then you should be easy going; if you demonstrate empathy, then you should be firm and tough; if you are tough, then you are seen as controlling. It seems that women are simply held to different standards of work behavior and leadership. By virtue of your position, you just cannot please everyone, every time. You learn and realize over time that some critical decisions, which later get accepted, are often taken in the face of a great deal of opposition from your colleagues who later come around. Then, there are times when you actually make genuine mistakes and errors of judgment. What then? You stand alone in facing the criticism or ridicule at the hands of others, that prompts people to wonder, does she have what it takes to be a boss?

There have been many times when I have felt different from other people in the conference room or in the meetings of the petroleum industry. I then realized that I embody diversity, often being the only woman or Asian sitting around a table of senior executives. I attended plenty of meetings where people assumed I must be representing my boss, because I possibly could not be the boss (although I was).

Having mostly worked in the male-dominated, macho petroleum industry, I was assumed by men to be secretary to a high-powered boss. Amusingly, I was often addressed as Mr Anjali Hazarika in correspondence emerging from India as well as abroad. Although such reactions existed only on the surface, they resulted in additional pressures on me to establish my competence. One way to respond to such pressure was to do extremely well and to be aware that others might underestimate my worth. I thought I should do good work and the work will eventually speak for itself. I learned everyday not to count on others' validation as a measure of my worth. To hold a leadership position in a traditionally male-dominated industry, I had to be "twice as good as a man." As a woman, I was not given the benefit of doubt. If there were doubts, they were about my competence or my warmth—a typically feminine quality—or sometimes resentment at my very presence. I had to establish myself as competent and collaborative at the same time. Often, one's own personal experience shapes one's attitude towards diversity and inclusion, and plays a significant role in defining one's priorities as a leader.

It is for this reason you have to have strong feelings of self-worth and self-esteem. In order to be a successful boss or a leader, you must define yourself in strong, positive terms and actions. It is especially important not to define yourself solely in terms of your job, because too many people over whom you have little control can have a negative impact on you and your job. In some sense, women do suffer the disadvantage of leadership roles having a masculine aura, especially in settings like business, engineering, manufacturing, and science that are considered male domains, and at higher levels of power and authority.

Women, of course, must prepare themselves both intellectually and educationally to meet the challenges of leadership positions. The most critical areas for this preparation are image, exposure, and education. Developing a proper image requires a solid understanding of the kind of projection (body language, dress, etiquette) one will need to assimilate into the business environment. One could develop a style that minimizes gender differences, yet defines individuality, integrity, and effectiveness. In terms of exposure, women must be open to the kinds of events and opportunities that allow them to learn the behavior it takes to be successful in business. And women must be prepared with a solid education and skill set to compete with others when seeking high positions in organizations. After all, reputation and image are based on solid performance.

For women to become "good bosses," organizations must first recognize that women have a contribution to make; and that recognition must come from the understanding that, if they are trained properly and have the skill, their contribution may provide competitive leverage. If an organization is committed to objectively working to hire the best and the brightest in a diverse culture, many inequities will be taken care of. Then, organizations need to legitimize women's authority, because women lack the built-in legitimacy which men possess.

When I was appointed as the director of the National Petroleum Management Program, I was subjected to extra scrutiny and intense performance pressures. I used to work extra hard for meetings and presentations in front of committees and boards. I was well aware that, if I showed any weakness in domain knowledge, I would never be forgiven. I had to strike a delicate balance between assertiveness (without offending people) and influencing in an indirect manner. It was very fortunate that the then secretary to the Ministry of

Petroleum and Natural Gas signaled his confidence in my leadership. That made things easier.

All things being equal, leadership effectiveness depends on the fit between the work setting and the gender of the role holder. Thus, working in a leadership role congruent with one's gender appears to make one more effective, or at least perceived as being more effective. For instance, the transformative, participatory style of leadership associated with women may backfire in traditional male settings such as the military, sports, or manufacturing industries. Conversely, the command-control style associated with men may backfire in a retail, fashion, advertising, or social service agency.

## Ambivalence Is Everywhere

There is a great deal of ambivalence in attitudes towards not only women's careers but also their leadership positions. There are continuing uncertainties about their ability to lead. This is due to the mental models people have about women and leaders. When people's ideas about leadership do not match their view of women, they evaluate women less favorably as leaders. By and large, leadership roles are culturally masculine. As a result, women are at a disadvantage for such positions even when they are identical to their male counterparts in all respects except gender. It is a common perception that women do well on challenging tasks because of their hard work, but that men do well on them because of their competence. Similarly, it is believed that while women fail on challenging tasks due to a lack of ability, men fail on them only when they are lazy or plain unlucky.

Some leading headhunters were asked recently whether they encountered any resistance when recruiting male executives for positions in which the recruits would be reporting to women. It was confirmed that there is apprehension because of a great heritage of male superiority and male dominance across cultures. There has been a consistent pattern of male advantage in hiring except in traditionally feminine domains [2].

Polls in America have asked people to respond to the question: "If you were taking a new job and had your choice of a boss, would you prefer to work for a man or a woman?" Americans are still more likely to say today that they would prefer a male boss (33 percent) to a female boss (20 percent) in a new job, although 46 percent say it doesn't make a difference to them. Gallup first put this question to Americans in 1953. At that time, 66 percent of Americans said they preferred a male boss. Five percent said they preferred a female boss. While the percentage who prefer a female boss has grown over the last 60 years, it has never crossed 25 percent [3]. An Indian poll also suggests that most people prefer male bosses to female ones, and that view includes a significant majority (79 percent) of female respondents [4]. Employees are often reluctant to have a female boss or superior, at least in the short run. Some men feel threatened by the entry of women. They feel uncomfortable with female colleagues or fear that the presence of women will drag down their own performance. Some men find it difficult to identify with a female boss and may not be as loyal or cooperative with her as with a male boss [5]. As a result, women experience a less supportive work environment, and this is borne out by research [6]. In fact, as studies have demonstrated, men, on average, disapprove of high levels of competence and authority more in women than in other men, and resist women's influence more than women do. This resistance is further intensified if women hold positions of authority in masculine domains.

There is a general feeling that there may be more problems working with a woman than working with a man. However, if the direct report has confidence in her own self, she tends not to be concerned, especially once she knows that the woman boss is competent, knowledgeable, and has the right credentials.

The instinctive male response to a female superior is to doubt her worthiness to boss him. A man will take order from a "superwoman." But work for a female who is not extraordinary? Many men would instinctively recoil at the idea. The assumption a man makes when he goes to work for a woman is that she would not be in the job if she was not qualified. He could also take the diametrically opposite view that "she is there because of all the (wrong) reasons except competency." At the root of this fear or resistance is the age-old stereotype of the superiority of men, which makes them more suited to positions of authority. A woman is indecisive and can't make tough decisions. A man, therefore, feels threatened by a woman in charge. All said and done, women face complex issues rarely encountered by men when it comes to leadership.

Part of the problem may be the failure to notice when a man projects his other relationships unconsciously on to a woman boss, or when he perceives the woman not as his leader but as his mother, wife, friend or even as a threat. The good news is that there are women who also command loyal, happy troops composed of both genders, and there are men who say they would not think twice about following a woman leader. Equality then is not when a Sheryl Sandberg or an Indra Nooyi gets promoted to head a company. Equality is when a mediocre female executive progresses as far as a mediocre male executive.

## Ambivalence due to Gender Roles

This ambivalence can also be attributed to the fact that women's status is inferior to that of men in most societies. Practically, in all cultures young girls have limited access, if at all, to and control over tangible or intangible resources (knowledge, power, prestige, and decision-making authority), whether within the family, in the community, or in society at large. Even in organizational life, the status of women continues to be derived from prevailing patterns in the family and the stereotypes regarding gender roles, and not so much from their abilities. As women entered the business world, they found themselves in positions consistent with the roles they played at home, supporting the work of others in communications, in human resources, in staff positions with relatively small budgets and few people reporting to them.

With the increasingly high cost of living, dual career families have almost become the norm. Married women who seek professions that demand long hours or travelling away from home, experience some form of role conflict. They feel guilty about not being good mothers when they work outside the home. Women also face role conflict when they select professions or occupations that are not considered "feminine," such as engineering, the armed services, construction, stock markets, etc., and which require engaging in discussions, conflicts, and controversies. Frequently, role conflict is resolved by avoiding occupations or situations that challenge conventional definitions of femininity. Sometimes, one decides to put up with this conflict throughout one's life. As can be seen, ambivalence about holding positions of power is also in women's own minds.

This ambivalence can lead men to ask the following questions:

## What is it like to work for a woman boss?

How does a man who has never worked for a woman boss before behave with one? Let us examine some of the apprehensions he may have. Highly cooperative female leaders may be criticized for not being direct and dominant enough. On the flip side, female leaders who are assertive and dominant may be criticized for lacking warmth. This double bind creates a barrier to successful women's leadership. Warmth begets likeability and competence leads to gaining respect. Effective leadership requires competence and warmth as well as likeability and respect.

## Will she facilitate my growth or be a roadblock?

Men, in particular, resist female leadership because men possess higher social status than women and view women as having less power and authority. People prefer to work for bosses with power, connections, and resources more than for bosses who practice good human relations or give a good performance appraisal. What good is praise without the organizational power to back it up and make something significant happen?

One myth or stereotype held by men about a professional woman is that she may not be well networked or integrated into the organization. The fear is that she herself is less likely to be promoted and less likely to take a stand for them. They say they are reluctant to work for her, because they feel their opportunities to move upwards will be less. Men feel competitive towards women, especially in higher-level leadership roles traditionally held by men, where men have more to lose from a woman's advancement. The challenge of being a woman in a leadership role is managing the delicate balance between addressing these unarticulated doubts and concerns and creating an enviable track record.

## Will she delegate or try to do-it-all herself?

Often women are very committed, prefer to be perfectionists, and are task-oriented. They want to do everything well, so well, in fact, that they end up doing it all by themselves. Overcommitment, a high sense of responsibility, and feeling overprotective of their teams constitute some of the major factors that block delegation. These strengths can be a serious impediment to development and time management. Learning to delegate is a major transition skill first-line executives need to learn in order to get promoted to the second level. A manager who does not delegate may make critical mistakes that thwart her success. Researchers report that men delegate more often than women [7]. If women want to become future leaders, they need to leave the tactical and short-term to their juniors and get more into the strategic role as they move up. Just as this is good for their own development, it is equally good for the development of their subordinates.

## Will she provide challenging assignments?

Women managers often report difficulty in obtaining appropriately challenging assignments that are critical for development on the job. Meeting the challenges inherent in tough assignments and learning new behaviors or skills in overcoming them are necessary for further advancement. Whatever the causes of women's lesser access to challenging assignments, this is the prevailing stereotype about women managers. The stereotype is the reason why male subordinates can have doubts and concerns about their own advancement under a woman leader.

## Will she communicate directly and straightforwardly?

Many men feel that women are too indirect and convey even important messages in a roundabout way. When feedback is to be given, many women soften the blow of constructive criticism by couching it in positive comments. A man may have difficulty figuring out what the female boss or colleague is actually saying. He may want to know exactly what the problem is and what he needs to do to remedy it.

A second important point is that sometimes women managers spend an inordinate amount of time worrying about hurting or alienating subordinates. This can cause problems for all concerned. Sometimes, women have to be firm and decisive to the point of being aggressive to bring about changes. They must, however, learn to use their anger or assertiveness constructively. Clearly women's leadership and communication styles sometimes do not fit with the prevailing model of top management communication in their companies.

Under such conditions, any imperfections can get magnified, imperfections which would have been easily ignored in the case of male leaders. In response to these pressures, when women leaders succeed by performing well, sometimes they ironically increase doubts about their competence. Is she a case of preferential hiring or advancement, men might wonder. Most of these fears can be dealt with by bringing them skillfully out into the open, and by carefully selecting and preparing women to hold leadership positions.

It is equally important from a woman's point of view, because new women bosses are often watched and criticized, and their performance is cited as evidence that women cannot be good bosses. For some reason, an inexperienced male boss can be tolerated. But an inexperienced female boss? No way. Not yet. This may well continue until women reach a critical mass. Until then, women may still have to live up to a higher standard of performance than men, and an individual female boss will be seen as representing her whole sex.

## Performance Review: Key Leadership Challenge

One of the most sensitive times for a woman boss is when she does the performance review of a male colleague/subordinate. Although men accept evaluation and criticism more positively than women do (women tend to take it more personally), I am not sure if they accept that criticism well from a female boss. I have always undertaken a great deal of preparation to marshal the facts of a man's performance or failings if any, so that his desire to improve is bolstered at the end of the performance review. However, it is tough dealing with older subordinates (as issues of gender get mixed up with those of age), and tougher still to deal with an insubordinate employee who fails to respond to warnings. Firm lines have to be drawn in terms of what is acceptable behavior and this has to be communicated effectively.

Some men react by trying to play on a woman's emotional sensitivity or empathy. For instance, "My wife is pregnant," "She has a difficult pregnancy," or "My son has his board examination," etc. People assume women are kind and gentle at home and expect the same of them at work. Women's acceptance of this expectation that they should be nice, kind, and nurturing may deter them from assertively claiming leadership and may make them uncertain while reprimanding others. The indirect style of communication is often misinterpreted by male peers. In fact, some of my female clients have been accused by peers of being political and having hidden agendas. A woman leader should be aware that her indirect style can engender distrust among certain kinds of men. What she calls diplomacy, he calls politics. In all these matters, women must act with fairness and, above all, get their own feelings under control so as to not precipitate an emotional battle.

The very worst circumstance in which a woman is placed in a managerial position over men occurs when she has not had much managerial experience, lacks confidence, and is not supported by her corporate bosses. It is, therefore, important to convey that a woman in a leadership position has been chosen on the basis of demonstrated ability. Some suspicion may still remain. Underlying this suspicion is the mismatch between the typical qualities of a woman and that of a typical leader.

In the meantime, there are other techniques that can be acquired for the unfamiliar role of being a boss. These are based on experience as well as on understanding effective human relations. The following tips might prove handy:

- Approach the discussion with good preparation and attention to detail. Review his past performance, any recurring themes that reveal strengths, challenging people or situations, and knowledge and skills that need to develop. Outline SMART goals for the forthcoming period.
- Be specific when you deliver a reprimand.
- Do not reprimand your male colleague/subordinate in public. Do it privately but be firm and timely. Do not save it for later.
- One does not have to play the "one up on you" game with him every time. One could go to his desk once in a while to talk to him.
- Avoid scenes by anticipating situations. Review his work, project report, draft, whatever. Don't let him give a presentation that may be so bad that you may have to rescue him in the middle. Preview the presentation, otherwise you, as well as your team, can lose face.
- Do not be defensive about being tough. If he acts in a manner that is not productive tell him this behavior will not be accepted or rewarded. Sometimes, women bosses spend an inordinate amount of time worrying about hurting or alienating subordinates.
- Don't be afraid of your own aggression or anger. Sometimes, anger can be used constructively to bring about changes.

- Don't set up a competition with your male colleagues in which they are forced to try to show you that women are not superior. Don't let anything become an issue of his manhood versus your womanhood. Hit a problem head on. Deal with it directly.
- It may be an effective technique to try to be flexible and mirror the behavior of the people you are dealing with. You may need to change your approach depending on the situation.
- Approach discipline delivery events constructively with more sensitivity to recipients' potential reactions and socialization processes. Take special training in discipline delivery in case warranted.
- Most importantly, give praise, appreciation, or positive feedback as soon as possible after a good performance.

This should by no means be interpreted to mean that one has to abandon traditional feminine behaviors. Women may have to supplement their concern for relationships with more focus on results. Depending on their interpretation of the situation, they could learn to become more assertive, depersonalize some situations, use more instrumental methods, and overall increase their behavior repertoire for managing conflict and dealing with power.

## Resistance to Women's Leadership, Authority, and Expertise

During my tenure as the president of WIPS, a few cases were referred to me for confidential consultation. One of them was a complaint of sexual harassment by a woman employee (secretarial support staff) about a male messenger in the department.

Normally, the victim is in a subordinate position, but in this case the accused was in a subordinate position. The episode was immediately reported to her female boss and also an office-bearer of WIPS. From the victim's distraught condition, her boss did not doubt her statements. However, to her dismay, she found out that instead of being sympathetic to their young female colleague, the five other male employees in the department (officers and subordinate staff alike) entirely supported the version of the male messenger and called the woman in question "a flirt." Both the parties, the accused as well as the victim, were on contractual jobs for over a year and a half. But greater effort was made to retain the male employee, while simultaneously suggesting the female employee be dismissed. The atmosphere at the workplace was vitiated, undermining morale and mutual trust. The whole group also tried to pressurize their boss so much that, in the beginning, she lost all confidence to take disciplinary action against the accused. She was afraid of using her own power and authority. It was almost as if she had to make a choice between being correct and being liked. To top it all, she did not know how to handle the accusation that being a woman it was expected that she would support the woman in question without even considering who was right and who was wrong. Suddenly, the female boss with no hidden agenda whatsoever started getting viewed with suspicion only because the victim was of her gender. The normal process of enquiry was also perceived as giving "undue" attention to the "favorite" party. After going through a lot of turmoil, she realized that she had to deal directly with the undue blame, thereby rejecting her own feelings of suffering and victimization. She had to learn to be invulnerable to destructive feedback. After two enquiries and discussions, when she was absolutely certain of the facts, she decided to take effective action against the accused by discarding her defensiveness. She held a departmental meeting to clearly state what was acceptable behavior in the office and what wasn't, and what would happen if anyone transgressed the limits, irrespective of their gender. By doing so, she used her leadership position effectively and set up an example in assertiveness and in the exercise of her legitimate authority. It is noteworthy that, despite companies adopting and enforcing policies to protect employees from sexual harassment, women are still susceptible to harassment, and sometimes even third-party harassment. It is also remarkable that, when women assume leadership positions, and lead in a supposedly masculine (authoritative and directive) manner as required for disciplinary action, then they are devalued when the evaluators are men.

All said and done, subordinates resent being disciplined by women managers. Indeed, a study of gender and discipline at work [8] by Atwater—a professor at the School of Management, Arizona State University—found that women dislike being told off by other women even more than men do. Men and women alike would rather be scolded by a male boss. The study examined recipient's perception of workplace discipline. Women managers delivering discipline were perceived to be less effective and less fair than males.

Atwater and her colleagues interviewed 163 workers from a broad range of professions who had been disciplined in a variety of ways, from being fired to being ticked off. In about 40 percent of cases, they found subordinates changed their behavior as a result of their reprimand and female bosses were as successful in this as men. However, male bosses were much more severe than women. They were three times as likely to suspend or sack a subordinate and only half as likely to give merely verbal scolding. Even so, when female subordinates were asked if they felt responsible for their bad behavior, 52 percent disagreed when a female boss read the charges against them. The figure was only 18 percent when the boss was male. This could be explained by the fact that the arrival of women in managerial roles is a recent phenomenon and, therefore, their authoritarian role receives less legitimacy than men. If women managers become aware of how they may be perceived, they can approach disciplining events more constructively and with sensitivity to the recipients' potential reactions.

## When your competence is not enough

I will share an interesting experience here. I was once facilitating a developmental program on "Rediscovering Creativity" with a mixed group of men and women executives. For one of the experiential activities, the group of 30 participants was divided into two groups of 15 each. In a treasure hunt they were given the task of finding resources to complete a task in an allotted time. The group coordinators identified an expert in each group, a participant whose ideas surpassed those of the rest of the group. About 50 percent of the time, the expert was a woman. After the completion of the task, when group members rated each other's expertise, they rated female experts as having less expertise than female non-experts but rated male experts and non-experts equally. How could female experts appear incompetent? Apparently, women who display unusual competence in competitive settings can sometimes increase doubts about their competence. It is difficult for people to determine who has the best ideas, particularly in situations involving complex problems that do not have typical or obvious solutions. Under such conditions, which are common for real life problems, people rely on stereotypes to evaluate performance. In such situations, it is possible that expert women will be discredited but expert men will be given the benefit of doubt. An interesting study draws attention to similar findings that even when women have knowledge and expertise, what they know is not considered good enough in task groups [9]. It is in such situations that women must stand up to challenges and demonstrate and stake a claim to their full potency and sovereignty.

## Reclaiming One's Own Power and Authority

The case in point was an International Workshop of Women Managers from SAARC countries as Change Agents organized by the Indian Institute of Management Ahmedabad in collaboration with the Canadian International Development Agency. During the course of the program, one of the participants, the head of an NGO from Pakistan, whom we will call Fatima, mentioned her difficulty and distress in dealing with male subordinates and maintaining office discipline. She stated that they clearly resented the fact that they had to take orders from a woman and made no bones about it. They openly resisted her leadership because they firmly believed that men possess higher societal status than women in their country, and saw her attempt to wield influence in work situations as competing with them for power and authority. One of them made his contempt more apparent by adopting a "damn care" posture of resting his feet on the office table, when she walked into the office every morning. What was surprising was that she never took any objection to this unacceptable behavior or, at least, never let her displeasure be known to the concerned employee. Nor did she realize that, by tolerating this behavior, she was sending out a wrong signal to other employees that she did not mind this undisciplined behavior and there was no such thing as office decorum.

The participants were shocked to hear about this scenario. A role play was enacted, so that Fatima could practice assertiveness and learn to demonstrate her displeasure in an authoritative way. Considering that she was very docile, soft spoken, and friendly by nature, this was a tough call. In fact, these very qualities had earlier won her public approval. I know of some women who bask in the approval that traditional feminine qualities can bring. However, these qualities do not do justice to the role of leadership. A label like "Women are wonderful," in fact, deters women from assertively claiming leadership, and may make them feel awkward while performing regular managerial behaviors such as reprimanding others.

Until that workshop, Fatima did not know how she came across as a leader and how others experienced her. She realized that she had to be powerful and forthright and have a direct, visible impact on others. Two or three rounds of role play were conducted to familiarize her with the new role-taking behavior and how to have a challenging conversation. However, what came through the role play was that, instead of being firm and authoritative, she sounded apologetic and appeasing. She came across as someone who was pleading with and begging of her subordinate to "behave." This critical feedback was a turning point for her. By her own admission, her management style was often long on compassion and short on task-orientation. In fact, she had been savoring the approval her feminine qualities—friendly, caring, warm—had accorded her for a long time. This approval was now competing with the responsibility and obligations of leadership. Added to this was the fact that, in her culture, she also felt uncomfortable holding a position of authority, since women had seldom held such positions in the past. She lacked the required confidence in herself and in the system, and was not ready to risk failure. But surely women should be allowed to fail the first time—as men are—and learn from that failure. That is part of the secret to success.

Despite the fact that Fatima, selfless and compassionate, was committed to her mission, she lacked the ability to grab the attention of a room by making a powerful entry and forging quick personal connections. An ability to command a room is a cultivated behavior, where one projects confidence, decisiveness, and the ability to influence people. It also needs communication in a clear language and a confident tone. It is accompanied by a body language which conveys professionalism and power, an erect posture, steady eye contact, etc. In short, Fatima lacked "executive presence," as she was too conditioned by her "nice girl," seen–not–heard style of communication.

While helping her to craft a satisfactory response to this type of resistance, it became clear that the prescriptive stereotype of how a woman should behave was directly competing with her role as a leader. She also experienced an identity crisis as she perceived an incongruity between her gender and professional roles. She was well aware that her influence was challenged by doubts about her competence. This double standard was impeding her ability to lead and influence her team. The awareness of these subtle dynamics led her to practice new leadership behaviors and wield influence.

We learnt a valuable lesson from this experience: that practical leadership experience is crucial for developing leadership identity.

Similarly, women need to recognize that not every leader is universally liked. Women need to lead in an assertive, competent manner, accompanied by friendly, warm behavior only to the extent that it does not undermine their authority, and is appropriate for the situation.

## Crystallizing Leadership Identity

A workplace can only be diverse if the people who work there can be themselves, bringing their whole selves to the table, and being permitted to retain various components of their identity. It is important for anyone in a leadership role to combine and integrate the various components of their personality into a coherent whole that provides the foundation for one's values, thoughts, actions, and behavior [10].

"When you leave for work every day, what do you leave behind? Your opinions? Your uniqueness? Your religion? Your political affiliation? Your native language? Your gender? Your children?" asked a powerful advertisement of PriceWaterhouseCoopers on a billboard in New York many years ago. When we go to work with our professional identities, do we leave our nonprofessional identities at home?

Each of us has a sense of personal identity that comes from individual personality traits and interpersonal relationships. Then, there is a layer of social identity that comprises the parts of our identity that come from belonging to particular groups, including nationality, religion, gender, language, community, socioeconomic status, etc. A person can simultaneously be a professor, a writer, an active community member or an office bearer, wife, mother and daughter. This awareness serves us well, as it introduces us to different perspectives and enhances our ability to accurately read situations that require leadership ability. Just as a leader needs to understand the impact of her identity on others, she also needs to understand how the identities of others color the lens of how they view her as a leader. Becoming a leader then involves internalizing and crystallizing a leadership identity where tentativeness withers away and its place is taken by clarity and a sense of purpose.

Research [11] confirms that the development of a leader requires the integration of personal, social, and professional identities. Leaders must know who they are as leaders, how they deal with others, and how others deal with them, and how to respond to situations effectively. Followers tend to identify with a top leader who combines and represents many aspects of different social identities in a leadership role. Developing an integrated identity is easier for someone who is a member of the dominant group; for instance, in business, being a male and a top leader in the corporate sector, or in politics as a successor of a top political leader by virtue of being his son. Forging a leadership identity can get much tougher for someone who does not belong to a dominant group or is perceived to be different from the dominant group on the basis of surface qualities. It is, therefore, important to be seen as a leader by significant others or to see oneself as a leader.

The Chairman of PepsiCo, Indra Nooyi, is a star in the US corporate world. She is an Indian woman, born in a Tamil-speaking family, who played cricket and a guitar for a rock band in her growing years, studied in an Ivy League business school in the US, is a mother of two daughters, and a philanthropist who has given an endowment to her alma mater. She is a top executive at work just as she is a top executive at home. She is an architect of her own identity, and this will be appealing to those who share aspects of her various social identities. The leaders of today are vastly different from the leaders of yesteryear. They no longer come in a particular color or gender. It is, therefore, critical to understand one's leadership identity and its implications for leadership development.

## Developing Leadership Brand

How am I coming across as a woman leader? Is this the brand identity that best represents who I am and what I can do? Does this brand identity create value in the eyes of my stakeholders? These are very important questions to ask in different phases of the leadership journey. Leadership is not so much a position we hold, but a disposition of values and vision we possess. This is because, whether we realize it or not, we all have a leadership brand. How we interact with others, how we get our work done, and how and when we deliver is all about building a brand identity.

A leadership brand is not static. It evolves in response to the different roles and responsibilities one holds and the different expectations one faces at different times in one's career. One needs to have great clarity and focus in choosing one's leadership brand, because it is about delivering results in response to the expectations of the role. To that end, the process of choosing a leadership brand has an outward focus.

> I once worked with Natasha—a very well qualified and competent executive—who was promoted as a senior vice-president, finance. Her successful stints in previous roles such as internal auditor, chief finance manager, etc., had earned her this promotion. A few months into the role, she expressed her complete bewilderment at being scored low on "thinking strategically," a competency very important at her level. I advised Natasha to have a conversation with her boss as well as peers to figure out what was expected of her role and how she could demonstrate she was meeting those expectations. Her new role required her to create and communicate a clear vision of her role, linking it with business objectives and developing an effective strategy to achieve that vision. In short, in this leadership role, she needed to develop a brand identity as a strategic thinker. Once this was clear, she proceeded to take certain initiatives that could demonstrate how she thought strategically. In the process, she had to involve people in decision making, ask challenging questions, and take tough decisions about priorities and positioning of the initiative. In a quarterly review, she found out that the scores on "thinking strategically" were better than before, but there was still scope for improvement.
> 
> I wondered whether the problem was in the presentation of the brand, and whether she expressed herself convincingly and effectively. She needed to tailor her presentation to her audience, so understanding their needs was very important. In our sessions together we worked on her body language and how her voice could be used as a strategic tool. Then it was time to find out how others experienced her in the departmental meetings. The feedback was encouraging. While working with the senior leadership team, she made an effort to reframe conversations so seniors could follow her logic, reasoning, and position, and also see how her initiatives were linked strategically to the objectives of the organization and were generating better financial outcomes. Months later she was actually outscoring others in strategic thinking.

Advancing up in a male-dominated hierarchy requires a strong, skillful, and persistent woman who does not internalize diffidence and avoids the wavering of confidence that further fuels the doubts of her peers or colleagues. Such a woman is truly competent. She is also truly vulnerable, because her gender will be blamed for any shortcomings or failures. Despite this, competent women do succeed and their achievements break down boundaries and shatter stereotypes for the women who come after them. As a matter of fact, women leaders are better placed to understand and appreciate the constraints faced by women in the workplace, thereby leading the change and helping them realize their full potential [12].

As we have seen, the leadership journey of women can go through many trials, tribulations, and triumphs. It is a journey that mirrors the reclaiming of spaces and the redistribution of power, and women have achieved it in many spheres. In the process, they might wonder whether it is worthwhile being on the board of a company? The road to restoring the natural order in boardrooms is a similar journey they need to make and the time starts now.

## Is It Worthwhile Being on a Board?

India is one of the few countries to mandate an appointment of women directors on the board of listed companies. Section 149 (1) of the Companies Act 2013, mandating that every publicly listed company must have at least one woman board director, has brought this issue to the forefront. The categories of companies which need to comply with the requirement of having at least one woman director are as follows:

a. Listed companies
b. Public companies with a paid-up share capital of INR 1 billion or more
c. Public companies with a turnover of INR 3 billion or more

While there is a lead time in this coming into effect (one year after the law takes effect in case [a] and three years in cases [b] and [c]), it is critical to start thinking about this issue actively today.

A significant number of companies have inducted a woman member from the promoter family to comply with the rule within the deadline. Even public shareholders at annual general meetings are demanding better representation of women on boards. However, some of the largest public sector enterprises have not yet met the requirement of at least one woman director on their boards, even a year after the rule came into force.

Why? Because companies are finding it difficult to find qualified women in traditional business settings. The reasons are all too familiar. The primary reason is the late entry of women in the corporate sector. It also takes a good 20–25 years to painstakingly build careers. Many drop out of the workforce due to family responsibilities. As a result, women are too underrepresented in the workforce to be able to enter the board pipeline. Even for those who are eligible to be on the board, the percentage stays stagnant.

The 2016 Global Board of Directors Survey [13] indicates that there is a gender as well as generational divide at play here. Male directors, especially older respondents, said that "the lack of qualified female candidate was the primary reason." Women cited that diversity is not a priority in board recruitment. Younger male directors (age 55 and under) said the reason was that traditional networks tend to be male dominated.

This is confirmed by a new report from the Equality and Human Rights Commission (EHRC) that suggests that "old boys' networks" are barring women from the boardroom at some of the UK's biggest companies. The report reveals that more than 60 percent of the UK's largest firms have failed to meet a voluntary target of 25 percent female board members. The problem is particularly acute at the executive level, with 90 percent of FTSE 250 firms having no women at all in executive posts. Perhaps the most disconcerting finding by the EHRC is the fact that during the period 2012–14, fewer than half of the UK's largest 350 companies increased their female board representation at all.

This may be partly explained by the other problem highlighted in the report: the method companies are using to find and select new board members. Nearly a third rely on personal networks, rather than publicly advertise such roles. No wonder then that those all-male golfing trips and long lunches take on an extra layer of significance [13].

Even then those who are qualified and eligible would not like to be mere rubber stamps. Company boards need to get women because they are good and not because they are women. Tokenism is a very valid reason for women to be wary of being on boards. Moreover, tokens are perceived negatively, sometimes with downright derision, and often doubted, and, as a result, not trusted. Being labeled as a mere token creates discomfort, isolation, and self-doubt [14]. Being perceived as a token can also interfere with performance [15]. In fact, because of their high visibility, tokens are subjected to intense scrutiny, face additional performance pressures, and are singled out because they are different, rather than because of their own particular accomplishments. In such situations, there are perceptions that even small mistakes can be fatal, and tokens feel they have to work harder to receive recognition for any individual achievements. These reactions to tokens seem to occur whether the token is a woman or anyone from any minority group.

Such treatment of women limits their options and makes it difficult for them to rise to positions of responsibility. Having a critical mass of women in executive positions can lessen this problem. When women are not in the minority, their identities as women fade into the background and colleagues are more likely to react to them in terms of their individual competencies.

Half a dozen women board members I interviewed said they would like to be invited on a board for their expertise, experience, and track record, rather than on a gender card. They would like to act as key influencers in shaping opinions, sharing ideas and perspectives, and making significant contributions.

Despite the appeal of joining a board, there is a small category of women who are apprehensive due to the demands of board service, and are concerned about the risks and liabilities involved. For instance, significant fiduciary responsibilities can be perceived as daunting and due diligence on the company in consideration can be seen as an additional effort.

## From tokenism to critical mass

To reduce the element of tokenism, research on women directors investigates how many women a board should have to have a bearing on corporate performance. Evidence suggests that when the size of the minority group increases it gains trust and the majority benefits from the resources women bring to the organization [16]. In other words, when the minority group reaches critical mass, a qualitative change takes place in the nature of group interactions.

So what number represents the critical mass? Research on women on corporate boards [17] suggests that the tipping point or critical mass is reached when a board has at least three women. In fact, a critical mass of three or more women creates "normalization," where gender is no longer a barrier to communication, and where women directors are more likely to feel comfortable, supported, and freer to raise issues and be active participants.

While one woman on the board can, and often does, make a difference, increasing the number of women to two or three ensures that women's voices are heard and their contributions noticed [18]. Three or more women creates a critical mass, and they are no longer treated as outsiders. Any woman member of the board is then less likely to feel neither pressurized to alter her behavior nor simply be her own self in order to fit the norm set by men [19]. When companies are struggling to have even one woman director, three is a huge number. At least for now!

Despite all the legislative efforts to create a critical mass of women on boards, the percentage of women on boards remains quite low throughout Europe and the US. The Russell 3000, an index that measures the performance of the largest 3,000 companies in the US, in 2012 showed the number of women on boards in a chart as shown here [20].

**Russell 3000 index: Number of women on boards**

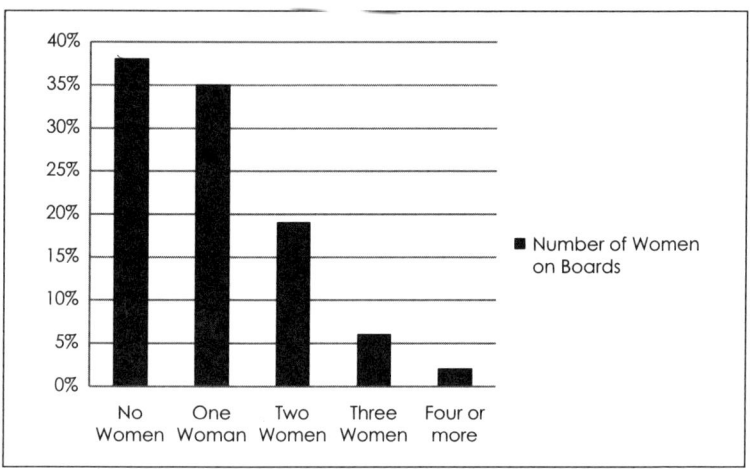

As can be seen, a full 94 percent of the boards with gender representation have less than the critical mass of three needed to make a true difference. The perspectives of multiple stakeholders, which enrich the diversity of thought, problem-solving, and decision-making, are still missing.

Here is the good news. One study of 22,000 profitable global firms indicates that the impact of having more women in the C-Suite is bigger than that of having a woman on the board or as the CEO. Similarly, from having no women in corporate leadership (the CEO, the board, and other C-Suite positions) to a 30 percent female share is associated with a one-percentage-point increase in net margin, which translates to a 15 percent increase in profitability for a typical firm [21].

As one company secretary mentioned,

> Having one woman director as a "representative of diversity" on a board of 12–15 members will not make a difference. But if you have more than that, and if they are working on significant committees and formulate policies that filter into the

executive arm of the company, then you can begin to correlate diversity with performance because these people will implement policies.

Clearly, a great deal of work needs to still be done to create a critical mass of women on boards to ensure that difficult issues and problems are thrashed out, resulting in better problem solving or more informed decision making. Let's examine women's position in boardrooms across the world.

## Women in boardrooms across the world

Nordic countries have been trendsetters in advocating women's rights. Norway became the second country after Finland to grant women the right to vote in 1913 and is today one of the top 10 countries in terms of percentage of women in parliament [22]. In 2005, Norway's parliament mandated gender representation on the boards of public companies and that at least 40 percent of board members must be women. Today, Norway is at 40 percent, with the highest representation of women on boards. This strategy is justified not on the grounds of gender equality, but on the grounds of improving decision-making ability at the top. If those at the top share the same background, experience, and probably similar perspectives, then it will stifle innovation.

Today, in the US, for example, when women make up 57 percent of the labor force one would expect to see a greater proportion of female directors, if a meritocratic system were truly and objectively being implemented [23]. Yet, women today hold only 19.2 percent of the board seats of S&P companies, according to Catalyst, a nonprofit organization focused on advancing women in the workplace [24,25]. In Europe, women account for 20.2 percent of the board members of the EU's largest publicly listed companies [26]. Japan fares even worse, with only 3.1 percent of board seats held by women. Multinational automobile, electronics, and computer companies, which represent Japan's primacy in the global market, are completely male dominated, while those that have opened up board seats for women tend to be medium-sized firms.

## Trends in gender diversity by country

### 2016 Egon Zehnder European Board Diversity Analysis, Percentage Board positions held by women in 2016

| | |
|---|---|
| France | 37.3% |
| Germany | 22.2% |
| Norway | 39.7% |
| Sweden | 37.7% |
| Switzerland | 29.2% |
| United Kingdom | 26.3% |
| *Western Europe overall* | *26.2%* |
| Russia | 7.5% |
| Australia | 26.8% |
| China | 9.6% |
| India | 12.2% |
| Japan | 5.3% |
| South Africa | 20.8% |
| New Zealand | 23.1% |
| Brazil | 6.7% |
| Canada | 25% |
| United States | 19.9% |
| Global overall | 18.5% |

## A Case for Diversity on Boards

The American poet Ezra Pound once said, "When two men in business always agree, one of them is unnecessary." This, in essence, justifies bringing diversity to boards. The case for expanding board diversity is by now well known. Attracting and retaining the full range of the best available talent to oversee, govern, and advise companies in an era of unprecedented challenges and change is one of the top challenges for companies around the world. Diversity is a key to making boards more consistently effective than ever before. Diversity is vital not only because it is the right thing to do, but also because it actually enhances shareholder value. The best ideas can flourish only when an organization embraces individuals with different views and experiences. True diversity of thought reduces "group think" and unlocks fresh perspectives, innovation, and creativity. To effectively fulfill both governance and advisory functions in a global world, boards must actively include broad viewpoints that originate from differences in a wide range of perspectives on many issues, including product design and selection, advertising, public relations resulting in a more favorable public image, and industrial relations.

One of the CEOs who is an ardent votary of diversity once mentioned,

> Often what a woman board member can bring to a board is some perspective a company has not had before—adding some stark reality to the deliberation process. These perspectives are of great value and can represent the aspirations of the diverse workforce of the company. These perspectives are often missing from all male gatherings.

Clearly, diversity is important but in itself it's not enough. It must be accompanied by inclusiveness—a company culture that genuinely welcomes, values, and leverages the advantages of diversity. Diversity then is about counting the numbers and inclusion is about making the numbers count. What can women as potential directors do?

The business world has changed beyond recognition. Boards look for individuals with specific skill sets and experience to address these changes. Specific requirements are different for each board functioning in different industries. However, some broad themes and patterns are as follows:

1. Increase visibility. Women need to excel in certain areas of expertise and need to be known for specific competencies or expertise in that domain. They need to build up their reputation as thought leaders and create successful track records. Modest self-presentation on the part of women is warranted. It is important to convince the seniors and the peer group that women are worthy of advancement.
2. Start by exploring what the boards are looking for. Boards are looking for individuals with general management perspective and relevant industry experience. Those who have driven revenue growth through digital sales and marketing experience are equally valuable. CFOs and CIOs who have led technology transformation are of interest to some boards. Boards of companies who are seeking to grow overseas are interested in executives with business experience of international markets such as BRICS countries.
3. Educate yourself on what it means to be a director and how to add value to board discussions. Familiarize yourself with the company, its business, industry, financials, management team, and, not least, the board, its ethics, and values. Learn about governance issues and regulatory requirements.
4. Develop a target list of companies that best fit your skills, expertise, and interests. Where the profile of other directors is attractive, and the time commitment and remuneration are consistent with expectations, there is a good fit between the individual and the company.
5. Develop a high level of credible networks and relationships that can be potentially leveraged for the benefit of the potential board.
6. Sharpen soft skills, including the ability to offer constructive criticism, collaboration and influencing skills, and the confidence to share independent views.
7. Help other women develop by mentoring them for leadership roles to fill the diversity vacuum at the top.

# What can companies do to increase the number of women on boards?

1. As company boards seek to replace retiring directors, they need to ensure that a diverse slate including women and others representing different backgrounds is given due consideration. This should be a priority for the Chairman, CEO, chief human resource officers and nominating/governance committee chairs as well.
2. Companies need to reach out beyond the regular industry networks to find talented women leaders working in government, non-government or not-for-profit organizations, including law, academia, and the social sector, to create a rich balance of perspectives at the table. They may not be savvy about all aspects of the industry but will learn the ropes soon. This is the whole point of diversity, after all.
3. Companies need to set up a formal recruitment process. It is paradoxical that when an increasing number of companies are concerned about diversity and equality, many still fail to tackle concrete practices such as board-member selection methods that have a demonstrable impact on the problem. After doing a detailed competency mapping and skill requirement analysis, a search committee should be identified, which further finalizes a recruitment strategy and acts on it.
4. Companies can consider seeking help from professional services firms to include suitable women on their shortlist of candidates.
5. Companies need to create an enabling environment for women to grow into board positions. This is a long process and will not happen overnight. Many companies are offering career confidence-boosting workshops, or training women in negotiation skills.
6. Introducing temporary quota policy. The objective is to provide an opportunity to build up experience and network

mechanisms, set up training for subsequent cohorts, and increase exposure to female corporate leaders. Once a cadre of women is well prepared for leadership, the quota can be removed. The Netherlands introduced this and then removed it in 2013 [27].

7. Lack of general management or line experience is seen as the primary obstacle for women. CEOs consistently indicate that when seeking successors—particularly for Chairman and CEO slots or even board-level executives—they look for people with high-level profit-and-loss experience. A study which evaluated the leadership effectiveness of 7,280 executives found that, at every management level, women were rated higher than men. At the same time, data showed that the higher the level, the higher the proportion of men. CEOs need to ask, are the best people being promoted? [28]

8. Professional technology experience could prove to be women's stepping stone to the corporate boardroom. Directors need a robust understanding of technology. That's where professional technology experience can be a differentiator for women to close the gender gap on boards [29].

9. Companies need to carefully develop a diverse slate of candidates to whom enough challenging assignments are given or mentoring opportunities provided, to ensure that capable women rise to the top. At the same time, companies need to provide enough flexibility so that women can balance family commitments with a full-time executive role.

10. Companies need to take the lead in creating a databank on qualified women candidates with industry associations such as FICCI, CII and NASSCOM.

11. Companies should initiate mentoring programs to identify potential women directors and get them board ready. A mentor can be attached to them and, as part of the mentoring process, potential directors can be sent on secondments

to boards or board committees after signing confidentiality agreements to gain hands-on experience in policy formulation, strategic decision making, and corporate governance. These are some of the ways by which companies can create a conducive climate for women to flourish in the corporate world.

The next chapter looks at the best practices introduced by gender-responsive organizations that have created hospitable environments for their women employees. You will get a peek behind the scenes of some successful Indian multinationals, allowing you to learn from their experience which caused them to make real changes that blended and amplified the voices of men and women.

## References

1. Morrison, Toni, *Beloved*, as quoted in Devaki Jain, 'Women, Public Policy and the New World Order', May 2006: 22.
2. Davison, H. K. and M. J. Burke, 'Sex Discrimination in Simulated Employment Contexts: A Meta-analytic Investigation', *Journal of Vocational Behavior* 56, no. 2 (2000), 225–48.
3. Riffkin, Rebecca, 'Americans Still Prefer a Male Boss to a Female Boss', *Gallup.com*, October 14, 2014, http://brain.gallup.com
4. Datta, Kanika, 'Male or Female Boss: Does it Make a Difference?' *Business Standard* 12, no. 23 (May 21, 2015), http://inwww.rediff.com/business/report/column-male-or-female-boss-does-it-make-a-difference/20150521.htm
5. Ellemers, N., D. de Gilder, and S. A. Haslam, 'Motivating Individuals and Groups at Work: A Social Identity Perspective on Leadership and Group Performance', *Academy of Management Review* 29, no. 3 (2004): 459–78.
6. Eagly, A. and B. T. Johnson, 'Gender and Leadership Style: A Metaanalysis', *Psychological Bulletin* 108, no. 2 (1990): 233–56.
7. Oshabemi, T. and R. Gill, 'Gender Differences and Similarities in the Leadership Styles and Behavior of UK Managers', *Women in Management Review* 18, no. 5/6 (2003): 288–98.
8. Atwater, L. E., J. A. Carey, and D. A. Waldman, 'Gender and Discipline in the Workplace: Wait Until Your Father Gets Home', *Journal of Management* 27, no. 5 (2001): 537–67.
9. Thomas-Hunt, M. C. and K. W. Phillips, 'When What You Know is Not Enough: Expertise and Gender Dynamics in Task Groups', *Personality and Social Psychology Bulletin* 30, no. 12 (2004): 1585–98.

10. Day, D. V., M. M. Harrison, and S. M. Halpin, *An Integrative Approach to Leader Development: Connecting Adult Development, Identity and Expertise*, New York, NY: Taylor & Francis, 2009.
11. Lord, R. G. and R. J. Hall, 'Identity, Deep Structure and the Development of Leadership Skill', *Leadership Quarterly* 16, no. 4 (2005): 591–615.
12. Dasgupta, Brinda, 'Women Leaders Focused on Excelling in Workplace: Survey', *Economic Times*, July 29, 2016.
13. Spencer Stuart, Boris Groysberg, Yo-Jud Cheng and Deborah Bell. '2016 Global Board of Directors Survey', https://www.spencerstuart.com/research-and-insight/2016-global-board-of-directors-survey (accessed on June 18, 2017).
14. Bates, Laura, 'What Use Are Women's Networks? We Need Less Talk and More Action from Businesses', *The Guardian*, March 25, 2016, www.theguardian.com/lifeandstyle/2016/mar/25/what-use-are-womens-networks-we-need-less-talk-and-more-action-from-businesses
15. Kanter, R. M., *Men and Women of the Corporation*, New York, NY: Basic Books, 1977.
16. Powell, G. N., *Women and Men in Management*, Newbury Park, CA: SAGE Publications, 1993.
17. Kanter, R. M., 'Some Effects of Proportion in Group Life', *American Journal of Sociology* 82, no. 5 (1977): 965–90.
18. Erkut, S., V. W. Kramer, and A. M. Konrad, 'Critical Mass: Does the Number of Women on Corporate Boards Make a Difference?' in *Women on Corporate Board of Directors: International Research and Practice*, edited by S. Vinnicomb, V. Singh, R. Burke, D. Billimoria, and M. Huse, London: Edward Elgar, 2008, 222–32.
19. Konrad, A. M., Kramer, V. W., and S. Erkut, 'Critical Mass: The Impact of Three or More Women on Corporate Boards', *Organizational Dynamics* 37, no. 2 (2008): 145–64.
20. ———, 'Critical Mass on Corporate Boards: Why Three or More Women Enhance Corporate Governance', 2006. http://www.wcwonline.org/pdf/criticalmassexecutivesummar
21. Noland, Marcus and Tyler Moran, 'Study: Firms with More Women on the C-Suite are More Profitable', *Harvard Business Review*, February 8, 2016, https://hbr.org/2016/02/study-firms-with-more-women-in-the-c-suite-are-more-profitable
22. Grant Thornton, *International Business Report 2012*, Grant Thornton, http;//www.gti.org/files/ibr2012%20%-%20women%20in%20senior%20%management%20master.pdf.page9
23. U.S. Bureau of Labor Statistics, *Current Population Survey*, US Bureau of Labor Statistics, http://www.bls.gov/cps/cpsaat03.htm
24. Catalyst, *2014 Catalyst Census: Women Board Directors*, New York, NY: Catalyst, 2015.
25. Catalyst, *The Bottomline: Corporate Performance and Women's Representation on Boards*, New York, NY: Catalyst, 2011.

26. Egon Zehnder, *Global Board Diversity Analysis*, London: EGON Zehnder, 2016. https://www.egonzehnder.com/files/2016_gbda_digital.pdf (accessed on June 18, 2017).
27. Noland and Moran, 'Study: Firms with More Women on the C-Suite are More Profitable'.
28. Jack Zenger and Joseph Folkman, *A Study in Leadership: Women Do it Better than Men*, Utah, 2012.
29. Accenture, *Getting to Equal: How Digital is Closing the Gender Gap at Work* (Report), Accenture, 2016. https://www.accenture.com/...w__/ar-es/_.../Accenture-Getting-To-Equal.pdf, (accessed on June 16, 2017).

# 8
# Creating Sanctuaries in Workplaces

In the early days of coal mining, miners often took canaries with them below ground to serve as "air detectors." When the canaries stopped singing, it was an early warning that the environment was getting too toxic. Women may be to business what the canary was to coal mining. Like the canaries, women who work in today's corporate environment may be serving as an early warning system to alert the organizations about certain disturbing trends. I rather like this insightful metaphor from Carol Frenier's essay, "Love At Work" [1].

Despite all recruitment efforts, if women fail to join an organization in significant numbers, if they hold "low-visibility" jobs in what are termed as "women's departments," if they have fewer resources—manpower, funds—to accomplish major tasks, or if there is a constant exodus of women at alarming rates, then these are indications that all is not well with women in that organization. No wonder, in its *Global Gender Gap Report 2014*, the World Economic Forum estimates it will take until 2095 to achieve global gender parity in the workplace [2]. That's another 80 years till companies and governments are led equally by men and women, 80 more years of leaking talent pipelines and unfulfilled professional promise.

Even then, one still has to admit that, in many ways, now is a better time to be a woman than 50 years ago. By and large, women everywhere (barring a few exceptions) have got the same legal rights as men: to vote, to work, to do as they please. They have equal access to education at all levels, although only those in urban areas mostly make use of it. The qualitative argument for having more women in the workplace is also becoming more widely accepted. If they are working, they are protected (only up to a point) by equal pay and equal opportunities legislation. Yet, sooner or later, any discussion on women's progress in the workplace seems to lead to the same inevitable conclusion: "Women have come a long way, but they still have a long way to go."

Looking at the current scenario, it is impossible to disagree. So, do women find their organizations great places to work at?

Linda Wirth, a gender expert with the International Labor Organization (ILO), says,

> A lot of the stories you hear are that the women don't 'lean in'. But there are just as many stories of women who say that they've done everything to climb, but [have] ultimately been frustrated because they do not get appointed by the men around. This is one of the reasons why women leave the corporate world to start their own businesses [3].

The hurdles facing women aspiring to management jobs can be so formidable that they sometimes abandon efforts to make it to the top of large firms, taking their energy and know-how to smaller and more flexible companies. Many more women than men report that they have dealt with gender-based barriers by leaving employers or changing careers. This implies that talent will move to companies who are better at encouraging gender diversity.

Some set up their own businesses. They are "opting out" to strike out on their own. According to the Center for Women's Business Research, from 1997 to 2004, the number of women-owned businesses grew twice that of all firms in the US. One in 18 adult women in the US is a business owner. As of 2016, it is estimated that there are now 11.3 million (11,313,900) women-owned businesses in the United States, employing nearly 9 million people (8,976,100) and generating over US$1.6 trillion (US$1,622,763,800,000) in revenues. Between 2007 and 2016, the number of women-owned firms increased by 45 percent, compared to just a 9 percent increase among all businesses [4]. These women and their accomplishments are inspiring. Each one's story is different and offers a variety of lessons, whether it is on how to spot a marketable idea, how to distinguish oneself from the competition, how to hire and train the right people, or how to put customers front and center.

A new study by a multinational corporation shows that the rate of turnover in management positions is 2.5 times higher among top-performing women than it is among men. The standard explanation for why women are leaving is always rationalized as work–life balance. It is not entirely wrong, because women often cite "personal" or "family" as their reason for leaving. They never say that the working environments are not welcome or the organizational culture is suppressive, but that could be out of fear of burning bridges. Several newspaper articles [5] point to the disturbing trend of a large number of highly qualified women dropping out of mainstream careers. In developed markets, women at the senior level do not leave to go back home. They leave to be entrepreneurs, or go to not-for-profit or smaller organizations. Many think that this is in favor of seeking greater work–life balance, but this is rarely the case. Instead, they are seeking to be part of or creating their own working environments that value their ideas or contributions or allow them greater creativity. No wonder, women-owned businesses are growing all over the world. From the US to Latin America and from Europe to Asia, women today own or operate a third of all private businesses, and this percentage is growing at a faster rate than that of private businesses owned by men [6]. Women are becoming more entrepreneurial. Women own 36 percent of all businesses, according to the 2012 US Census, a jump of 30 percent over 2007 [7].

In a *New York Times*/CBS News/Kaiser Family Foundation poll of non-working adults ages 25 to 54 in the United states, conducted in November 2014, 61 percent of women said family responsibilities were a reason they were not working, compared to 37 percent of men. Of women who identified as homemakers and had not sought a job for a year or two, nearly three quarters said they would consider going back if a job offered flexible hours or allowed them to work from home. For many women with children, it seems the decision about work involves weighing a particularly complex set of benefits and challenges. The challenge is insurmountable in part because there is a dearth of programs and policies that support women in their prime career and childbearing years.

In Europe, family friendly policies have continued to expand and evolve in recent years. They include subsidized childcare, paid parental leave, part-time work, and taxation of individuals instead of families, which encourages women's employment [8].

In emerging markets, the burning question is, "Am I getting enough excitement or fulfillment that I leave my family to do this job?" In India, one can see a stark difference in the level of awareness among women regarding their rights at the workplace and in society, depending on the geography. In metro cities like Delhi, Mumbai, and Bengaluru, we find women who are empowered and confident of their place at work, as well as in society. In contrast, women from Tier-II and Tier-III towns are so overwhelmed by old conditioning and societal pressure that they fail to realize their full potential. These women have the same aspirations and ambitions when it comes to career and family, but they simply do not get the right support due to gender biases and social norms. We also know that women have a greater tendency and compulsion to interrupt their careers for reasons beyond work, in ways that limit their growth and development.

It's encouraging that many women want to be entrepreneurs and know that digital fluency will help them achieve those goals. This is particularly true in the emerging markets, where women are more than twice as likely as those in developed markets—61 percent versus 29 percent—to say they want to start a new business in the next five years [9].

In a 2011 survey commissioned by the Associated Chamber of Commerce and Industry of India [10] in 14 cities, work–life balance emerged as the single-most important issue and the single-most quoted reason for career breaks and disruptions. Eighty two percent mothers with young children prefer flexi-hours and childcare facilities at the office. Think of what a 45–55 hour work week means for work–life balance. Even without any extra responsibilities (out-of-town-trips, client meetings and dinners, work functions, conferences), this kind of schedule makes it extremely difficult for any professional to manage work and family. There is unspoken belief and apprehension among employers that, although they need to provide more meaningful policies to suit the changing needs of their employees, it might lead to other problems such as reverse discrimination, resentment from male colleagues, and issues about adjusting compensation packages. There are also no studies to prove that the introduction of such policies has actually brought about the desired results, in terms of reduced attrition rate of qualified women. However, Catalyst's *2010 India Benchmarking Report*, that studied 56 organizations from eight industry sectors, suggests that corporate India has a wide array of initiatives and well-defined strategies to help build a pipeline of women leaders in the workplace. Mentoring, sponsorship, and engaging men as champions have all seen some positive impact. However, more action and accountability on the part of companies is required [11].

Until then, what are the options?

## Jumping Off the Career Ladder the Only Option?

Clearly, women are compelled to consider stepping off the career track due to a combination of pull and push factors. The pull factors are family related, such as the needs of growing children, care of elderly parents, and, at times, personal health. But the actual culprit beneath the pull factors is the conventional division of labor, where only women are expected to deal with family issues.

Then there are a series of push factors that literally drive women out of the door: meaningless work, underutilization of their potential, lack of opportunity for advancement, long hours, unsympathetic superiors, insensitive corporate culture, etc. It is often said that women join companies, but leave managers. In a typical 9-to-5 workday, women actually cope with a combination of pull and push factors. No wonder, when women feel blocked by rigid policies or the proverbial glass ceiling at work, they are likely to respond to the pull of the family, especially when they are in the 40–44 age group. Even those with excellent career prospects make time for family responsibilities by relinquishing their jobs entirely.

Many employers and industries still prioritize long, continuous, traditional work hours rather than flexible schedules, a preference that tends to put women with children at a disadvantage [12]. The share of mothers who do not work outside the home rose to 29 percent in 2012, up from a modern-era low of 23 percent in 1999, according to a new analysis of government data [13].

## Is the pain worth the gain?

Many stay-at-home and part-time working mothers who want to return to the full-time workforce may encounter a "motherhood penalty" that extends beyond the actual time out of the workforce. Experimental studies have documented that employers are less likely to hire mothers (including mothers who never left the workforce) compared to child-free women, and when employers do make an offer to a mother, they offer her a lower salary than they do to other women [14,15]. Fathers, in contrast, do not suffer a penalty compared to other working men. Many fathers actually receive higher wages after having a child, known as the "fatherhood bonus" [16,17].

While coming to terms with the turmoil of leaving a job, many women promise themselves that they will return to work as soon as possible. After all, work has provided structure, fulfillment, and direction to their lives, given them self-esteem and identity, as well as ascertain position in society. Despite every intention to return to work after all the family responsibility is over, the reality is that many find it very difficult to do so. Clearly, leaving is easier; rejoining is harder, as well as expensive, both for the women and the organizations.

Incredibly, very few companies have ever studied the costs and statistics of maternity leave and, as a result, have not analyzed the investment made by the companies in recruitment, training, and development of women, and the returns it could have brought. We need to learn the right lessons from these studies. The studies will be harmful if all they teach us is that women are expensive to employ. What we need to learn is how to reduce that expenditure and how to stop throwing away the investments we make in talented women by exploring novel ways of retaining them. We need to learn how to become more responsive to the needs of working women by creating hospitable environments within the corporations that employ them.

The gender differences that impact work primarily fall into two categories: (a) those related to maternity and a spectrum of issues related to childbirth, nursing, bonding, child-rearing and (b) those related to different socializations, expectations of behavior of the sexes, and stereotypes that can impact male corporate culture and masculine rules of career development.

Let's face it. We cannot alter the biological fact of maternity. But can we not reduce its impact on the workplace or, at least, eliminate its negative effect on employee retention and development? This can be achieved to an extent by addressing the second category that relates to male and female socialization.

For instance, men continue to perceive women as the rearers of their children, so they find it entirely appropriate that women should renounce their careers to raise families, or take career breaks or extend maternity leave as long as possible. Just as they see parenting as fundamentally female, they see careers as fundamentally male. No wonder, working women who compete like men are considered unfeminine, yet women who emphasize family are considered uncommitted. However, it is not fair to box all women into one category. There are women who are totally dedicated to career and there are others who are forever balancing career and family. Clearly, the motivation, talents, training, and priorities of women are different.

## The best men in the organization

I know of some women who are extremely career minded. They are ready to make compromises in their personal life in order to seek leadership positions. They do not mind putting in extra hours, traveling at a short notice, working over weekends, and relocating as and when necessary to make the most of every opportunity for career development. Moreover, they do not mind remaining single or, if married, remaining childless until their careers are well established. These women are seen as "macho," but the reality is they are like the best men or employees you can get in any organization.

It is, therefore, important that these women are recognized for what they are through a neutral lens, identified early as high-potential "employees" and given the same opportunity any organization gives to talented men, to grow, to mature as all-rounded professionals and contribute to organizational objectives. Such women need to be accepted as valued members of the management team. They bring unique perspectives and styles of functioning to the table, despite the fact that the business environment is more stressful for them than their male colleagues. They often find themselves in the minority, often the only woman in the department or in intercorporate meetings. They are never quite sure or secure about the perceptions of their male colleagues, which can be a mixture of admiration, resentment, skepticism, attraction, competitiveness, pride, and anxiety all at once.

The majority of women, however, would like to balance both career and family. These women are just as serious about their careers as they are about being active, responsible parents. These women are willing to trade some career growth as well as compensation for freedom to spend more time at home when their babies are young. These women seek some understanding from the corporations that employ them. If you force such women to choose between family and career during the early child-rearing years, they will simply walk out of door with all the training, experience, and exposure the management has given them in the first 10 years. Even if they are forced to return after extended maternity leave due to nothing but financial considerations, what guarantee is there that they will return with the same vigor and commitment as before, now that they are torn between the needs of the baby left at home and the constant pressures of work? These women require a breather from a full-time work schedule. These women require part-time assignments and flexitime considerations, affordable high-quality childcare, and so on. Once this phase is over, they can reenter the competition wherever they left off. In addition, they will give back to the organization in terms of increased loyalty and productivity as a token of their gratitude that can result from such arrangements.

Work environment plays a critical role in women's careers. When the culture is "inclusive," where women are treated fairly, valued for who they are, and included in core decision making, benefits such as increased satisfaction and lower attrition of not only women but the entire team can be seen [18].

## Level the Playing Field

The first step to managing diversity effectively is to understand, rather than deny, the differences and be willing to deal with its implications and consequences. As Dr R. Roosevelt Thomas, Jr tells us, diversity is not synonymous with differences, but encompasses differences and similarities [19].

It is a paradox that equal opportunity means differential treatment. Nothing makes this point as well as the game of golf. Whenever I go for a round of golf this becomes amply clear. In golf, one does not object to handicaps. It's a system designed to even the playing field for golfers with different levels of experience and expertise.

The same is true for people from disadvantaged backgrounds. Reservation of a certain number of seats in hiring means just that differential treatment is provided to bring everyone on board. There are people who never picked up a job after completing graduation due to lack of experience. There are people who were denied other opportunities due to what group they belonged to. Otherwise, these people are bright, ambitious, and willing to learn. Today, smart minds don't come in a single color, shape, or gender. They come in all ranges of diversity.

What adjustments would you be willing to make to level the playing field for such smart people? More briefing? Stretch assignments? Committee exposure? A little more patience, direction, and engagement? The key thing to remember is that this entire disadvantage was not the fault of the person applying for the job you advertised. He or she now wants to break free of that, and have an equitable chance to learn and perform. You can provide the opportunity if you understand unequal treatment is necessary to reach equal opportunity.

After recognizing the problem, the next step is remedial action through dialogue and discussion. Often, the conversation with women starts only when they have decided to leave, and it's too late by then. It also needs an objective diagnosis of the situation. Such diagnosis involves senior managers probing an organization's practices and beliefs to uncover its deeply embedded sources of inequity.

It is equally important to understand the underlying reasons why employees do not want to prioritize gender diversity. For some, it means placing a lower priority on individual performance. For others, it means favoritism to some people over others. Some think diversity efforts will focus more on differences than commonalities.

An effective first step is often one-on-one interviews with employees to uncover practices and beliefs in the corporate culture. For example: Which practices affect men differently from women? How work gets done? What kinds of work and work styles are valued in the organization? What kinds are invisible? What are the assumptions for competence? What aspects of individual performance are discussed the most in evaluations? How is competence identified during hiring and performance evaluations? The answers to these questions can help identify cultural patterns and their consequences, and help keep the process on track.

## The Power of Small Change

The next step is designing the small initiatives or incremental changes that introduce positive change. Each small initiative is merely a means to an end to make the system better. These new initiatives can make sense even at companies that have formal gender programs. In fact, they make more sense at companies with formal gender programs because with such programs the management may tend to develop an attitude of complacency and they need to be vigilant and alert so that dysfunctional, old practices do not creep in.

There is a simple test to determine whether the new initiatives, policies, or programs are serving their purpose. The test consists of these questions: Does the program, policy or principle give special consideration to one group? Will it contribute to everyone's success or will it only produce an advantage for either men or women? Is it designed for "them" as opposed to "us"? Whenever the answer is yes, you are not on the road to managing equity.

This does not rule out the possibility of addressing issues that relate to a single group. It only underlines the importance of determining that the issue you are addressing does not relate to the other groups as well.

The small change strategy identifies unequal practices and assumptions so subtle that they are rarely noticed, let alone questioned. This approach also helps those involved in small change see how their efforts affect larger, systemic change. One small change begets another, and eventually these small changes add up to a whole new system. Most importantly, this approach routes discrimination by fixing the organization, not the women who work for it. The strategy, therefore, benefits not just women but all employees and the organization as a whole. Indeed, those companies enjoy a substantial competitive advantage which understand that money spent on making employees happy—that is, intellectually stimulated, emotionally fulfilled, and physically nurtured—is one of their wisest investments [20]. Organizations can deal with attrition of women by drawing the right conclusions and doing the right thing.

## How to win buy-in for gender-sensitive programs?

Introducing gender-sensitive programs is fashionable in today's organizations. Too often, however, they are not managed well, because managing gender or diversity programs is fraught with challenges and difficulties. Programs that address the underlying attitudes that prevent change have a better chance of succeeding than those that tackle only the symptoms of resistance.

As an internal change agent, responsible for initiating gender programs, I have seen employees wonder: Is the purpose of this program simply to comply with the law? Does this program mean that there are problems in the organization among men and women? Is the whole effort just about being correct and in vogue? Has this program been launched to suppress an actual conflict between male and female colleagues? How will it benefit the other gender: men?

It is in this context that two gender programs stand out in my mind among a host of programs I conducted or was associated with. I still remember the thrilling sensation I had—and the glow of that sensation continues to stay with me—when I walked into a conference room to address a session on "Harmonizing Diversity" expecting a room full of women. Instead, to my pleasant surprise, I found men in the majority (17 male managers to 13 female ones) in one session and 7 male managers and 33 women managers in the other. The only common factor was that both these programs had been organized in collaboration with SCOPE. I found the men not only sensitive, but also very supportive of women's issues. They spoke about the need for amending the Factories Act, which prohibited women from being posted on the shop floor during night shifts, and also expressed a need to start common crèches for babies in office complexes. While narrating how useful this would be for their women colleagues, I got the clear impression that they spoke from first-hand experience, either through dealing with their junior colleagues or with someone in their social circle. One could only dream about such an ideal scenario.

It is, therefore, important to find out what people in the organization think about the gender initiative, because it means different things to different people. For example, to some people it means diversity differences and not gender differences. This is why one must ensure that everyone feels included in gender programs. They are not only of women, for women, and by women. They must be built on the recognition that everyone—not just members of the minority group—has an identity and a story to tell, and will get a reasonable chance to tell his or her story. One has to try different approaches in line with the organizational culture, and an understanding of what will work in certain systems.

## Making a Business Case
### Customer focus

If you're having trouble making a difference in your company, try thinking about how customer focus might help. If women can make the bulk of the decisions in the marketplace, why can't they take decisions in the workplace?

Almost 80 percent of consumer decisions are made by women and minorities. Women do not buy brands; they join them. If the products of any company are purchased in large part by women, then the organization should have a meaningful representation of women running strategic business units or heading departments that help connect to the marketplace. It makes perfect business sense to increase the voice of women in senior decision-making roles. For example, research by MasterCard suggests that the percentage of buying choices made by women across the globe is more than 85 percent. It is for this reason that MasterCard has added more women to its workforce [21].

Therefore, you should make a sound business case and know the facts pertaining to your market. For instance, in corporate America, US$15 trillion in sales are generated by women-owned businesses. Also, women and minorities are starting business at twice the rate of anyone else.

American women constitute the largest economy in the world; followed by Japan, and American men. Why would you not have women helping you run the company? In India, women outspend men in online shopping and are also proving to be the more aggressive internet- and tech-savvy gender [22]. As Shipman and Kay suggest, the age of "womenomics" has arrived. There is an upcoming paradigm shift in the way individuals and companies approach work, due to an increase in the value of women in the workforce, and changing attitudes of women towards priorities of balancing work and personal life [23]. The economy is governed by women, which may have a ripple effect elsewhere in the world. As the *Economist* claims, "Forget China, India and the internet, economic growth is driven by women [24]. It is women who constitute the third largest consumer market in the world." It is, therefore, extremely important for businesses to realize that, if they form teams in the workplace that mirror the marketplace, there will be a strong consumer connect and sales will be sustainable.

## Higher financial returns

Research by Catalyst shows that Fortune 500 companies with a higher percentage of women in board positions outperformed companies with a lower percentage, and posted the greatest value to shareholders, besides higher financial performance in three measures:

1. Return on equity: on average, companies with a higher percentage of women board directors outperformed those with the least or none by 53 percent
2. Return on sales: by 42 percent
3. Return on invested capital: by 66 percent

Research clearly shows that boards with women are more likely to be particular about and pursue best practices like board evaluations, codes of conduct, conflict-of-interest guidelines, executive remuneration policies, all the areas that build company reputation and culture [25].

A more recent non-academic study conducted by an asset management firm in the UK looked at those companies with a threshold of at least 20 percent female representation across FTSE-listed boards. They found that operational and share price performance was significantly higher at one- and three-year averages for those companies with women making up over 20 percent of board members, than those with lower female representation [26].

## Talent retention

Furthermore, the presence of female directors symbolizes career possibilities to prospective recruits and also contributes to increased retention of women [27]. The number of women corporate directors on Fortune 500 boards is positively related to the number of women officers, the number of women holding line management jobs, and the number of women holding high ranking titles [28]. Women directors also provide mentoring and networking opportunities for junior women to develop their careers. These interactions increase the potential for women to find a wider variety of role models, and enable them to emulate behaviors from a number of women role models.

In companies where 30–50 percent of the workforce is women, a woman board member can provide a perspective pertaining to women employees that men can't begin to think about.

## Strategic importance of diversity

Women can enrich corporate life by bringing a different approach to an issue. Women have a different experience of life from men. They often bring a perspective a company has not had before, adding reality to the deliberations. Organizations that serve women as clients, customers, and employees can have better relationships with these groups when women are among those who hold leadership positions.

The best way for a company to get a competitive edge is to have a pool of talented men and women employed on the single criteria of merit, regardless of background, religion, ethnic origin, nationality, or sexual orientation. As companies become more global, they need a more heterogeneous labor force that is sensitive to social, economic, political, and cultural differences. The potential benefits of diversity include better employee morale, less absenteeism, improved client relations, new ideas for top management, and superlative decision making. This approach appeals to the consumers and shareholders who are fast becoming more diverse, and who expect the fact to be reflected in the companies they deal with.

McKinsey's research in a multi-sector, multi-country study indicates that companies with the highest share of women outperform companies with no women. In terms of return on equity, the more gender-diverse companies exceed by 41 percent and, in terms of operating results, they exceed by 56 percent when compared with companies with no women [29]. Variety is not only the spice of life but increasingly also the source of business success.

## Risk management

The *2016 Global Board of Directors Survey* was compiled through anonymous inputs from 1,067 directors from 58 countries. The key findings are quite startling and suggest that women directors report higher concerns about risks than male directors (concerns about activist investors and cyber security to regulatory risk and the supply chain) [30].

## Corporate governance

A Canadian study of private sector, public sector and not-for-profit boards [31] reveals that boards with three or more women are significantly different from all-male boards. Women on boards explicitly monitor the implementation of conflict-of-interest guidelines and ensure a code of conduct for the organization. Furthermore, boards with women place more importance on the use of recruitment consultants which is likely to reduce the influence of old boys' networks and increase transparency of selection. In addition, such boards are significantly more active in promoting non-financial performance measures such as customer satisfaction, employee satisfaction, and gender representation, as well as considering measures of innovation and corporate social responsibility. Better corporate governance is achievable through sharing a broader range of experiences and opinions. Women have different experiences of the workplace, marketplace, public spaces, and the community, and, therefore, bring a different perspective to debates and decision making [32]. Companies lacking board diversity tend to suffer more governance-related controversies [33].

## Ethical values

In today's world, with heightened concerns about ethics and integrity in business and politics, women with ethical considerations can have an advantage as a board member. There is evidence to suggest that women disapprove of unethical business practices such as the use of insider information, or unscrupulous negotiation tactics such as misrepresenting facts or making false promises. Similarly, a survey of values in 43 nations found that, in most nations, women were less tolerant than men of dishonest or illegal behavior such as taking bribes [34]. What's more, some management researchers have even suggested that including more women among executives can decrease fraud by top management [35].

Research over the past few years has confirmed that there are greater advantages to having women on boards. There are at least five–six areas where a big impact on corporate performance can be made, as we have seen from the examples above.

# Different Strokes for Different Organizations

Each organization has its own culture—shared beliefs, values, symbols, and its own social structure—regular patterns of behavior, norms and practices. Owing to both cultural and social barriers, women generally have had less access to leadership positions in organizations. Most of the barriers that exist today are so deeply embedded in organizational life that they have become invisible and subtle. It seems to me that gender inequity has simply gone underground.

However, it exists in prevalent work practices and cultural norms that appear seemingly unbiased. That is why most people don't even notice them, leave alone question them. But they create a pattern of systemic disadvantage which blocks women from career advancement. Even though women have gained much greater access than in any other period in history, the conclusion holds. Considerable change would have to take place in organizations before women will enjoy equality in organizations.

## Three approaches based on three assumptions

It takes all kinds of employers to make the corporate world. Some employers actively promote greater equality at work. Many are only sympathetic and sincerely believe that is enough. Others concede in theory but find women unsuitable to their sort of business or to work which they regard is more appropriately done by men. The majority of employers believe that they are already doing all that they should to treat all employees equally. Many employers have not given adequate priority to equality issues. This does not mean that they oppose the concept. Only a very few consciously resist any idea of equality. They believe that men will stay and women will go, that the gender of the employee is the best indication of competence, that women prefer not to be promoted as nobody will accept a woman boss, and so on. Clearly, lack of knowledge, information, and misinterpretation both of purpose as well as motivation have proved to be serious problems on the path to equality.

### The first approach based on the assumption of equality

As seen in the first chapter, this approach is based on the assumption that men and women are similar, therefore they are equal. This paradigm was supported for well over 200 years, and, as a result, many consider it the *only* way to conduct business or manage people. In this environment, women are expected to "fit in," learn to adapt as best they can, and learn the game men play in corporate life.

Since women have not been socialized to compete successfully in the world of men, so they must be taught the skills their male counterparts have acquired as a matter of course. "Fixing" women perpetuates the belief that women's contributions and competence are inferior to those of men. This approach is used when organizations ask women to minimize the differences by learning male corporate behavior, attributes, practices, and styles of functioning, and by rejecting the feminine behavior which comes naturally to them. In such organizations, the orientation or developmental training would center on assertiveness, leadership, decision making, and crisis management. Women are encouraged to speak up in meetings and to take tough, critical assignments on the shop floor. While the skills training is helpful, it does not remove the deeply entrenched systemic factors which hold women back.

## The second approach based on the assumption of difference

The second approach accommodates the unique needs of women through supportive policies. The organizations recognize the systemic barriers that block women's advancement. They are even willing to create separate tracks for women who find it hard to cope with the demands of faster tracks. These organizations offer mentoring programs, alternative career tracks during childbearing years, extended maternity leave, flexible work arrangements, and even crèches. These provide comfort and benefits to women all right, but they don't level the playing field. Launching a family friendly program does not challenge the belief that balancing work and home is fundamentally a woman's problem. It also does not address the gender bias that plays out in hiring, retention and promotional decisions. Utilizing women's assets, they post women to HR, public relations, marketing products to women, or to hospitality departments. Despite the work women do, which is mostly "invisible" like coordination or holding the team together, etc., when crucial assignments are given or rewards/promotions distributed, women typically are left out.

## The third approach based on the assumption that women are equal but different

In the third approach, organizations "value the differences" women bring to the workplace. They realize the value of diversity, and harness different people instead of trying to beat them into one mold, one system. They recognize that fitting women into the same mold as men might produce some level of efficiency for some time but will also stifle creativity. They sensitize their male managers to appreciate unique skills such as collaboration, listening, team building, and participative decision making that women bring to the table. They appreciate the fact that women leaders bring different leadership styles and score high on inspiring, role modeling, teaching and mentoring, and offering rewards and recognition. They initiate a culture of valuing diversity, valuing differences. They recruit and retain the best talent across a number of industries, ready to break out of the old patterns of behavior and awaken their organizations to new possibilities to ensure that their best and brightest are reaching their potential. They provide mentoring, coaching, and other developmental opportunities. But simply mandating to "value differences" doesn't mean that people will. It is important to hold executives and managers accountable for the implementation and results of these initiatives. There are various accountability mechanisms that organizations can employ to showcase and reward the progress of successful efforts, as well as track those that fail to meet critical diversity goals. Connecting particular goals with consequences—either rewards for progress or penalties for a lack thereof—is one of the ways in which organizations reinforce the importance of diversity efforts.

## What is in it for men?

It is a common observation that men are less likely than women to see value in diversity initiatives and more likely to believe that too many measures supporting women are unfair to them. This is particularly true in case of those men who are not familiar with the complexities of women's careers. So they may wonder what there is in it for them.

- For CEOs—who are mostly men—diversity is a source of creativity and innovation. The best minds are needed to address complex business challenges. A diverse workforce prevents an organization from becoming too insular and out of touch with its increasingly heterogeneous customer base. Diversity of leadership styles can contribute to more effective decision making, and the leadership behaviors that women typically display can have a positive impact on many dimensions of an organization's performance and health.
- Senior leaders—mostly men again—when staffing complex projects, look for a leader who is collaborative, more team oriented and empathetic. Often, such leaders are found to be women, who know how to identify things that have gone well and then drill down to find the person—visible or invisible—who it is responsible, as opposed to those who are merely managing impressions. Women leaders can make the contribution of invisible people visible in complex projects.
- Aspiring managers need to make themselves available anytime, anywhere. The stress that is generated by the implicit 24/7 mentality is felt by men and women alike. Although, it impacts women more than men due to their dual responsibilities, but men have families too and they too would like to devote time to family commitments and other interests. So men will also benefit from flexibility programs.
- Men as direct reports can learn one or two things from the female leadership style that focuses on bringing people together to get things done.

Therefore, diversity programs have to be broadened beyond women in educating both men and women about subtle gender biases and how they manifest themselves in unintended but unconscious ways and get imbedded in a company's culture. If men constitute 80 percent of the workforce, then they have to be part of the solution. They have to be definitely engaged in finding solutions on diversity at the workplace. They need to be enrolled in gender sensitization programs. Many men take equal responsibility at the family front, so they need to be equally involved. Some solutions are more appropriate in some companies, some countries and some cultures. It is the responsibility of the top leaders to reflect on what measures and mechanisms would be appropriate to their culture. However, at the core, the issues for women are similar in the corporate environment everywhere: the challenge of recruiting, retaining, and advancing women.

## The Best Practice Organizations

To find companies at the forefront of the diversity movement, I first identified companies with a reputation for successfully leveraging diversity After identifying these companies, I sent a structured questionnaire to them to get comprehensive data about employment statistics, policies, and third-party recognition from a public source. These companies represent different industries and regions, as well as different stages of inclusivity. For instance, some companies have well established practices for leveraging diversity, while others were in the process of setting them up.

They have not only committed leadership, but have also set up accountability mechanisms to monitor progress on projects targeted towards four areas of improvement: work–life balance, mentoring, flexible work arrangements, and women's networking. To support these projects on an enduring basis, these organizations have initiated women-friendly practices and policies. All of these organizations belong to the service industry, which employs a large number of women. We will look at four organizations: Wipro, ICICI Bank, NSE, and TCS, and their whistle-blower policies and innovative practices.

## Wipro: Towards a new paradigm

In today's complex and evolved workplace, talent is the critical driving force behind the success of any organization. People are a company's assets and, if managed correctly, the right assets always create lasting value. This is especially true in the service industry.

Wipro Limited is an Indian multinational digital strategy, IT consulting and system integration services corporation headquartered in Bengaluru. Meritocracy is at the core of its business. Driving innovation, accessing the full talent pool, and curbing attrition were the business goals that led to the evolution of the gender-diversity initiative at Wipro.

### A culture that nurtures talent

Wipro is approaching gender diversity not only as an important business strategy, but also as a deep culture change. The spirit of inclusion is deeply embedded in a Wipro culture that is open and collaborative. Wipro recognizes that men and women bring different and equally valuable perspectives to the table and need to benefit from each other's perspectives in order to sustain growth and success. The company has designed employee-friendly benefits, policies, and processes in line with this philosophy. Strong communication channels and training programs convey this message, and key metrics measure programs and initiatives.

### Life stage-based approach to gender diversity

Women constitute 32 percent of the workforce at Wipro. They make up 7 percent of the management group at the vice-president or higher level and 20 percent of managers overall. These women require different interventions at different stages of their career, as can be seen below:

- Wipro launched Women of Wipro, a forum that works towards making Wipro an inclusive workplace. This global program is now covering the 170,000+ workforce of Wipro. This forum was set up in response to the recommendations of an Employee Response Group Research that proposed a life stage-based holistic approach to gender diversity, which is unique anywhere in the world.

- At the Entry point, women benefit from a wide variety of exposure to challenging roles and role models. As a result, Wipro has begun offering a range of mentoring experiences, career advice blogging, and programs that invite guest speakers to share their experiences.
- At the Middle level, women with family priorities/responsibilities need flexibility. Along with paid maternity leave of three months, women can avail of extended unpaid leave up to six months. During this time, Wipro offers an "IN TOUCH" program to keep women abreast of company developments. The statistics show that this has helped 75 percent of the women with extended leave to return to the job. Wipro also has tie-ups with good daycare centers near Wipro campuses that offer subsidized rates to Wipro employees.
- At the Senior level, Wipro has revamped its Annual Succession Planning Program to bring more women into the leadership pipeline. The company's succession plan is reviewed by the Chairman every year, covers every managerial role, and includes a section on women.

## Mechanisms to raise awareness

- Raising gender sensitivity and awareness of inclusivity are vital components to building an inclusive culture in the organization. Wipro spreads awareness through a digital newsletter, Diversity Appreciation Workshop and Gender Sensitization Workshops across businesses. In addition, online training courses (mandatory) on Diversity and Inclusion have been introduced and Prevention of Sexual Harassment workshops were designed and conducted across the organization. Women Leadership training, self-defense workshops, and Employee Assistance Programs are other areas that have been extended to reach more employees in different locations.

- One novel initiative is onsite vacation camps for employee's children across locations. It is a boon for mothers who face long daily commutes and offers an alternative childcare option during long school holidays.

## Commitment to diversity and inclusion (D&I)

Wipro provides equal opportunity to employees of every nationality, caste/religion, gender, age, GLBT (Gay, Lesbian, Bisexual and Transgender) persuasion, and disability in various global markets. This commitment is translated into action, both at a business level as well as at an employee level.

### The diversity council

- The Diversity and Inclusion initiatives are spearheaded by the Diversity Council comprising of senior leaders of Wipro across businesses. It is implemented through and integrated with HR. It meets twice every quarter to review the various initiatives under the diversity umbrella. The Diversity Council reports the progress made every quarter to the Corporate Executive Council as well as the Board of Directors of the Company. As part of the KRAs, it is connected to measuring performance and associated rewards on the same.
- The quarterly Wipro Meets which are addressed by the CEO have a D&I agenda.
- Regular mailers on various programs such as Women of Wipro series, Kids at Wipro and the Induction Program cover the D&I agenda. In addition, during the International Women's Week, relevant communication is done both internally and externally.
- The Diversity and Inclusion initiative is truly embedded in the inclusive culture of the organization. D&I is everybody's business. As a result, no SBU head ever treats it as an HR activity.
- The diversity initiatives have been reported consistently in the past three years in the sustainability report of Wipro [36].

## Innovative approaches

- The mentoring initiative for high-potential women piloted in 2010 is considered innovative as it helps in the career development of high-performing women.
- The safety and security measures go beyond compliance and provide a safe environment where employees feel comfortable to work both at the workplace as well as during business travel.
- The online grocery shopping made available for all employees is especially useful for working moms who don't have support systems to take care of everyday grocery at home.

## Wipro as signatory to women's empowerment principles

Wipro has pledged its support to strengthen women's role in the organization and has joined six other leading firms as a Signatory to Women's Empowerment Principles. The consortium will conduct research to identify gaps within corporate policies that limit women's participation and involvement in the workplace [37].

All these initiatives are paying rich dividends. Although women's advancement to senior management positions is still lagging behind, and there is a considerable dip from the number of women at junior level to middle management level due to family responsibility (marriage and maternity), the number of voluntary resignations by women in the financial years 2013, 2014, and 2015 were nearly 60 percent less than the number of men in the same year. It is nothing but a vote of confidence by women employees in favor of their organization. It is also testimony to the fact that Wipro has delivered a differentiated value proposition that enables them to retain the best and the brightest. These initiatives have been duly recognized by winning many corporate awards. Wipro has also been the winner of the globally acclaimed Diversity Council Honors Award (2011), the NASSCOM Corporate Award for Diversity and Inclusion (2016), and the Excellence in Diversity and Inclusion Award at SHRM India HR Awards, 2016.

Wipro has also been included in the Dow Jones Sustainability Index (DJSI): World and Emerging Markets for the seventh time in succession and has also been named as one of the World's Most Ethical Companies by the Ethisphere Institute for the fifth successive year.

## ICICI Bank: Gender-valued, sensitive meritocracy

It is a great compliment to any institution if it is considered as a veritable nursery for providing top women talent to various institutions in the banking or the financial services sector. ICICI Bank is one such institution which is known for nurturing and grooming top women talent, promoting gender equality and creating a strong leadership bench. From its early days, building a culture of gender diversity was in the DNA of ICICI Bank. The trend was set in 1980 by extraordinary visionaries like S. S. Nadkarni and N. Vaghul with a focus on brilliant execution. K. V. Kamath continued the tradition and now Chanda Kochhar is taking it forward. The number of senior women bankers that you see today within the Bank is a testimony to this fact. ICICI Bank is renowned for being a talent magnet for grooming women leaders.

Some facts about ICICI Bank:

- ICICI is a diversified, Indian multinational, banking and financial services company headquartered in Mumbai, Maharashtra.
- ICICI Bank is the country's largest private sector bank by consolidated assets.
- It offers a wide range of banking products and financial services to corporate and retail customers through a variety of delivery channels and through its specialized subsidiaries in the areas of life and non-life insurance, venture capital, asset management, securities brokerage and private equity.
- The bank has a network of a number of 4,850 branches and 13,882 ATMs in India (as on March 31, 2017) and has a presence in 17 countries, including India.

- It employs around 82,000 employees; around 30 percent of them are women. Women occupy 17 percent of the senior management positions in the bank and 40 percent of ICICI Bank's executive board members are women.

## A business case for diversity

This is what Chanda Kochhar, Managing Director & CEO, ICICI Bank, who is counted as one of the most powerful businesswomen in India, has to say,

> The answer to achieving diversity and access the female talent pool lies in creating a truly equal opportunity workplace, which is completely gender neutral: where management is in fact blind to gender while selecting people for job positions and promotions. For instance, we at the ICICI group have a large number of women in leadership positions—but we notice the high proportion of women in our top management team only when outsiders point it out to us! Being an equal opportunity employer and a complete meritocracy, where performance alone is the criteria for recognition and growth, has produced a number of outstanding business leaders, both men and women. We just focus on selecting the best candidate for a particular job, then offer them a fair atmosphere where merit is recognized and rewarded. Women are attracted to ICICI Bank because they have seen equal opportunities in practice here, not just as a slogan or mission statement.
>
> While creating a gender-neutral workplace, we must not lose sight of the fact that women do have special responsibilities and, therefore, special needs at times. Organizations must be creative in addressing this issue, with flexible work schedules, longer leave periods and full use of technology to reduce the need for women to be physically present in the office for work. Most importantly, all this should not be seen as a favor

to women; it should be an integral part of the organizational processes and should not impact performance evaluation or assessment of growth potential [38].

## Gender neutral organizational culture that nurtures talent

- For ICICI Bank, diversity has always been linked with the company's core philosophy of meritocracy. Regardless of gender, employees are promoted and given higher responsibilities based on their credentials. There are absolutely no compromises made on merit.
- ICICI Bank follows a recruitment policy of competency-based hiring which is different from the traditional practice of hiring people largely based on functional expertise. This practice of hiring from across sectors helps to expand the supply pool of applicants.
- The Bank's Probationary Officers' Program has consistently seen women's participation at around 35 percent. The principle of meritocracy espoused by the organization precludes all considerations other than performance and potential. Meritorious employees are given higher responsibilities and challenging assignments. Women employees in ICICI Bank have broken the proverbial glass ceiling on the basis of performance and potential shown in the workplace.

## Dealing with unique challenges faced by the banking sector

"The main challenge is in securing adequate number of applications from women candidates given the smaller representation of women passing out from academic institutions. Now this trend seems to be changing as academic institutions are trying to achieve a healthy mix," says T. K. Srirang, Head, Human Resources, ICICI Bank. With an unbiased recruitment process, this changing trend of a healthier gender ratio in academic institutions should translate into a better gender ratio in organizations.

## Dealing with functional bias

ICICI Bank has consciously tried to address the bias about certain functions such as Sales and Debt Management. It was earlier believed that the aforesaid functions are not meant for women. So the Bank defined the skills set for both these functions and invested into training the candidates for these roles. Similarly, for the role of Branch Manager in the Bank, ICICI started hiring from across different industries, clearly stating that past experience is not the sole criteria. This was a big shift as it provided access to talent pools across the segment.

Women employees also have to deal with societal bias or negative perceptions about certain roles such as customer engagement, sales, and debt management. In addition, they also need to manage the delicate balance of their own equations at home in order to function effectively. The scenario is different with younger women who are willing to experiment and also are more comfortable with front-end assignments.

## Addressing the hump in the middle

The other major challenge faced by the Bank is attrition of women employees at their critical life-stages like marriage, childbirth, motherhood, etc. The current nuclear family set-up does not provide the support available in a traditional joint family which takes care of the various life-stage needs. Thus, women in the age group of 28–35 years show higher attrition, which consequently results in slower career progression. This statistic is not specific to ICICI Bank only, but is true across the employment market in the country.

## New initiative: iWork@home

To address the challenge of retaining women who drop out from the workplace due to various life-stage needs, ICICI Bank announced an initiative on International Women's Day in March 2016 that will benefit many young working women professionals. It is a great career enabler in that it uses technology to enable women employees to work from home for an extended period of time depending on their needs.

Employees are provided access to their required operating system in a safe and secure manner to create an office-like environment, initially for a period of up to one year. The bank will roll out the facility across several core functions and at the same time ensure that there is no loss of productivity. The system has a three-level security protocol to ensure that only the concerned employee can access the system. The Bank has also designed a unique facial recognition technology to ensure that no one can impersonate the employee and get access to its applications. Chanda Kochhar says

> We wanted to create a stronger support system for women to ensure that they do not leave the workforce due to family responsibilities at key life stages. We decided to use technology to make life simpler for women managers. This will help the young women managers to focus better on their work without carrying the guilt and the emotional stress of staying away from their children.

This initiative clearly shows that ICICI Bank is willing to support and sustain women employees so as to help nurture and fulfill their ambitions and dreams [39]. The ability to offer opportunities for highly talented women after understanding their priorities and needs in the context of Indian culture is what sets ICICI Bank apart.

## Mechanisms to track accountability

Some specific mechanisms to track progress of these initiatives are

- Specific checks and controls on performance ratings of women, to ensure that they are not discriminated against.
- Protection of Women employees on maternity leave from any bias arising out of their absence from duty for a long period by checking rating shifts for employees on Maternity/Long Leave.
- Priority consideration for transfer requests post marriage, coupled with rating checks for undue drop in the performance rating of transferred employees.

- Considering that ICICI has an all-India presence, the organization takes extra effort in accommodating the transfer requests by women to join their husbands posted elsewhere.
- Liberal leave policy (Maternity Leave, Adoption Leave, Child Care leave, Fertility Leave), flexi-time, and flexi-place facilities. Facility of working part-time with half pay for two to three years.
- A robust policy on sexual harassment and inappropriate behavior towards women at the workplace.
- ICICI has set up a Gender Neutral committee with a significant representation of women to help a woman employee report issues in confidence.
- At the induction program itself, the Gender Neutral Policy is explained in an Open House. ICICI ensures that the internal working environment is safe, women employees are protected, and people do not cross the line.
- It also takes care of the external environment. ICICI has a policy that, if women are staying late or travelling late, it is the responsibility of her boss to ensure that she is accompanied by a male colleague who needs to ensure that she reaches home safe.

In the final analysis, having women at the top certainly helps attract young women from business schools. The message is that this organization will treat them fairly. This is a huge motivating factor, besides providing a big boost to brand reputation. ICICI Bank's brand is built among others on a deep understanding of the priorities and needs of working mothers. As good employers of women, companies such as ICICI Bank add to their credibility with key stakeholders (employees, investors, customers, regulators). They not only minimize the risk, but also build brand equity and goodwill.

In September 2016, ICICI Bank was awarded as one of the top 10 'Best Companies for Women in India' by Working Mother Media, a US-based company, in partnership with Avtar Group, an Indian organization focusing on Diversity and Inclusion in the workplace.

## National Stock Exchange (NSE): Creating a great place to work

NSE's success stems from a visionary leadership team that recognized the shortcomings that then existed in the trading, clearing, and settlement infrastructure and overcame these by leveraging technology and adopting a new set of business rules that placed significant emphasis on market integrity, transparency, and fairness. NSE was promoted by leading financial institutions, banks and insurance companies and incorporated in November 1992. In the ensuing years, NSE has become one of the leading exchanges in the world, ranking third globally in terms of transaction volumes. These efforts contributed to India's market capitalization rising from INR 3,63,350 crores in 1994 when trading started at NSE to INR 67,53,614 crores in 2011 for NSE-listed companies. NSE enjoys 76 percent market share in the cash market and 99 percent share in the derivatives market. NSE has its headquarters in Mumbai and regional offices in Delhi, Chennai, Kolkata, Ahmedabad, and Hyderabad.

### Equal opportunity employer policy

- NSE is an equal opportunity employer and treats people as its greatest asset. It is the policy and practice of NSE to comply with all applicable fair employment practices and equal opportunity laws in every state where NSE employees work.
- NSE prohibits discrimination against any employee or applicant based on language, race, color, religion, sex, origin, ethnicity, age, disability, marital status, sexual orientation, gender identity, or any other category protected by law.
- The current share of female employees in NSE is 33.45 percent and the same is monitored regularly through monthly Human Resource Management Information System (HRMIS).
- NSE has been certified as a Great Place to Work, by the Great Place to Work Institute, USA and assessed as an organization in the "Best Culture" quadrant, i.e., the highest level an organization can achieve.

## People philosophy at NSE

- Talent management and creating a talent pipeline at all levels is a key focus area at NSE.
- NSE makes a concerted effort to facilitate aspiring women to reach higher levels of leadership through focused development and coaching initiatives.
- NSE seeks employee feedback through the annual Employee Engagement Survey and informal work groups. This feedback is then used to develop people-related policies/practices.
- A formal feedback mechanism is available to prevent and report harassment of female employees. To that end, a sexual harassment policy and grievance handling mechanism have long been in place.

  The annual online Great Place to Work survey done by an external agency includes questions related to fair treatment of female employees. It is completely anonymous, and it is in fact a validation of their people philosophy by a neutral agency.

## Talent acquisition

- No discrimination is made while selecting candidates for any role and the only selection criteria is the requirement of knowledge/skill and the right attitude for the defined role.
- It is noteworthy that women constitute 50 percent of the selection panels.

## Talent management

- Women employees are key members of all work groups, i.e., Innovation, Customer or People, and Business Excellence.
- They are given well-rounded exposure, as per the competency matrix under the talent management framework.
- To ensure growth and development in their respective careers, women are advised to take up roles like Branch Head/Region Head, which requires liaising with senior government/non-government officials.

## Dual-ladder career policy

- Considering the unique needs of women employees, a dual-ladder career policy has been developed, for an employee to choose a full-time or part-time career with flexi-time.
- Further choice is also given either to become a Specialist or Generalist, based on competency, potential, personal interest, and needs related to maintaining work–life balance.
- What is unique about this policy is that, once the needs in a certain phase of life are satisfactorily met, conversion from one status of employment to another—i.e., part-time to full-time, or generalist to specialist—is possible.
- International exposure is also provided by nominating women employees to training/seminars/conferences and visits to other exchanges around the world.
- If a woman employee is in the family way, special care is taken during promotions and job rotations to ensure that she is comfortable discharging her new role/responsibility and, at the same time, not losing on growth or any learning opportunity. Additional manpower support is given to departments on a temporary basis to ensure smooth functioning of the department when female employees take additional leave during pre- post-pregnancy or during any other medical emergency to take care of their children or family members.

## Executive coaching

- NSE is one of the very few organizations where executive coaching is hardwired into the company's talent management philosophy. This is with an objective to prepare women managers for high-level positions, increase their exposure to senior leadership, and maximize their workplace contribution.
- An executive coach is also assigned for high-potential women executives for their continuous development. No wonder, three women sit on the board of NSE when the board size is of 10 members.

## Work–life balance and best place to work initiatives

- Online Social Counseling is made available for both personal and professional issues.
- Doctor on Campus is made available and various health camps are regularly organized.
- Annual medical check-up has been designed with special tests for female employees, like mammography, etc.
- Informal social groups of female employees are encouraged in the workplace to support/counsel/resolve/report any professional/personal issues.
- Fitness initiatives for female employees like Zumba dance classes and healthy diet food in the cafeteria have been introduced.

## Ensuring safe commute

- NSE runs shuttles to and from the office from designated pick-up and drop-off points.
- For those working after office hours, the company offers car service to and from their homes. This provides reassurance to employees and their families.
- During national emergencies like riots, floods, etc., female employees are transported from home with appropriate security or given excellent accommodations in nearby starred hotels, if they need to stay back.
- Flexi timings are available during hours of need to support family.
- Transfer requests are accepted to lighten jobs without hampering women's future career prospects.
- Women are encouraged to accept interstate transfer request if they want to join their spouse after marriage. If NSE does not have an office in the desired location, then women employees are encouraged to take up temporary assignments from home, if possible.

As a result of all these initiatives, the trend of attrition at NSE is gradually decreasing, as per this data: 19 percent in 2014–15, 13.95 percent in 2015–16, and 13.07 percent in 2016–17.

It is beyond doubt that NSE will attract the best women and men in the industry, and their collaboration will create better products, communications, and customer service to serve changing and competitive markets and an increasingly female workplace.

## Tata Consultancy Services (TCS): Innovative workplace

With its headquarters in Mumbai and presence in 49 countries, Tata Consultancy Services (TCS) is a global leader in IT services, and digital and business solutions. TCS is a part of the Tata Group, one of India's largest industrial conglomerates and most respected brands. It is one of the largest private sector employers in India and the second largest among the listed Indian companies with the highest retention rate in a globally competitive industry. TCS remains the most valuable company in India with a market capitalization of over US$73.9 billion (2016–17). Dedicated to ensuring the highest levels of certainty and satisfaction through a deep-set commitment to its clients, and a global network of innovation and delivery centers, TCS has been recognized by Brand Finance as one of the Big 4 Global IT Services Brands.

TCS has over 380,787 employees as of Q4 FY17, of which 34.7 percent are women who also occupy 11 percent of senior management positions.

### Diversity and inclusion

At TCS, diversity is not only about women but also about a workforce that comprises unique individuals from different nations, cultures, backgrounds, skills, and abilities who bring their varied experiences and ideas to the workplace.

Inclusion is about creating a conducive environment that embraces diverse opinions and empowers all employees to reach their highest potential. The spirit of inclusiveness provides equal opportunity to all.

A module on D&I appreciation and sensitization deals with real-life challenges of handling diversity with solutions to overcome the challenges.

The company's focus on diversity is not restricted to Indian shores. TCS has also been certified the Top Employer in Britain, the Netherlands, Belgium, Switzerland, Germany, Sweden, Denmark, and France. No wonder TCS has been ranked as No. 1 Employer in Europe by Top Employers Institute.

## Enabling work environment

TCS provides a conducive environment for its employees and offers a wide range of creative initiatives from the benefits package to well thought-out development programs in line with the corporate culture. The key to this success and recognition is the unique way in which TCS organizes country-specific cultural workshops as mentioned in the following.

The "Culture Meter" program helps associates take the first step toward imbibing cultural sensitivity and promoting awareness and appreciation of diversity. It provides information on a host of topics about various geographies and regions to create awareness. For instance, if APAC is working toward organizing the workplace parents group with planned meetings and outings with children, then Europe is organizing work–life balance programs. If UK and Ireland are celebrating supplier-side diversity and conducting diversity audits, then USA and Canada are initiating women-led projects that ensure equal opportunity and inclusion across cross-functional teams, setting up women's subcouncil and local hires' subcouncil. The D&I function in emerging markets is busy in creating health awareness and promoting learning languages.

## Progressive HR policies

The HR policies of TCS are employee-friendly and dynamic. They are reviewed on a regular basis to include relevant feedback from various sessions, online platforms, and discussion forums. Some of the employee-friendly policies are as follows:

- Global D&I policy
- Equal opportunities and non-discrimination policy
- Night shift policy
- Safety and security guidelines
- Policy for eldercare
- On boarding program for foreign nationals visiting on assignments.

As a result of these policies, TCS has been able to sustain highest retention rates in the IT industry besides creating a world-class learning and training organization.

For wider exposure, TCS allows flexibility of roles through global job rotations across businesses, practices, and functions. Recognizing that life-long learning is key to competitive advantage, a platform is provided to expand the professional network and an industry benchmarking study is commissioned with focus on best practices and leadership.

### Responsiveness to customers and markets

It is well recognized by TCS that creating an inclusive culture is the only way to succeed for a customer-centric organization. The diverse workplace teams need to mirror market realities in order to provide service in innovative ways. Gender-blended teams in design, development, marketing, and sales ensure that products and services satisfy the most diverse markets.

### A wide range of programs for every level

Although the core agenda is clearly aimed at nurturing and supporting high-potential women who want to move through the management pipeline, the range of programs offer something for everyone at every level.

The initiatives introduced in 2008 under the Diversity and Women's Network (DAWN) are remarkable and meant to address attrition. TCS found out that their women employees were leaving at an alarming rate, not because of competitive reasons but for family reasons. That is when TCS reviewed its HR policy and processes and made a paradigm shift from offering leave without pay policy to crafting a progressive policy on childcare leave.

Further, an internal support group for workplace parents was built by bringing them together on a common platform to share experiences. The group organized "Daycare Tie-ups" with childcare service providers close to the workplace with good amenities and discounted rates for TCS employees.

Aware that off-ramped women are a rich talent target, TCS made special efforts to engage and reintegrate associates returning postmaternity or long weave with the "Stay Connected" program that provides mentoring opportunity and "reorientation" through mailers sharing TCS news and updates sent once or twice a month.

Further, "Be Inspired" sessions are organized for associates at the junior and middle levels where leaders share inspirational success stories and get a chance to connect with young associates at a personal level. Considering that in the case of most women careers "just happen accidentally," these sessions provide a long-term perspective on developing careers while managing various stages in a life cycle. It also provides an excellent opportunity for peer networking.

## Empowerment of talented women: iExcel

iExcel is a unique executive education program tailored to develop women leaders in middle management; it offers a multitude of benefits for the participants. The women not only get an opportunity for the self-development and enhancement of leadership capabilities but also a chance to build learning partnerships and networks with other leaders, thereby gaining confidence and visibility.

The session covers a host of topics ranging from self-awareness, personal effectiveness, global etiquette, effective communication, customer delight, creating business impact, developing business presence, and visibility to living a balanced life and being a global leader.

The faculty consists of a diverse range of internal and external speakers, role models, thought leaders, and expert consultants. By the end of the program, each participant comes up with a robust and sustainable action plan, both for her own career and for supporting those of others. Needless to say, all these initiatives overall create a culture where women are not only treated fairly but also provided equal opportunity.

Diversity brings its own challenges. Successful gender integration requires good planning and management to skillfully mitigate the subtle resistance, miscommunication, and frictions that can occur. Managing diversity to reap its potential advantages is one of the most important challenges faced by any modern organization. Needless to say, TCS is showing the way.

As we have seen from the previous examples, many forward-looking companies are introducing inclusive practices and programs. Their leadership is committed to it and they have put mechanisms of accountability in place that help them to watch women's careers. This enables them to acknowledge the full potential of educated and talented women. In a rapidly evolving business environment, it is the surest guarantee of gaining a lasting competitive advantage.

Moving forward with progressive proposals requires enlightened activism on the part of those who desire organizations with greater gender integration and families with more equal male and female roles. Companies alone cannot be expected to craft all the policies that will make a difference to women's lives. Governments too need to take action. When business, academia, and policy leaders collaborate to address these proposals, they create an enabling, inclusive environment and an interdependent ecosystem. We will look at this in the last chapter.

# References

1. Frenier, Carol, 'Love at Work', in *When the Canary Stops Singing: Women's Perspectives on Transforming Business*, edited by P. Barrentine, San Francisco, CA: Berrett-Koehler Publishers, 1993: 17–21.
2. World Economic Forum, *The Global Gender Gap Report 2014*, World Economic Forum, Geneva. http://www3.weforum.org/docs/GGGR14/GGGR_CompleteReport_2014.pdf, (accessed on June 18, 2017).
3. *Grant Thornton International Business Report 2012.*
4. *The 2016 State Of Women-owned Business Report*, Commissioned by American Express Summary of Important Trends, 2007-2016. http://www.womenable.com/content/userfiles/2016_State_of_Women-Owned_Businesses_Executive_Report.pdf, (accessed on June 18, 2017).
5. Overholt, Alison, '25 Top Women Business Builders', *Fast Company*, no. 94, New York, NY: Jahr USA Publishing, May 2005.
6. Ernst & Young, *Scaling Up: Why Women-owned Businesses Can Recharge the Global Economy*, Ernst & Young, 2011, http://www.ey.com/Publication/vwLUAssets/Scaling_up_-_Why_women-owned_businesses_can_recharge_the_global_economy_-_new/$FILE/Scaling_up_why_women_owned_businesses_can_recharge_the_global_economy.pdf
7. Stengel, Geri, 'Why the Force Will Be With Women Entrepreneurs in 2016', *Forbes.com*, January 6, 2016, http://www.forbes.com/sites/geristengel/2016/01/06/why-the-force-will-be-with-women-entrepreneurs-in-2016/#5e53392a4ce2
8. Miller, Claire Cain and Liz Alderman, 'Why US Women are Leaving Jobs Behind', *The New York Times*, republished in *Economic Times*, December 15, 2014. https://www.nytimes.com/2014/12/14/upshot/us-employment-women-not-working.html, (accessed on June 18, 2017).
9. Accenture, *Getting to Equal: How Digital is Closing the Gender Gap at Work*.
10. *Hindustan Times*, '82% Women Prefer Flexi Hours at Work: A Survey Commissioned by the Associated Chamber of Commerce and Industry of India', New Delhi: *Hindustan Times*, May 24, 2011: 4.
11. Bagati, Deepali, *2010 India Benchmarking Report*, Catalyst, 2011. http://www.catalyst.org/system/files/2010_india_benchmarking_report_web.pdf, (accessed on June 18, 2017).
12. Goldin, C., 'A Grand Gender Convergence: Its Last Chapter', *American Economic Review* 104, no. 4 (2014): 1091–119, scholar.harvard.edu/files/goldin/files/goldin_aeapress_2014_1.pdf
13. Cohn, D'vera, Gretchen Livingston, and Wendy Wang, 'After Decades of Decline, a Rise in Stay-at-Home Mothers', Pew Research Center Social and Demographic Trends, April 8, 2014, www.pewsocialtrends.org/2014/04/08/after-decades-of-decline-a-rise-in-stay-at-home-mothers
14. Correll, S. J. and S. Benard, 'Getting a Job: Is There a Motherhood Penalty?' *American Journal of Sociology* 112, no. 5 (2007): 1297–338.

15. Kricheli-Katz, T., 'Choice, Discrimination, and the Motherhood Penalty', *Law and Society Review* 46, no. 3 (2012): 557–87.
16. Killewald, A., 'A Reconsideration of the Fatherhood Premium: Marriage, Coresidence, Biology, and Fathers' Wages', *American Sociological Review* 78, no. 1 (2013): 96–116.
17. Budig, M. J., 'The Fatherhood Bonus and the Motherhood Penalty: Parenthood and the Gender Gap in Pay', Washington, DC: Third Way, 2014, content.thirdway.org/publications/853/NEXT_-_Fatherhood_Motherhood.pdf
18. Westring, Alyssa, 'New Research: A Supportive Culture Buffers Women from the Negative Effects of Long Hours', *Harvard Business Review* February 24, 2014. https://hbr.org/2014/.../new-research-a-supportive-culture-buffers-women-from-the-n, (accessed on June 18, 2017).
19. R. Roosevelt Thomas Jr, 'Affirmative Action to Affirming Diversity' in Harvard Business Review, March–April 1990; no. 90213: 5–15.
20. Meyerson, D. E. and J. K. Fletcher, 'A Modest Manifesto for Shattering the Glass Ceiling', *Harvard Business Review* 78, no. 1 (2000): 126–36.
21. Bhattacharyya, Rica, 'We Need More Women as it's a Business Case for Us: Ron Garrow, Chief HR officer, MasterCard', *Economic Times*, June 14, 2016.
22. Sarkar, John, 'Women Outspend Men in Online Shopping: Study', *Times of India*, April 12, 2016.
23. Shipman, C. and K. Kay, *Womenomics: Write Your Own Rules for Success*, New York, NY: Harper Business, 2009.
24. 'Women in the Workforce: The Importance of Sex: Forget China, India and the Internet: Economic Growth is Driven by Women' in *The Economist* London, April 12, 2006.
25. Carter, Nancy M. and Harvey M. Wagner, 'The Bottom Line: Corporate Performance and Women's Representation on Boards', *Catalyst*, 2007, http://www.catalyst.org/knowledge/bottom-line-corporate-performance-and-womens-representation-boards
26. Bhogaita, M., 'Companies with a Better Track Record of Promoting Women Deliver Superior Investment Performance', *New Model Advisor*, 2011, https://www.gov.uk/government/uploads/system/uploads/attachment_data/file/31480/11-745-women-on-boards.pdf
27. Billimoria, D., 'Building the Business Case for Women Corporate Directors', in *Women on Corporate Boards of Directors: International Challenges and Opportunities*, edited by R. Burke and M. Mattis, Dordrecht, The Netherlands: Kluwer Academic, 2000, 25–40.
28. ———, 'The Relationship Between Women Corporate Directors and Women Corporate Officers', *Journal of Managerial Issues* 18, no. 1 (2006): 47–61.
29. Desvaux, G., S. Devilland, and S. Sancier-Sultan (Eds), *Women Matter: Women at the Top of Corporations: Making it Happen* (Report), McKinsey and Company, 2010.
30. Groysberg, Boris, Yo-Jud Cheng, Spencer Stuart, and Deborah Bell, *Global Board of Directors Survey*, 2016. Harvard Business School and the Women Corporate

Directors (WCD) Foundation. https://www.spencerstuart.com/research-and-insight/2016-global-board-of-directors-survey, (accessed on June 18, 2017).
31. Brown, D. A. H., D. L. Brown, and V. Anastasopoulos, *Women on Boards: Not Just the Right Thing...But the "Bright" Thing* (Report), Ottawa: The Conference Board of Canada, 2002.
32. Zelechowski, D. and D. Billimoria, 'Characteristics of Women and Men Corporate Inside Directors in the US', *Corporate Governance: An International Review* 12, no. 3 (2004): 337–42.
33. Lee, Linda-Eling, Ric Marshall, Damion Rallis, and Matt Moscardi, *Women on Boards: Global Trends in Gender Diversity on Corporate Boards* (Report), MSCI, November 2015, www.msci.com/documents/10199/04b6f646-d638-4878-9c61-4eb91748a82b
34. Dollar, D., R. Fisman, and R. Gatti, 'Are Women Really the "Fairer" Sex? Corruption and Women in Government', *Journal of Economic Behavior and Organization* 46, no. 4 (2001): 423–29.
35. Zahra, S. A., R. L. Priem, and A. A. Rasheed, 'The Antecedents and Consequences of Top Management Fraud', *Journal of Management* 31, no. 6 (2005): 803–28.
36. http://www.wipro.com /investors/Pages/sustainability-at-wipro.aspx.
37. Wipro, *Times of India*, December 24, 2012.
38. Talk delivered by Ms Chanda Kochhar, MD and CEO of ICICI Bank, at YPO Women's Retreat, Goa, March 29, 2012.
39. *The Economic Times*, 'ICICI Bank Rolls Out iWork@home for women employees', *Economic Times*, March 8, 2016: 8.

# 9
# The Ecosystem of Empowerment

Once I spoke at a conference on "Diversity and Change," painting a scenario about transforming organizations into hospitable environments or ecosystems that are populated by groups of like-minded people who share ideas, values, respect, and trust, and then proceed to celebrate the diversity of styles, competencies, strengths, religion, gender, and belief systems. A place not so much a physical location, but a way of life with reverence for all the people and things within it. At the end of my speech, one of the delegates said how she too yearned for the kind of ideal restructuring that would transform her workplace. "But where is such a place?" she asked in anguish, "Are there any models?" Another delegate voiced the same opinion about how she and her colleagues longed for such a change. "So what can be done? Who can make a difference?" she asked in a rather militant tone.

"The answer is ... all of us," I said with conviction, "It's you and me. It's women and men. It's governments, companies, and NGOs. It's academic institutions, business schools, and civil society. This work requires collaboration around a jointly shared collective agenda with multiple partnerships. No single partner can implement sustainable change in achieving equity and effectiveness. So the burden of succeeding cannot fall on any one stakeholder's shoulders."

This can only happen in an environment where the collective capacities of all people can flourish, and where differences between different individuals and between different groups are nurtured and their rights matched by their obligations. A community needs to be created by common purpose rather than common location with a spirit of cooperation, collaboration, of independence and interdependence, and sharing the great adventure together.

Is this a mythical place? Are we talking about imaginary companies where, one fine day, the playing field will be leveled for everyone? Certainly, no one is there yet, but some companies are at least trying to get there, by being sensitive and responsive to women. These companies of the future are run by men and women who have examined their own preconceptions and shaken off those vestiges of old-fashioned, outdated thinking that prevent progress. They have an earnestness to implement the new thinking in letter and spirit. These companies are capacious and commodious, and have the remedial, restorative, therapeutic qualities that lesser companies lack.

The task of such a renewal and organizational transformation often looks daunting, not only to us as individuals, but also to companies, governments, non-governmental organizations, and the civil society of which we are a part. It is for this reason that creating such sanctuaries or ecosystems will not be possible without equal partnerships and interdependence among all the ecosystem partners while managing the delicate balance between the competing demands of value creation and obligations. Enhancing the linkages and collaborations among these stakeholders can enrich the entire ecosystem. This facilitates in finding long-term solutions to the most intractable problems facing us environmentally, socially, as well as economically; because no one party is capable of solving them. There are many success stories of this kind. For instance, while dealing with the challenge of creating a learning ecosystem for the Indian hydrocarbon industry, the competing oil and gas companies used collaboration as a strategy for mutual advantage between each other and other industry players. The knowledge network helped to successfully execute large-scale industry change [1].

## A Confluence of Opportunities

These are the best times to realize that vision. A confluence of opportunities suggests that a new generation of women are pioneering new roles in politics, business, and entrepreneurship, and demanding a full partnership with men. These opportunities are, to a great extent, mutually complementary and tend to reinforce each other's reach and use. The critical factors are globalization, demographics, and technological advancement.

Will the trend greatly alter the gender equations in organizations? It is unlikely that even the most favorable economic conditions will be enough to rapidly bring significant numbers of women into positions of true economic power. However, the forces of the market economy are doing more than any movement to propel women into positions of power. Working women are one of the most important engines of the great burst of economic growth in the post-war era. *The Economist* has dubbed the feminization of global gross domestic product, "womenomics," and, in a striking analysis, found that during 2000s, increased female participation in the paid labor force has contributed more to the growth of the world economy.

This calls for an integrated understanding and a basic restructuring of the distribution of power in society. Such restructuring, however, is ultimately achieved through the accumulated daily negotiations of social change occurring in the various arenas of society. Women's progress depends upon global, regional, national, and local contexts. Each country has to develop its own approach based on national realities, historical factors, and sociocultural mores.

It is important to remember that there are different shapes of women's struggles, just as there are different stages of women's development. Any strategy to reduce gender bias has to be centered on work, not welfare; not only because work provides independence and an income, but because it also provides order, structure, dignity, and opportunities for growth. It is important to recognize, therefore, that empowerment is both the primary objective as well as primary means of development. Whatever the approach, it would do well to include two simultaneous alternatives: assimilation into the mainstream and/or special categorization, depending on the case. Gender mainstreaming is valuable for development of public policy; at the same time, separate categorization is necessary to focus the spotlight on hitherto "invisible issues." It is for this reason that one has to go beyond an either/or strategy to include "either" *and* "or" positions in a complementary fashion. Approach to women's development, therefore, would do well to include both these perspectives [2]. We need both cultural transformation and government action—a change in values and a change in policies and in practices—to promote the kind of society we want.

This requires acknowledging the interdependence of all major stakeholders in a community. To that end, no one agency can be expected to craft all the policies or provide all the benefits that will make a difference to women's lives. All the stakeholders have a shared responsibility to make the environment as enabling as possible in reducing the gap between women and men as corporate leaders, employees, entrepreneurs, suppliers, consumers, and community stakeholders. Linkages in five areas, therefore, are essential:

1. National governments can act as a catalyst, provide direction, and shape policies to create a holding/enabling environment. (For instance, extending maternity leave to workers in the unorganized sector and providing tax incentives to companies offering flexitime, or providing 5 percent tax cut to medium-sized companies with 50 percent women on boards.)
2. Business enterprises need to cooperate closely in a competitive industry and invent new practices or models that are not only good for women but also for business.
3. Not-for-profit organizations need to provide services such as quality childcare, which cannot be provided by the corporate sector.

4. Academic institutions need to align education with industry needs.
5. Women's associations need to actively promote legislation that eliminates perverse incentives for companies to subject their employees to long hour weeks. Women themselves need to rethink their roles and careers and put the new attitudes to work.

Although all the stakeholders have a role in creating change, business has a major role and can, therefore, act as a cardinal influencer. Despite the considerable efforts made by many companies, a large number of women are still languishing in the pipeline. As a result, much of the hard work needs to be done by the companies. In fact, enriching partnerships will provide many perspectives to promote the right kind of values, policies, and institutions to shape up the gender ecosystem in a new world.

## Harnessing the Ecosystem

Ecosystems are intrinsically local. In an ecosystem, knowledge and capabilities are dispersed. But a vibrant ecosystem can enable assets, capabilities, and roles to be constantly arranged and adjusted in response to unexpected challenges and through self-organization. Although initiatives need to be taken in each part of the ecosystem, a principle actor can catalyze the emergence and subsequent development of an ecosystem. The principal actor would take on the role of an orchestrator who shapes the ecosystem indirectly rather than through command and control. The principal actor would also contribute one or more assets necessary to deliver value, and could forge multiple bilateral alliances with complementors to improve efficiency. In the gender ecosystem, the principal actor would be the corporation. In each region, multiple change agents—government institutions, *gram panchayat*s (village administrations), educational outfits, NGOs, civic advocacy groups—with shared interest in enhancing local quality of life, can come together to have a dialogue in order to enrich the entire gender ecosystem. In fact, evidence suggests that regional collaborations can accomplish things that are difficult to achieve at the national level, because the institutional practices of regions could be specific to each region. Therefore, this need not be state-managed.

Enhancing the links and collaboration among these regions can enrich the gender ecosystem and point to an agenda for leaders in each domain. A multi-sectoral gender institutional architecture needs to be fostered at the national, state, and local levels. The architecture needs to be supported by five fundamental elements—governments as enabler, companies as principal actor, NGOs as influencers, and civil society as complementors, and women and men as the change agents themselves to create a fertile environment or enriched ecosystem. To that end, digital platform and networks can be leveraged to facilitate connectivity and interaction between stakeholders. Such an ecosystem will be self-sustaining.

## The Five-sector partnership model

### How can governments (policy-makers) make a difference?

No economic progress can occur without human progress. Gender equality should be understood as an immediate policy priority of central importance for women, societies, and economies as a whole. Creating a gender ecosystem would require equal contribution from political leadership, thoughtful introduction of economic and educational enablers, public resource allocations, tax incentives, prevention of gender-based violence, judicial and legal provisions, and the creation of a gender-sensitive media. In fact, all macroeconomic policies, especially monetary and fiscal, need to be modified to have a desirable impact on women.

- Governments can encourage the corporate sector to reserve a certain percentage of their CSR spend as gender component. A recent study of 217 companies in India indicates that, although companies are blending CSR with responsible growth, their CSR spend on women's empowerment is nil [3].

- Governments can facilitate women's leadership by building both the legal and physical infrastructure to help them prosper. This means taking stock of whether or not there are laws in place that protect women from discrimination in the workplace and reviewing laws that might treat women differently to men on a range of issues such as the ability to register a business, to travel, to open a bank account, to hold property rights, etc. Infrastructure is also critical for allowing women to participate in work and advance in equal measure; simply getting to and from work is highlighted as a major issue for working mothers in emerging economies such as Brazil. Contributions to women-supportive infrastructure by institutions or individuals can be suitably incentivized through income tax benefits. In Sweden, legislation guarantees parents of young children the right to part-time employment with proportional fringe benefits. Throughout Europe, governments have required companies to treat the parenting of babies as a special circumstance of employment and have invested heavily in programs to support the children of working parents. Governments should also look at how to cut nursery costs, which are prohibitively high in many economies and, following the example of Eastern Europe, encourage more women to enroll in science courses. Without such infrastructure in place, women (and men) will find it hard to juggle competing priorities [4].

Governments could also consider making it easier for women to combine work and having children. That means lower taxes or tax allowances for children or better public services such as affordable quality childcare together with generous maternity or parental leave facilities. For instance, the German government has agreed to give women a year's paid maternity leave and their partners two months, in a bid to boost one of Europe's lowest birth rates. It means the mother will be entitled to 67 percent of her salary for 12 months. The complement of paid parental leave is the right of employees to demand a time-out of their employment contract. Parents may demand an unpaid parental leave up to three years after the birth of the child [5]. Whatever the reason, such facilities augur well for working mothers.

Research has indicated that there is a correlation between the representation of women at the top and both the overall employment rate of women and government support in certain European countries such as Norway, Sweden, Denmark, etc. [6].

To remain competitive in the global economy, developing countries are transitioning from industrial production-based to knowledge-based economies. During the transition to knowledge-based economies, human capital development becomes one of the central concerns for policy makers, business executives, and human resource experts. An important part of overall human capital strategy is the development of policies related to gender equality and the creation of equal opportunity for participation in the workforce. Women need not remain outsiders to the reform process. The breakdown of the joint family system in India has led to a situation where most of the work related to childcare and family falls on the shoulders of women. Once they finish at work, they start a second shift at home [7]. In an open economy such as India, the government is duty-bound to focus on equity. At the same time, the government cannot ignore or neglect the efficiency dimension. Resources must be used efficiently, competitive pressures are to be maintained in all markets, and the productivity of resource utilization has to be increased. Hence, a judicious mix of equity and efficiency considerations is required in policy initiatives.

## Integrated policy interventions to achieve gender equity

India has enshrined gender equality in the constitution as a Fundamental Right and Directive Principle, and empowered the states to adopt measures of positive discrimination in favor of women to neutralize the cumulative socioeconomic and political disadvantage faced by them in all spheres.

- The National Commission for Women was set up by an Act of Parliament in 1990 to safeguard the rights and legal entitlements of women.
- The 73rd and 74th Amendments (1993) to the Constitution of India have provided for reservation of one-third seats in the local bodies of *panchayat*s (village administrations) and municipalities for women, laying a strong foundation for their participation in the decision-making process at the local level.
- In 2009, an amendment to Article 243D of the Constitution raised the one-third reservation provided to women in *panchayat*s to 50 percent, a major step towards gender equality at the grassroots level.
- Provision for reservation of women in the police forces of union territories in 2015 [8]. India has also ratified various international conventions and human rights instruments committing to secure equal rights for women. Key among them is the ratification of the Convention on Elimination of All Forms of Discrimination Against Women (CEDAW) in 1993, Beijing Platform For Action, and the UN Convention on Rights of the Child.
- The endorsement of the ambitious 2030 Sustainable Development Goals by India will further change the course of development by addressing key challenges such as poverty, gender equity, good health, quality education, decent work conditions, etc., which are critical for the local and global success of goals.
- The National Policy for the empowerment of women was introduced in 2001 to bring about the advancement, development and empowerment of women in the mainstream of national life. It is time to do a review and see what gaps there are in implementation, how they can be addressed by strengthening the evaluation mechanisms, and what the

emerging areas are that can facilitate the participation of women in entrepreneurial activities and help them to take up leadership roles in all sectors of the economy.
- "Beti Bachao, Beti Padhao" (Save and educate the girl child) Scheme—to ensure the rights of the girl child and help bridge sex ratio gap [9].
- Trade Related Entrepreneurship Assistance and Development Scheme for Women (TREAD) during the 11th Plan. The Government of India grants up to 30 percent of the total project cost to non-governmental organizations (NGOs) to promote entrepreneurship among women. Further, the government grants up to INR 1 lakh per program to training institutions/NGOs to impart training to the women entrepreneurs.
- Government together with private and public sector can focus on closing gender gap in secondary and tertiary education and lower barriers to job creation and expand skill training for women in key sectors.

## An Agenda for Action: Burning Questions

### Representation on public bodies

In order to reverse historical gender discrimination, some of the questions governments can consider to bridge the gap between policy and practices:

- What is the proportion of women on elected (and non-elected) governing bodies? Are issues prioritized by women adequately addressed in governing bodies?
- What is the proportion of women standing for and winning parliamentary seats? Are there particular constraints—e.g., financial or high levels of intimidation—on women standing?
- Are the mechanisms for a party's nomination and selection of candidates gender neutral or are they biased towards male candidates?
- Do long working hours and related constraints, such as mobility, militate against women entering positions of

political authority? What can be done to make conditions more women friendly?

- What is the proportion of women taking up formal and non-formal leadership positions compared to men?

Such questions are a reminder that a lot needs to be done. As the number of women on these public bodies increases, qualitative changes will be visible.

The myth about women not suited for politics is shattered by sheer number of female presence. It has demonstrated that only "quota" will get women in; without such legal enablement, men will not accommodate women. The importance of quota or reservation of seats for women has been an eye-opener for the men and women of upper echelons. Women are also reshaping the operation of markets, the use of new technologies, and the formulation of economic policy at the national and international level.

Consider the example of Bangladesh. The Grameen Bank there pioneered micro-credit societies consisting entirely of rural women, who traditionally had no property, purchasing power, or creditworthiness. The Grameen Bank proved that poor rural women could be relied on to repay loans with commercial interest and hardly any default. Micro loans were first used for improved consumption, and then for starting female-owned businesses. From Bangladesh to Kenya to Jordan, there is evidence to show that when it comes to repaying loans, women are very responsible, with a 98 percent repayment rate [10].

Closer home, women's Self-Help Groups (SHGs) in Andhra Pradesh have also shown that, if poor and marginalized people are given the opportunity and confidence to improve their lives, they can increase their family incomes within months. Poor, rural communities in Uttarakhand and Kerala have shown how their participation in setting up and maintaining drinking water schemes has reduced construction costs, improved construction quality, and greatly enhanced the prospects for sustainability. These are promising examples to build on with a common theme of empowerment.

## Civil service/public sector institutional reforms

Similarly, leadership at the top and middle level of the income spectrum needs to ask:

- How can the reform process strengthen institutional commitment to equal opportunities?
- Are women more likely to lose their jobs or suffer cuts in pay due to downsizing and restructuring initiatives?
  Is the reform process cutting back on services mostly used by women and children, e.g., healthcare, education, etc.?
- Are appropriate safety nets being established to protect particularly vulnerable groups?
- Do institutions deliver services which meet the needs of women as well as men? Are there constraints on women's access to particular services?
- How can decentralized structures create opportunities to increase women's participation in the labor force and responsiveness to women's needs?

## Female labor participation

Global research has shown that there is a close correlation between female labor participation rate (FLPR) and fertility rates. India's FLPR was an estimated 26.7 percent in 2014 [11]. The fertility rate in India between 1980 and 2001 has dropped from 5 to 2.9 per woman, and between 2010 and 2015 is 2.5 live births per woman. Although, in India, women's employment is heavily skewed towards low-paying, low-skilled dead-end jobs, the fertility rate has dropped sharply whenever women have been employed in quality jobs with clear career prospects that require and generate commitment, and offer alternative interests and achievements to domesticity and motherhood.

The experience of developed economies also shows that the fertility rate can drop only when the conflict between women's productive and reproductive roles significantly raises the opportunity cost of having children. So, it is not women's entry into the labor force as such, but true economic empowerment, that is linked to reproductive decision making.

Some of the most important factors that can affect fertility are: economic development, female education, and female participation in the labor force. As Amartya Sen tells us, "soft" factors such as empowerment of women, education, and health have an effect on "hard" numbers such as GNP [12]. However, it is to be acknowledged that having children reduces labor force participation for women and increases it for men. Women's less consistent labor force participation and fewer hours of employment contribute to their lower wages and lesser workplace advancement and authority.

## *Mandating quotas of women on boards*

The business world remains broadly split on the introduction of quotas. However, there is a growing sense that the underrepresentation of women in business requires an extraordinary solution.

Findings from Carleton University in Canada suggest that legislation and political reform can reverse women's underrepresentation. They found that electoral systems, without quotas, will not reach a level of 40 percent legislative participation by women until near the end of the 21st century. But, in the 26 countries they studied that met or surpassed a target of 30 percent, 21 have some form of proportional representation, and 13 of the 26 either use quotas or have reserved seats for women [13].

Quoted companies should be required to disclose each year the proportion of women on the board, women in senior executive positions, and female employees in the whole organization. The old adage, "what gets measured, gets done," remains true. Transparent reporting will help Chairmen and CEOs to better understand the composition of their workforces and monitor attrition rates [14].

US companies generally lag behind their European counterparts when it comes to the percentage of women on their boards, but US companies are far more likely to appoint a female CEO or CFO. India and Malaysia are the only countries that impose mandatory quotas for gender diversity in Asia. The implementation, however, is not highly effective, particularly in India.

Quotas may not be the correct solution in every country, but encouraging signs from Israel, France, and Norway suggest that legislation can create the "step change" required to facilitate future female advancement, by forcing business leadership teams to think about the relevant barriers. Although strict quotas need to be avoided to ensure that only the best are selected, setting targets could undermine the credibility of women at the top. Not setting them could be problematic too. But when softer measures to enhance diversity leave no impact, then it is the only way to make a change, at least initially. But the more fundamental point is this: not every board should follow the exact same road to diversity. Nor should they all advance at precisely the same pace. Every culture and every company is unique, and each one has to find its own way.

### Women in Parliament

Women's political empowerment and equal participation in political decision making are likely to feature in the new sustainable development agenda taking over from the Millennium Development Goals in 2015.

In 2015, parliamentary elections were held in 58 countries. Some form of electoral gender quota was used in 28 countries, where elections were held for 34 chambers. Women hold 28.3 percent of the seats in these chambers. No form of quota was used in 30 countries, where elections were held for 36 chambers. In those chambers, women represent a mere 13.5 percent of all members. In a total of 67, or 25.1 percent, of parliamentary chambers across the world, women now represent more than 30 percent of the membership. A slightly higher percentage of upper houses (27.6 percent) include more than 30 percent women, compared to single or lower houses (24.1 percent).

Results, therefore, confirm that the implementation of quotas leads to more women being elected. Quotas are necessary, but not sufficient. All political parties need to field women candidates [15].

The primary reason is that women's political participation transforms the process of setting priorities for public policy and helps make governance more egalitarian and inclusive [16].

Regionally, the greatest gains were made in the Americas, where, on average, women's share of parliamentary seats rose by 0.8 percentage points to reach 27.2 percent. Despite the very vocal women's movement, the glass ceiling in political leadership in the US shows that it has not been shattered yet when it comes to having women in powerful positions, either in public or corporate life.

In fact, evidence suggests that greater political representation often translates into more gender equality. In all the European Union countries, there is a unified and coordinated approach. In Sweden, for instance, women have achieved parity in government and parliament. In India, the similar case in point are the 73rd and 74th amendments to the Indian constitution, which make it mandatory for the state governments to conduct *panchayat* elections after every five years, keeping one-third of the seats reserved for women. With the amendment, women are getting elected to these bodies with one-third strength.

As *panchayat* heads, they have changed public agendas, reduced corruption, improved governance, helped draft policies sensitive to women, children, and families, and made better spending decisions on projects with high social returns [17, 18].

*Gender equality: Social and economic indicators*

The *Human Development Report 1996* of the United Nations states that human development, if not engendered, will be endangered. In HDR 1995, two additional indices were introduced. The first is the Gender-Related Development Index (GDI), which captures achievement through life expectancy, educational attainment, and income, and has been extended as a measure to 137 countries. The other index is the Gender Empowerment Measure (GEM), which has been extended to 104 countries focusing only on three variables, namely income-earning power, share of women in professional and managerial jobs, and their share in parliamentary seats. Notwithstanding the constraints in collecting and interpreting data, these indices have significant implications to minimize, if not eliminate, gender disparities through incentives, investments, and other methods, and provide a basis for national debate and public accountability.

## Gender-sensitive budgets

Clearly, macroeconomic policies, government expenditure, and taxation measures do not have the same impact on men and women. Given the generally different social or economic positions of men and women, gender budgets are, therefore, fundamentally about mainstreaming gender issues, about ensuring that women are not regarded as a "special category" interest group. In fact, they recognize that men and women play different roles as economic agents, both as contributors to economic growth and recipients of public expenditure benefits. It, therefore, requires a gender-sensitive analysis of fiscal policies.

India introduced a gender-sensitive budget as part of the Union Budget in 2004, with substantial increase in allocations. The initiative is supported by Gender Budgeting Cells in all ministries and departments. Although women's empowerment cannot happen overnight, at least a beginning has been made.

Looking at economies through the lens of gender produces a different analysis of economic restructuring. Conventional economic indicators may signal progress with more and more women entering into paid work and economic reforms (including liberalization and privatization) facilitating economic efficiency. But, they may obscure the transfer of real costs (as reflected through time and effort of people) from the public sector, where such costs are monetized and show up in government accounts, to households (the domestic sector) where such costs are not monetized and are, therefore, not visible. Gender-aware economic analysis suggests the need for a more holistic definition of "efficiency," which directs attention beyond financial costs.

## Tax incentives

It is beyond doubt that modern economics would not function without women workers and few women would want to function without jobs. The sort of incentives or disincentives governments can offer would make a big difference to the people and the way they organize their lives. If, for example, the tax system favors the traditional—"man as a provider and woman as a housewife"—type of family, fewer women will go out to work. If governments want women to be able to make a free choice about taking jobs, they need to tailor tax and social security systems to individuals rather than family units. This would necessitate reforms of the tax system and social security policies to eliminate the concept of the sole breadwinner in a dual-career family.

There seems to be a consistent message resounding throughout various studies that there are major gaps in policy, investment, and earnings that prevent women from performing to their full potential in social, economic, and political life.

## WEF gender gap study

The first-ever gender gap study of the World Economic Forum (WEF) in 1995 is extremely significant. The study measures the gap between men and women in five critical areas: economic participation, opportunity and empowerment, access to education, access to reproductive healthcare, and political indicators. The objectives of such studies or indices in the *Human Development Report* quoted above are essentially to allow countries to identify their strengths and weaknesses in an area of critical importance for the development process, and to provide opportunities for countries to learn from the experiences of other countries that have been more successful in promoting the equality of women and men.

The 2015 study, covering over 140 nations, puts Iceland, Norway, Finland, Sweden, and Ireland at the top of the list. India has been ranked 108 in 2015 and 87 in 2016. The *Global Gender Gap Report 2015* gives us a wealth of detail about the continued worldwide imbalance in gender equality and what it means for the future. In some areas, the news is good. Political representation, for example, has made great strides in the 10 years covered in the study. Overall, 50 percent of the countries have or have had a female head of state. And it's been shown that, once women attain leadership roles, the number of women serving in senior positions starts to rise. Scotland's Nicola Sturgeon, the country's first female head of state, has already achieved gender balance in her cabinet. Of course, progress can be made under male leadership, too: Justin Trudeau, who became prime minister of Canada in November 2015, named a perfectly balanced 15 men and 15 women to his cabinet. And, in African countries, the overall number of parliamentary seats held by women increased, on average, by 15 percent from 2000 to 2014. In education, too, there has been a good deal of improvement. More women than men are pursuing higher education in 97 of the 145 countries included in the WEF report, for example. And, in some places, such as the UK and the US, this issue has been so well addressed that the gender balance scale has swung the other way.

However, progress toward parity in the key economic pillar stands at 59 percent now, larger than what it was in 2008. The WEF, in a report released in 2016, says the economic gender gap could take 170 years to close, a number that is just unacceptable [19].

### Judicial/legal provisions

It is clear that legislation makes a difference, but it does not offer all the answers. New laws and progressive policies have succeeded in getting more women into the workforce, but looking beyond the statute book, it is clear that legislation has not enabled more women to take up leadership positions. In rich and poor countries alike, the infrastructure of justice is failing women. Legal reforms are necessary but they must also be implemented to translate into true equality. Across the board, existing laws are too often inadequately enforced, keeping many women from reporting cases of gender inequality, as indicated in a flagship UN report [20].

Both progress on implementation and compliance with the laws has been slow. While fighting gender bias in society, one must consider how both formal legal systems and personal laws, such as those related to marriage, divorce, maintenance, and guardianship, affect women.

- How can women's legal rights be strengthened?
- Are current laws gender equitable? If so, are they enforced with the same degree of fairness?

### *Removing gender bias from inheritance laws*

Truly civilized societies ensure that women's inheritance rights are more secure than those of men, for the simple reason that women take on the awesome responsibility of producing, nurturing, and providing a home for the next generation. By and large, women tend to have values that enhance governance. Recent research suggests that where women's influence in public life is higher, corruption is lower. However, unequal rights and low socioeconomic status limit women's ability to influence decisions in their communities. They are also underrepresented in national and local legislatures.

It is, therefore, heartening to note that, in a bid to legally empower women, the Government of India has initiated moves for determined enforcement of as many as 39 Central Acts which have remained dormant all these years. The laws and their enforcement need not remain an isolated success. They must succeed in changing mindsets.

Apart from ensuring their implementation, the government is also planning a few fresh legislations and amendments to several existing acts in an attempt to fight gender bias. The legal-judicial system needs to be made more responsive, assertive, and gender sensitive to ensure quick justice, especially in cases of domestic violence and personal assault. This needs to be supported by a sensitized judiciary, compassionate prosecutors, and more ethical defense lawyering. A better system would be to nominate specially designated judges in every district court assigned for a period of three years to undergo mandatory gender sensitization for a period of three years at the state or national judicial academies. One pathbreaking role model of sensitive judiciary is the creation of the Vulnerable Witness Deposition Complex and the guidelines for operationalizing the facility in three district courts in Delhi between 2012 and 2016. This system prevents revictimization of the victims due to lack of privacy, the pain, and trauma experienced in the presence of the accused. The sensitivity shown in dispensing justice is unparalleled anywhere in the world.

Simultaneously a training program captioned 'Making Courtroom Practices Responsive Towards Victims of Sexual Offences' for sensitization of all judges as well as some prosecutors, police officials, and legal aid lawyers was undertaken. By April 2017, 500 judges, 75 prosecutors, 135 legal aid lawyers, and 150 police officials had undertaken the program held in seven batches [21].

Governments need to support women's legal organizations, implement gender-sensitive law reforms, facilitate a gender-sensitive judicial system, invest in women's access to justice courts during and after conflict, and use quotas to boost the number of women legislators.

### Gender-sensitive press and media

Politics apart, there are other sectors where women allege gender bias. With regard to mass media, private sector partners and media networks need to be involved at all levels to ensure equal access for women in the areas of information and communication technologies. The press and media are major generators of change in society. Media needs to portray images consistent with the human dignity of girls and women. The media needs to specifically strive to remove demeaning, degrading, or stereotypical images of women. Considering that 80–90 percent of the people who are in control of media and advertising are men, we need more women in positions of power in the press and media, to influence political parties and governments and to make important contributions to society.

Why is gender equality so hard to achieve? There are several reasons for this, but the main reason is unconscious bias. The American film actor Geena Davis believes that it results in part from lopsided male representation in television and films, a long-standing trend observed by the Institute on Gender in Media that she founded. In family films, the ratio of male to female characters is 3:1. Shockingly, the ratio of male to female characters has remained exactly the same since 1946. Of the characters with jobs, 81 percent are male [22]. Sexism runs deep in Hollywood, with pay disparities, issues of ageism, and discrimination against female directors, who in any case are in minority (only 7 percent of Hollywood directors are female, even in 2016) [23]. According to British actor Keira Knightley, the gender wage gap in Hollywood is equally glaring, and needs to be addressed [24].

In a government-sponsored study, newspapers were criticized for not reporting on women's issues. Women journalists invited to discuss the report expressed helplessness at the apathy of news managers in projecting women's issues. What was not discussed is that women are equally responsible for this state; because every editor looks for a good story, whether it's gender based or not. Therefore, women reporters who see themselves as women first and journalists later need to do a reality check on the actual number of stories on gender which they have written but which have not been published. Instead of blaming news managers, women reporters need to be proactive and attentive to the reporting of relevant gender-based stories [25].

Gender sensitization and non-discrimination in the portrayal of women in all forms of media and use of gender-sensitive language has to be advocated to ensure that women are not represented in a demeaning or stereotypical manner. Particular attention has be paid to the sensitive reporting of crimes against women, as well as gender sensitivity in the reporting of seemingly gender-neutral topics such as politics, economics, culture, conflict, etc. Media campaigns creating awareness on gender equality and promoting the dignity and safety of women have to be encouraged.

Discrimination against women, entrenched in deep-rooted cultural beliefs and traditional practices, persists throughout the world. Although there has been some progress at the grassroots level, success has been largely invisible, since it has not been translated into improvements in women's daily lives. The cost of failure to achieve true gender equality to societies will be high in terms of slower economic and social development, waste of human resources, and loss of related progress.

## How can employers make a difference?
### Role of employers' organizations/chambers of commerce/industry associations

The employers' organizations, chambers of commerce, and industry associations need to come forward and use their lobbying and influencing ability with governments as well as the corporate sector, to push for action on social and institutional reforms.

The most important strategy of the employers' organizations would be to convince employers that gender equality is a best business practice from the perspective of economic, legal and social considerations.

| | |
|---|---|
| Economic Reasons | : The economics of equal opportunities makes good business sense and facilitates better utilization of human assets. |
| Legal Reasons | : Equality is a worldwide issue and relevant ILO standards and conventions related to this issue have been ratified by most governments, including the Indian government. |
| Social Reasons | : No enterprise, no business, functions in a sociocultural vacuum, therefore, the employers must integrate the principle of gender equality in the social fabric to bring about a multiplier effect. This will challenge patterns of behavior and assumptions established and entrenched over a period of time. |

Considering that members of the employers' organization belong to diverse sectors of industry such as financial institutions, transportation, infrastructure, petroleum and chemicals, steel, power, coal, and agro-based industries, etc., developing strategies and action plans that are implementable across the board, as given below, is absolutely important:

- Setting up of a database at the regional, national, and international level.
  Data, evaluation, and course correction are the cornerstones of an equitable new world. Data does not exist in many areas and, when it does, is often sexist and misses information on women entirely. The gender gap cannot be closed unless holes in the data gap are plugged. Gaps and biases reinforce the social stereotypes and cultural practices that do not value women. Data can be used to equip decision makers, corporate leaders, civil societies, and communities with clear evidence of what works and what does not in lifting women's underrepresentation in the corporate sector.
  It is important to gather sector-wise quantitative data on the company's experience with turnover of management-level women, occurrence and return from maternity leave, and level of organization attained in relation to performance. It is equally important to correlate this data with factors such as age, marital status, and age of children.
- To gather quantitative data on how women are perceived by both genders in the company.
- To collect benchmarks of best practices in maintaining work-life balance in developed countries.
- To conduct a cost-benefit analysis of the return on company's investment in high-performing women. To factor in the probable cost of the corrective measures and policies to rectify the imbalances.
- To find out the value of women to the company and to correlate this with the cost to recruit, train, and develop women.

If the value of women is greater than the cost to recruit, then the companies would want to do everything to retain the employee.
- Lobby with the government: The employers' organizations can act as pressure groups in influencing the government policies and legislative measures, as governments today are receptive to ideas and suggestions put forward by NGOs, employers' organizations and freelance experts while formulating policies on social and institutional reforms. Public–private partnership is required not only for enhancing physical infrastructure but also human infrastructure that delivers speedy justice to all and enables them to lead a life of dignity and respect. In the dialogue that the Indian government has with the industry or chambers of commerce at least twice a year—one before the Union Budget and the other for the Five-Year plans—these aspects of women's development must be discussed with action points and implementation timelines.
- Platform for disseminating information.
- Employers' organizations can disseminate information on gender equality through policies, programs, and activities such as seminars, workshops, and training programs with both men and women as participants in which equal opportunity policies could be subtly interwoven with management principles and practices and discussed.
- Upholding the dignity of women in media.
- Redressal of issues related to transfer, promotion, and protection of women in employment.
- To conduct surveys and research studies on areas that have been overlooked or are under-researched.

Studies on women's effectiveness as managers should be undertaken to gauge their contribution to the organization once they become managers, the distribution of female managers by size of firm, type of industry, type of ownership, etc. What percentage of women are entrepreneurs? What is the role of the informal sector and its contribution to GDP? Increasingly, women are setting up small businesses at home or working with their spouses in family businesses. How can their contribution be recorded and then augmented? Findings from such a research done by a neutral agency can provide valuable inputs for policy formation.

### Role of business/private sector

Just as government has a role in business, business has a role in government. Private sector accountability is especially important in forging partnerships with the government for development of a comprehensive national strategy for improving health, education, and social services, and for the setting up of training centers for skill building. Apart from this, how can an enabling environment be created? The only way to get companies truly interested in promoting women is to convince them it is good for business, for the reasons given below:

1. An equal distribution of talent pool

Women constitute 50 percent of the world's population. There is simply no evidence that the qualities—intelligence, energy, decision making or leadership, and professional qualifications—that make people perform well at work, are unevenly distributed between men and women.

A shortage of the right talent is a top concern for CEOs in all industries and geographies. WEF, in its 2016 *Future of Jobs* report [26], identified high skills instability across all job categories and noted: "Net job growth and skills instability result in most businesses currently facing major recruitment challenges and talent shortages, a pattern already evident in the results and set to get worse over the next five years." Because women are underrepresented in the workforce in most countries, they are a significant source of untapped talent. The report further notes that women hold fewer line roles across multiple industries.

How can you possibly get the best talent if you're not drawing from the fullness of the talent pool and depend solely on male graduates from 10 percent of the best schools in any country? If organizations only recruit men, they narrow the recruitment choice to only half of the brightest and best people available. Given the findings of overall effectiveness by many studies, dismissing any candidate on the basis of gender not only denies opportunity to talented individuals, but also dries up the management talent pool.

Many countries around the world are facing serious demographic challenges from shrinking and aging populations. Inviting and integrating women into the corporate world, therefore, makes sound business and economic sense. Empowering women boosts economic growth. Christine Lagarde, MD, IMF, in her address to the W-20 Summit in September 2015, had estimated that, if the number of female workers were to increase to the same level as the number of men, GDP in the US would expand by 5 percent, in Japan by 9 percent, and in India by 27 percent. These estimates, while tentative, are significant and large enough to be taken seriously. This applies particularly to countries where potential growth is declining as the population is aging [27].

2. Development of women as a segment of human resource

All companies hire men and women on the same exacting standards as they claim they hire only the best people with the right kind of executive profile from the best undergraduate or business schools. Why should women not be given a chance? In fact it is a losing proposition for both the organizations as well as women.

It is important for corporations to recognize that women have a contribution to make to the overall betterment of the corporation and that recognition must come from the understanding that, if they are trained properly and have the skill, their contribution may provide competitive leverage. If a corporation is committed to objectively hiring the best and the brightest and working towards retaining them, many incquities will take care of themselves. There are several companies in India who are paying more than lip service to creating a critical mass of women by proactively hiring a greater number of them. For instance, Tata Steel's thrust on diversity includes setting up of a gender intelligence cell, incentives to hiring agencies for identifying high-potential women candidates, flexible hours and enhanced paid maternity leave of 18 weeks, and appropriate changes in performance rating systems so that women on long leave don't lose out on seniority. The company is also taking up proposals with state and central governments to introduce changes in the Factories Act to allow women to work beyond 7 PM [28]. Accenture has a metrics-based recruitment process for hiring women that has pushed up the percentage of women to 30 percent, a special recruitment drive for women-only colleges, and a referral program for women. HSBC makes a conscious attempt to build a strong female executive pipeline by effectively using the graduates campus trainee program and building databases of successful female candidates in the industry at all levels. The percentage of women at HSBC is at 33 percent [29].

3. Treating women's issues as family issues

The last two decades have seen great social change, the emergence of nuclear families, and more women joining the workforce. The biggest and best-run businesses, therefore, increasingly believe that, to attract and retain the best staff, they need to accept that people have families as well. These family oriented policies need not be aimed exclusively at women, as they can backfire by inviting further discrimination. It is better to acknowledge that men also have families and they too need to spend time with them.

In fact, a new study by the Center for Creative Leadership (CCL) and Clark University shows that family commitments can help improve work performance among parents. Being a committed parent can enhance managerial ability, because child-rearing develops skills that are useful at work, such as negotiating, compromising, conflict resolution, and multitasking, which are all important traits of successful managers. Family experiences provide managers with positive feelings that carry over to the workplace and facilitate performance. They also help managers develop the ability to see others' views—a capacity which is critical to supervising others, working in teams, and relating to superiors. The study [30] contradicts conventional wisdom that parents are easily distracted by their responsibilities at home—in particular, their children—and are, therefore, more likely to be ineffective at work.

For this reason, it is high time "dependent care" is treated as a business issue. Study after study shows that most young working parents have trouble arranging child or elder care due to lack of information about available resources. Those with most difficulty also experience the most frequent work disruptions and the greatest absenteeism. Childcare needs differ from one employee population to another. In order to offer an effective childcare program, companies first need to study the location, the age of its workforce, and the competitiveness of its labor market in relation to the financial resources available to them. Considering that quality and affordable childcare is difficult to find, corporate programs could be helpful in providing some or all of the following:

- Help in finding existing childcare and elder care programs through referral services.
- Financial assistance or subsidy for childcare for entry-level/lower-level employees, or contract arrangements with external providers to operate onsite/near-site centers at very low or no cost.

North Carolina-based software company SAS Institute Inc. is a shining example. It provides free childcare services at an onsite center. The company reported its turnover rates to be less than half the industry average. The center's additional expenditure is considered fully justified as a result of the decrease in the extremely high cost of recruitment and training of new workers. Providing such facilities makes eminent sense, given the special role played by women in raising families.

4. Ensuring conducive environment
Research has also shown that, quite often, the career aspirations of highly talented persons are frustrated by institutional and bureaucratic

rules, policies designed to maintain the status quo. Inequity or unfair, even insensitive, treatment can have enormous costs. If the problem is systemic—i.e., most women are treated this way—then the company further suffers from decreased productivity and inefficiency as attrition among high-potential women increases.

High attrition has huge cost implications. Turnover concerns shareholders, can hinder production and service, and negatively affects customers. The rationale for work-life programs includes enhanced competitiveness in recruiting, removing barriers for employers to be more productive, reduced costs through decreased absenteeism and low medical costs, and improved retention. Female talent leaks out at every organizational level, but interventions at critical junctures can have a big impact.

Realizing this predicament, GlaxoSmithKline Consumer Healthcare increased its maternity and adoption leave to six months from the earlier three months, just like FMCG major P&G. The major objective behind the move is to be able to retain women, as well as to create a more inclusive workplace. Companies find it easier and less cost-intensive to take back their own employees after long breaks than hire and train new people [31]. Philips India has revamped its maternity related policies to include crèche tie-ups and monetary support for children below four years, options for part-time and remote working, and sabbaticals up to six months (for those who have completed three years of service) and one year for those with five years of service [32].

5. Seeking maximum ROI on recruitment/training

On an average, every company makes a decade-long investment in training and developing new recruits and in adapting their skills to specific organizational needs. When young working mothers are forced to make a choice of leaving because either the company does not provide parental leave or family support is inadequate, the company fails to amortize the 10-year investment they made in recruiting and training them. If the company makes a replacement with a new recruit, recruitment and training costs will be astronomical. The more highly trained the employee, the more expensive she becomes to replace. Worse still, if they leave to join a competing firm, the same experience will be put to work against the former company. Keeping staff turnover down can save a lot of money. This is critical when the economic cost of losing a well-qualified woman is estimated as at least 1.5 times the salary [33]. It makes economic sense, therefore, to accommodate women by offering family friendly benefits, rather than risk losing them and having to start all over again with someone else.

HLL offers a five-year career break that can be availed twice for a variety of reasons—for pursuing studies, bringing up children, or even to join a spouse posted in another location. HLL offers six months of maternity leave to women who have worked at least two years for the company. Companies also use differential leave strategy to retain and reward older employees.

Godrej Industries has modified its leave benefit policy to include fertility treatment, to allow women employees to claim sick leave for time taken off during fertility treatment. The company has also amended its healthcare policy—which was earlier limited to spouse, children, and parents—to include live-in partners. These initiatives come under the "whole self" pillar of employee branding [34].

Many women consider flexibility in when, where, and how they do their work to be more important than compensation. One must recognize that someone caring for young children or elderly people may have many hours of potentially productive time to contribute during the day, yet may not be able to leave home for long. In order to arrest post-maternity attrition levels—the single largest reason for women leaving their jobs—companies like GE, Motorola, Cisco, and Ford have set up crèches on campus or have tied up with them. Motorola, Accenture, and GE also set up office infrastructure— laptops and high-speed broadband and telephone connections at company expense—at the residences of new mothers to enable them to continue working. Accenture also routinely reschedules shift allocations for women in its business-process outsourcing business.

6. Developing corporate commitment

There are several things a company needs to do in order to create an environment where employees with dependents can do their work without sacrificing family interests. To begin with:

- It needs to develop a corporate policy that is constantly communicated to all its employees. For instance, Johnson & Johnson added the following statement to its 40-year-old credo: "We must be mindful of ways to help our employees fulfill their family obligations." DuPont has developed a mission statement that partly commits to "making changes in the workplace and fostering changes in the community that are sensitive to changing family unit and increasingly diverse work force."
- It needs to train and encourage first the supervisors and second the line managers to be sensitive, adaptable, and responsible. Formal policies and measures can only succeed if sensitization programs typically focus on making managers gender sensitive.
- It needs to develop and give specific training tools and programs to sensitize all its employees. Training is critical. IBM, Johnson & Johnson, and Merck have all established training programs to teach managers to be more sensitive to work and family issues. Such training typically lays the business case for flexibility, reviews corporate programs and policies, and presents best practice case studies to underline the fact that old systems and practices need rethinking. Organizations have a tendency to sustain rather than disrupt themselves due to hard-wired operating models that define how business is done. The company, therefore, needs to hold all its managers accountable for flexibility and their sensitivity to family issues and, most importantly, for women's advancement.

At times, corporate mission statements of most companies pay lip service to the value of family and community, while their day-to-day practices are a different story altogether. For example, in one company, maternity leave was counted against an individual manager when measuring absenteeism, a key element in their performance appraisal. The system, which was originally designed to discourage malingerers, actually ended up punishing young mothers. In the absence of new and forward-looking performance measurement systems, such systems coexist with explicit corporate messages to promote flexibility. The change will never take place unless the supervisors are actually evaluated for their sensitivity to family issues.

7. Removing stigma

Finally, the message top management sends to all employees is as important as it needs to be consistent. The management also needs to work towards removing stigma in availing work-life policies, which women frequently encounter. It is a paradox that, despite having work-life policies and arrangements, organizational culture punishes women who want to avail of such benefits. Women report encountering cultural and attitudinal barriers and tacit resistance when they want to take time off that they are entitled to. Only demonstrated commitment by the leadership of the company will set the tone for others to transform conventional attitudes and practices and provide appreciation and flexibility endorsed by corporate culture.

Women need inclusive culture to succeed. What is unique to any culture is how women's family issues play out in organizations as well as in the broader sociocultural environment. Yasmine Hilton, the former chairperson of Shell India, has gone on record to say that the strong inclusive culture of Shell helped tremendously in her career. Shell is gender neutral when it comes to assignments and promotions, and accommodates the unique needs of women and their cultural context by offering flexible working arrangements and personal sabbaticals of up to two years [35].

## Different solutions for different management levels

In concrete terms, what can companies do that reflects their understanding of the huge costs to businesses of losing highly educated women when they start their families?

A study of 72 large US firms showed that family friendly human resource practices increased the proportion of women in senior management five years later, after balancing other organizational variables [36]. In the Indian context, Wipro has been able to show similar results.

However, companies need to set clear targets for each part of their business divisions. That way more people can engage in change, taking individual responsibility for improving women's representation rather than seeing it as a human resource function.

For instance, at the *entry level*, IBM faced a shortage in the talent pipeline of women in technology. The tendency of young girls to opt out of science and math in school was identified as one of the causes. In 1999, IBM initiated a pilot technology camp called EXITE in the US and other countries staffed by IBM volunteers with technical backgrounds. The objective was to spark the interest of high-school students, so that they continued to take technology classes that would position them for future careers in these fields. After the girls attended the camp, they are assigned an IBM female scientist or engineer as a mentor. The EXITE camp program has grown tremendously since it was launched, and, annually, there are over 50 camps being held around the world. As a result, the proportion of women at the entry level has risen significantly [37].

At the middle management level, it is all about balancing career with family. The employers need to recognize that there is a time when people are prepared to go away from home and a time when they need to stay at home. Many highly educated, high-earning, high-achieving career women have indicated [38] that the following cluster of work policies would help them achieve balance in their lives over the long term:

*Flexible schedules:* There are two different needs for flexibility. One is the need for working hours that accommodate children's normal schedules and their predictable special requirements such as doctor's appointments, parent-teacher meetings, birthday shopping, etc. The other is the need to deal with emergencies and unanticipated events that are part of family life: a breakdown in childcare arrangements, sudden illness, an early/unscheduled closing of the school, etc. The most common response to both the needs is flexitime, that is, permit alterations of a basically rigid work schedule by 30–60 minutes or provide an allowance, which is to vary from one workday to the next. Hewlett–Packard pioneered flexitime in the US, and it is now quite popular with the large employers. It has a positive impact on late coming, employee morale, and absenteeism.

*Part-time employment:* It is a pity that even the term "part-time" seems to have a negative connotation. It is, therefore, quite common for managers to show great resistance to part-time work. However, contrary to popular belief, part time is not necessarily the same as half time. Most seniors seem to regard "full-time" work as sacred and perhaps cannot imagine that anyone working fewer hours could do anything productive or useful. Studies indicate that a third to half of women with young children would want to work less than full time for at least a while, despite the loss of pay and other benefits.

*A time bank of paid parenting leave:*

- Parenting leave is different from maternity leave, i.e., from pregnancy, childbirth or even disability leave. Companies need to formulate clear, comprehensive disability or sick and maternity leave policies as different from parental leave policies. This would allow for three months of paid leave which could be taken as needed until the child turns 18.
- If women are permitted to have flexible work schedules, then most women will opt to return early on part-time schedules. Such a leave of absence might span up to three years; unpaid all right, but with the assurance of a job when the time comes to return to work.

*Career-path alternatives:* It would take a lot of innovative thinking and cultural adaptability to design meaningful part-time work opportunities. But an even greater challenge is to find ways of fitting these flexible arrangements into a long-term career path. If commitment to family is not seen as lack of commitment to work, then the usual definition of fast-track career progression will require some modification. What needs to be done is to find ways of offering broad business experience to employees, which will then allow them to work in a range of departments. For example, Mobil created a wide range of facilities at hub locations, partly in order to allow its employees a greater variety of work experience without the need for relocation.

As we saw in the last chapter, NSE is a unique organization that offers career alternatives (i.e., part-time to full-time work or generalist to specialist cadre).

*Keeping linkages with former employees:* Analogous to active retirement, an alumni standing will help women who have left or are not active in their careers to stay in the loop. They could be tapped for advice and guidance and the company would pay their dues and certification fees so that they could maintain their professional standing. It is worth spending corporate time to explore the reasons for employee separation apart from the information exit interviews provide. The Tata Group of Companies launched a novel Initiative called Tata Second Career Internship Program (SCIP) in 2008. It invites talented women to resume their corporate career in select locations. It is for women with qualifications in management, accountancy, law or engineering, with a maximum of four years' experience and who have taken a career break of less than eight years. It offers 500 hours of flexi-office engagement spread over six months on live business projects with an attractive stipend. SCIP has been an ongoing program from 2011. The group on-boards an average of 80–90 women every year through the program. Several women have returned to full-time work not only with the Tata group but also other companies.

- GE India launched 'Restart' in 2008 with an objective to integrate women, who had taken a career break, back into the workforce by hiring them as full-time employees. Restart is targeted at women who have worked for at least four years with any company and have been on a career break of a minimum one year. Each Restart hire is given a support system to help develop skills and have a smooth transition back to work.

- In 2011, Hindustan Unilever (HUL) launched 'Career by Choice', a comeback program that provides a platform to women looking for real opportunities to work part time and flexibly after a career break.

The program aims at providing opportunities to women with more than two years of relevant work experience to work on live business projects ranging from six months to a year. This program is supported by a comprehensive portal, areUthewoman.com. While HUL has several initiatives aimed at promoting gender balance in the company, this initiative is available to both men and women [39].

*Creating avenues for voluntary work and community service:*
Many women professionals, who don't find their full-time work enjoyable and satisfying, give their time, skills, and energy to voluntary activities outside their jobs. For some, it is a way of giving back to the community what they received early on from it. The findings of a study presented by the Center for Work-Life Policy [40] suggests that the skills required to do community service can be a source of competitive strength if companies learn to develop new awareness about the work of minority employees, mostly women, and provide them opportunities to reflect on their experiences and generalize the lessons for application in other settings as well as cultivate their cultural capital. It is beyond doubt that substantial community involvement develops leadership and interpersonal skills, and builds organizational and communication capabilities, all of which are transferable to and highly valued in the workplace. Many corporations, for instance Chevron, Shell, Tata Steel, and Wipro, have created avenues for community service.

At a *senior level*, companies have to consider high-performing women and look for ways to create an environment in which they can contribute and succeed. Leadership training, succession planning, challenging assignments, mentoring, and sponsorship are critical factors here. The next step to increasing the representation of women and to attain the goal of organizational diversity, is to build the culture of sponsorship. This may neutralize the effects of maternity leave and ongoing family responsibilities on career advancement and may help in evolving the criteria companies use for promotions to include a diversity of leadership styles. In the final analysis, it is important to remember that transformation is neither easy nor quick. After an initial commitment from the top management, change may be visible only after 8 to 10 years, that too after continuous monitoring by the executive team.

## A word of caution: Stem the reform backlash

From my experience, I believe that no corporate policies, programs, or guidelines can cover all of the myriad work-life situations that are bound to arise. For example, the principle of flexibility has to run both ways: from organization to employee and employee to organization. To encourage this two-way flow, corporate leaders need to ask: "What can the corporation do to maximize your productivity? How will you feel valued and welcome?" Often, people come up with more creative and better solutions for meeting their needs for flexible work hours than their managers or HR department. A 2014 report shows that, by having flexible workplaces, women's career aspirations increased by nearly 30 percent and the retention of women improved by as much as 40 percent [41]. For employers, even small- and medium-sized enterprises, these schemes improved staff retention, motivation, and engagement, without detrimental costs or implementation challenges for business [42].

Despite the numerous advantages of flexibility (the freedom to take time off or to do some work at home and some at office), part-time employment (which enables women to maintain responsibility for critical aspects of their jobs, keeps them in touch with the changes occurring at workplace, etc.), and shared employment, flexibility can be costly in numerous ways [43]. It requires more supervisory time to coordinate and manage, more office space, and greater benefit costs to the companies. Therefore, it needs to be provided selectively.

The managements need to discuss the costs as well as the benefits. The managements also need to make abundantly clear that, in most instances, the rates of advancement and pay will be appropriately lower for those who avail of such policies than for full timers. Evidence tells us that most career and family women are more than willing to make that trade-off. In the final analysis, strategies to improve women's career prospects would work with total top management commitment, only if fully integrated into a sustainable, wide-reaching initiative adapted to the culture of the organization. They could be practices to identify invisible barriers blocking women, devising and implementing remedies such as sensitization of managers to gender and family issues, exit interviews to find out why women leave, development of programs that value employee diversity in recruiting, training, promoting, and introducing flexibility in time and places of work, creating opportunities for lateral mobility, and devising job mobility that does not necessarily involve geographical transfers. The range of options is wide indeed. The appropriate "package" will be specific and unique to each work culture and environment.

After HSBC implemented its Flexible Work Arrangement Initiative (which offers three options: staggered hours, part-time work and telecommuting), their attrition rate became the lowest in the industry [44]. Any reforms such as these may seem costly and inefficient in the beginning, but systematic analyses suggest that employers as well as employees can benefit from such policies. The benefits to individuals are obvious. The benefits to employers can include retaining and recruiting talented employees, enhancing employee motivation, reducing turnover, and gaining a favorable image as "a good place to work" [45].

### Role of the public sector: The CSR program

In the modern world, corporations are often called upon to play a larger role in society than was customary in an earlier era. Often, a corporation operates with the approval of the society in which it is established. It must, therefore, conform not only to the laws and mores of the society, but also to its changing needs. Increasingly, many corporations, and the society in which they operate, have come to realize that industrial activity has potential impacts that extend beyond the limited scope of business operations. These impacts include, but are not limited to, impacts on the local environment and the ecosystem. Many corporations have been involved in a wide variety of community development projects in coordination with local leaders, national government officials, and company executives. Such projects include the development of villages around the operational areas, construction of infrastructure (for example, schools, roads, power supply facilities), the study and preservation of wildlife habitats, the preservation of cultural and historic monuments, and the establishment and equipping of libraries, health clinics, primary schools, etc.

In the context of public-sector enterprises, Corporate Social Responsibility (CSR) is viewed as a way of conducting business, which enables the creation and distribution of wealth for the betterment of its stakeholders, through the implementation and integration of ethical systems and sustainable management practices. Stakeholders include employees, investors, shareholders, customers, business partners, clients, civil society groups, governmental and non-government organizations, local communities, environment, and society at large. Central Public Sector Enterprises (CPSEs) are encouraged to join hands and pool their resources and capabilities to create synergy for undertaking joint ventures for projects which have scalability and greater social impact that can trigger socioeconomic development through a ripple effect [46].

One such illustrative example is that of a self-help project that generated self-employment for women around Oil India's (OIL) operational areas in Duliajan (Assam) in India, in which I was involved right from the inception. With the national policy on CSR setting up a broad direction, OIL provided the sponsorship and funding. It invited Dibrugarh University to conduct a survey for identification of needs in 13 villages around the field headquarters' of OIL, developed a blueprint for the setting up of a Handicrafts Training and Production Center in consultation with the district's industry officers, and mobilized heads of local village administrations to recruit deserving women candidates for training. Post training, an innovative solution was also needed to tackle the continuing challenge faced by women of securing adequate financing for their small-scale manufacturing unit. OIL, as an enabler, facilitated bank loans for setting up their small-scale units. The production center later became a marketing channel for selling the products. OIL also became one of the institutional buyers, by picking up survey sample bags for the geological department and other accessories for company guesthouses. As of early 2017, 950 rural women have been trained under this scheme and 190 women have set up small-scale units post training.

As can be seen from this example, regional strategies work best when they focus on using underlying capabilities and local assets and skills, such as weaving in this case. OIL took on the role of an orchestrator in creating a vibrant ecosystem indirectly, rather than through control and command. OIL not only provided a leadership role, it also exhibited change readiness. This collaboration brought multiple actors in the region together to produce a multiplier effect in order to enrich the quality of life and the ecosystem.

## The role of multinational corporations in emerging markets

It is no longer useful to think in polarized "East" or "West" terms. It is more important to think about taking the best ideas from across the globe and incorporating them into a strategy for growth. Successful multinationals think in terms of interdependence, developing skills in both developed and emerging markets. At the same time, no one can afford to ignore the mounting issues surrounding sustainability and the environment, geopolitical risks, and the role of the government. The multinationals need to find ways of making those considerations a fundamental part of business. To that end, bonding with local communities proves to be vital in this effort. It is also important to understand the prevailing process of socialization in a given country and society. It will not do any good to blindly adapt western practices of management to local cultures and conditions. People want to identify with a company that resonates with local values and culture. It also helps in building a strong recruitment brand. For instance, for women in emerging markets like India, elder care and childcare play a significant role in their lives. It has the potential to limit their ambitions or stall a high-flying career. As an antidote to such pressures, HSBC has provided an option of telecommuting under its Flexible Work Arrangement (FWA) Program in 2008. This option enables employees to work from home or even from a location elsewhere in the country. HSBC provides the technology to access the company system. However, implementing the program required sensitizing the managers who thought they would lose control over their teams. Two years later, the program was a huge success. Approximately 600 employees with an equal percentage of men and women have availed of one or more of the FWA Options. Internal studies indicate that productivity has gone up in about 88 percent of employees and has remained the same in the rest of the workers [47].

## Partnering with universities/educational institutions

It is well known that women are underrepresented right from entry-level positions in certain sectors, such as automotive and industrial manufacturing, energy and basic materials, and technology. As a result, women are poorly represented throughout the talent pipeline. This problem usually arises from recruiting challenges or pre-pipeline problems, particularly the low graduation rates of women in industry feeder programs such as engineering (where they receive about 20 percent, 24 percent, and 23 percent of bachelor's, master's, and doctor's degrees, respectively) [48].

Leading companies today are partnering with universities to cultivate talent early. Facebook has launched an initiative called TechPrep to nurture talent in early education, often at points where girls abandon paths which were leading to STEM-degrees.

Google India started a pioneering "Women in Engineering" award program that promotes diversity not only within the company but across an emerging market. This program celebrates young women in college or graduate school who have chosen to pursue a career in engineering or computer science, traditionally male-dominated fields. The selected women are given the award of US$2,000 for their academic excellence and demonstrated leadership skills. The award has inspired the winners not only to stay in the field, but also to pursue higher degrees and mentor younger women. To be able to do that, the HR team for engineering at Google India worked hard to get a buy-in from the senior management and sensitized many Google engineers who served as judges for the competition [49].

### Nurturing Women Entrepreneurs

Women entrepreneurs require special developmental opportunities and exposure. In 2008, Goldman Sachs launched 10,000 Women, a global initiative to offer relevant management education to women entrepreneurs of small and medium businesses with an annual turnover of INR 5–50 lakhs and a minimum of 10 employees. In partnership with the Indian School of Business (ISB), the initiative claims to support deserving participants by providing full scholarships for the program. The 16 weeks of non-residential education program and 13 weeks of mentoring support on the job from ISB enables women entrepreneurs to further their business and their dreams. To date, it has trained over 1,300 women entrepreneurs in 13 cities in India alone.

In 2016, IIM (Bangalore) and Goldman Sachs together launched a Women Startup Program targeted at women with no entrepreneurial experience, but who were keen to set up ventures on their own. The program will offer a combination of online courses, classroom training, mentoring incubation, and support to selected projects [50].

## How can NGOs make a difference?

Demographic studies indicate that the economic value of education is increasingly being realized by young women who join occupations formerly reserved for men. As more women join the workforce, the support most men used to receive at home is lessening and women who work get as little, if not less, support as men. To many managers, the time they spend with family is precious. It is understandable if many women managers feel guilty about sacrificing this part of their life to the demands of work and if they also experience frustration at being forced to quit their jobs.

Such skilled women, who later have the time and inclination to contribute to society, run very active, effective NGOs. One of the reasons for the success of NGOs led by women is their decentralized structures. Women enjoy doing things together, in a democratic set-up where everything is linked to everything else. The hierarchy is not built on authority or competition, but on cooperative achievement; not on power over others, but in empowerment of others; not on ranking, but in linking.

In many women's organizations, hierarchy or class lines are easily blurred as women professionals share common cause around personal, economic, and social issues, including violence against women, poverty, job security, land rights, reproductive and health rights, and women's citizenship. Secondly, the mobilization of women into women's NGOs has occurred on the part of women with education and work experience, and represents their response to continuing common problems for women.

In fact, the corporate world would do well to invite community participation through NGOs to set up dependent care services (crèches for infants and childcare/daycare centers), elder care programs, and model consortium centers complete with a sick room for mildly ill children, etc.

Similarly, from property ownership to inheritance rights, from employment malpractices to domestic violence, from retirement plans to entrepreneurial skills, training and opportunities, NGOs can offer legal counseling and literacy classes on a variety of issues.

NGOs can play an important role in influencing business corporations to commit themselves to social responsibility and accountability in all their operations as well as influence the civil society around it. For instance, a major challenge in ensuring equality of treatment for the girl child is getting men to be sensitive to the issue. Plan India, an NGO, creates awareness on the issue by recognizing that men, as key players, have to be engaged to ensure gender parity. To garner the support of men, they need to be convinced about the benefits of gender equality [51]. Further, by the time boys and girls reach adolescence, attitudes about unequal gender roles are already formed, and large proportions of girls and boys express attitudes justifying the right of a man or boy to control the behaviour of or perpetrate violence against women and girls. Therefore, it is important to help young girls and boys, especially boys, to adopt gender egalitarian values. There is evidence to show that after the intervention of the Do Kadam Barabari Ki Ore (Two Steps Towards Equality) project, Gender role attitudes became more egalitarian and notions of masculinity became more positive in rural Bihar [52].

## How can we—men and women—make a difference?

After years of conditioning and subtle messages, it takes a woman to sit down and think through what she wants do with her life, to actually figure out whether she wants to break from the tradition. Many women seem prepared to accept traditional, gendered divisions of labor both at work and at home, even though their careers are being compromised. However, it is hard to say whether they are doing this by choice or because they think there is no alternative. Most women employees begin near the bottom of organizational hierarchies, so it is much easier for them to accept existing practices than lobby for change.

### Consciously choose career

Women need to consciously choose careers that will give them the gift of time. Certain careers provide more flexibility and can permit more interruptions. For instance, female entrepreneurs can be better off in combining career and family than corporate women. Corporate women are slightly better off than women doctors and surgeons.

### Sensitizing men

Tackling gender bias is not the sole responsibility of women. Research [53] clearly shows that men are less likely to see it as a barrier to female advancement. Fewer men acknowledge the challenges women face at work. Many corporate men, particularly among the older generation, seem to be insensitive to women's issues at work and at home, because it has been so convenient to them all these years. Even in organizations whose policies support women, prevailing attitudes and unrelenting job pressures undermine them. But women's entry into the corporate sphere has had a profound effect on the younger generation of men in business. This is mainly because they happen to be the other half of a dual-career couple. They often realize that, unless they take on a more equitable share of the domestic burden, they will find home a less peaceful place than they might have hoped. As Gloria Steinem [54] powerfully puts it, women have convinced themselves for the last 25 years, at least in America, that they can do what men can do. Now, they have to convince everyone that men can do what women can do. If they don't, the double burden of working inside and outside the home will continue to be a reality for most women. Until men are fully equal inside the home, women can never be equal outside it.

### Shifting gender roles of men

Increasingly, as men accept more responsibility for child-rearing and other domestic work, the ideal of a totally committed employee will become outdated. Work–life balance issues faced by high-potential men married to high-potential women can lead both groups to resist careers that severely curtail their participation in family life. It will need enlightened activism by men as well as women to convince organizations to review and revise practices that compromise family obligations rather than career obligations. Women with high earnings can always rely on domestic help or expensive childcare centers. But most families find such options difficult. Therefore, greater help from men at home would go a long way in balancing the demands of career as well as family.

We also have to rethink the logic that equates long hours with superior performance and corporate commitment. If we talk about quality time with children, then maybe we should apply the concept at work too. We should think less about how many hours we spend at work and more about what we do with those hours. Many parents need to be willing to challenge prevailing norms—which assume that a commitment to parenting makes you less valuable as an employee—and convince their employers.

## Sensitive parenting

New age parents need to groom their children well. They will be raising kids who will be possibly someone's future spouse or mother and father or someone's future employee or a boss. So they are not going to be respected unless they learn to be respectful. Early on, boys need to be encouraged to take on some the family responsibilities that usually fall on girls. Young boys and girls both need to be trained in homemaking, just as they need to be given training in career-making when the time is right. Hopefully, many young girls with talent and ambitions will seek the support of their fathers to realize their career aspirations. With such a change, the men of this generation will be less inclined than men of the previous generation to ignore or support discriminatory practices.

## Tackle your own gender assumptions

Mothers also have to help young girls in tackling their own gender assumptions, which are manifested in the subjects they choose to study at school and university, and the jobs they choose to apply for. Once recruited, they have to be mindful of the support they provide to female peers and mentoring to women who come after them and the ideals they hold on acceptable leadership models.

## Act as influencers

Beyond their personal lives, individuals can also take steps to influence employers and governments. There are more ways to make your voice heard than ever before; letters to your legislators and local papers, blogs, and tweets on social media are just a few examples. Joining an organization with similar objectives can make all these activities easier.

## How can civil society make a difference?

Gender equality is a social justice issue. Gender equality in society is linked with gender equality at work [55]. Therefore, at a deeper level, the members of any civil society should cherish the core values of genuine concern, sensitivity, consideration, and compassion towards all. An unjust society where the rights of some people are recognized and those of others ignored, will gradually create an environment of inequity, indignity, and injustice.

It is paradoxical that most companies or workplaces reflect 21st century challenges and opportunities, but societal expectations still belong to the 20th century. This creates tremendous stress for working women. That is why the traditional perceptions of masculinity and gender roles need to be redefined through specific media campaigns that provide alternative models of masculine behavior and suggest that you are more of a man if you share responsibilities equally.

Social rules governing the role of women are deeply entrenched and not helpful to female progression. As biases can begin very early in life, it is important to influence early emergence of inequity, since it is more difficult and costly to resolve over time [56]. Boys need to be taught to stand up for girls and stand up against boys who demean young girls. When grown up they will know how to stand up for women.

One of the real barriers to women's progress is the issue of balance: the stress caused by a culture or society which does not recognize the realities of combining work and family. For instance, the conviction that women are the primary caregivers of children needs to be altered together with the belief that men are the primary providers of the family. Making it easier for women means making it easier for men too. Men who choose to stay at home to look after their children are stigmatized too. Many parents want to play a more active role in their children's upbringing and, therefore, the quality of life offered by a job can become a deciding factor. It is important to recognize that women have multiple identities as professional, mother, wife, and daughter. A holistic and inclusive approach is needed to address the entire life cycle spectrum needs of a woman.

Transforming discriminatory social attitudes and mindsets is possible by building and strengthening stakeholder participation and inter-institutional partnerships with community involvement. Advocacy campaigns and public sensitization/awareness programs that focus on women's rights and entitlements must engage the men and boys of the community. It may be worthwhile to focus these efforts in states with low female labor force participation [57].

## Need for a Multi-sectoral Solution

All said and done, we have to recognize that there is no simple or single solution as there is no single path to equality; equality in itself is a path. This is because gender inclusivity is not about a set of simple initiatives that organizations need to undertake to increase their female populations, or policies to ensure women have a harassment free and secure work environment. It is a far more complex, multi-dimensional transformation journey with multiple stakeholders who must work together in order to create a holistic and empowered society, where men and women have different but equal roles to play. When the stakeholders operate in isolation, they are less effective as agents of change. They are more likely to be successful in their objective of achieving equity and parity when they are networked with pathways that allow free flow of ideas, programs, and resources. Enhancing collaboration among these stakeholders can create an ecosystem which is not only good for the growth of the economy, but also good for society.

Gender sensitivity, not gender, is the watchword, for patriarchy is endemic to any system, and not a trait of men alone. What matters today is the ability to think together and think imaginatively about matters of substance, integrating many perspectives.

Change can be unnerving and frightening, because the future is uncertain. But it also teaches a certain tolerance for uncertainty, and hones a certain capacity for trust and patience. To that end, change is timeless, unpredictable. It does not become the next standard operating practice in 90 days and it may not have a positive impact on the next quarter's financial statement. For change does not always come loaded in a truck. It may come in baby steps, one step at a time. It takes time to implement a program of renewal and change, and failure is part of the process.

The stakes for women are high. If we want a world in which inequality based on gender, class, caste, and ethnicity is to be erased out of every country, we need faith. If we want a world where fulfillment of basic needs becomes a basic right, and where progress of women is recognized as progress for all, we need trust. If we want a world where women's work of nurturing, caring, and weaving the fabric of family, is valued and equally shared by men, then we need lots of patience.

To all those who are impatient to see change happen overnight and who think it is too little, too late, let me share with you the bamboo story, which is a teaching in patience. I first heard it from a farmer in Hakone, one of the most scenic and beautiful places near Tokyo.

Do you know how the bamboo grows? After the seed falls to the ground, it is watered by the rains and nourished by the natural nutrients of the soil. During the first year, nothing happens. The rain and the earth continue to do their good work for the second year, but again nothing happens. This pattern is repeated during the third and fourth years. Suddenly, in the fifth year, during the span of not more than six weeks, the bamboo grows 90 feet. Did the bamboo grow to be 90 feet in six weeks or five years? If nature had become impatient and abandoned her nurturing duties at any time during those five years, the bamboo would have died. If the gardener had dug up the bamboo to see if it was growing, the bamboo would have died then as well. The bamboo grows 90 feet over five years, but during the first four years it appears not to grow at all. Nature teaches us wonderful lessons about patience and trust. Shouldn't we also try to resist the temptation to abandon the journey before we reach our destination?

An African proverb directs the way: "If you want to go fast, go alone.

If you want to go far, go together."

May we find our way together, as we go far!

## References

1. Hazarika, Anjali, 'Leading and Executing Industry Change Through a Learning Network', *Vikalpa* 33, no. 3 (2008): 63–77.
2. Jain, Devaki, 'Women, Public Policy and the New World Order', a talk delivered on May, 2006, New Delhi.
3. Majumdar, U., N. Rana, and N. Sanan, 'Blending CSR with Responsible Growth', *Economic Times*, September 15, 2016.
4. Grant Thornton, *International Business Report 2015*, Grant Thornton.
5. von Bröckel, Jan. 'Germany's System of Parental Leave', November 17, 2016. www.janvonbroeckel.de/english/parental_leave.html
6. Devillard, S., W. Graven, E. Lawson, R. Paradise, and S Sancier-Sultan, *Women Matter 2012: Making the Breakthrough* (Report), McKinsey and Company.
7. Hochschild, Arlie and Anne Machung, *The Second Shift: Working Parents and the Revolution at Home*, New York, NY: Viking and Penguin, 1989.
8. ANI, '13 Achievements of Narendra Modi-led Government's First Year in Power, as Listed by Him', ANI, New Delhi: May 30, 2015.
9. Vatsa, Manoj, 'Beti Bachao Beti Padhao Scheme', January 25, 2015.
10. Ellen Iskenderian, Mary, Dean Karlan, Tony Sheldon, Nelun De Silva Wijeyeratne, and Andrea Levere 'Can markets help the poor?' *Yale Insights*, New Haven, CT: Yale School Of Management, October, 20, 2007, http://insights.som.yale.edu/insights/can-markets-help-the-poor (accessed on June 28, 2017).
11. United Nations Department of Economic and Social Affairs, 'India', *World Statistics Pocketbook*, New York, NY: Statistics Division, United Nations Department of Economic and Social Affairs, 2016, data.un.org/CountryProfile.aspx?crName=INDIA
12. Sen, Amartya, *Development as Freedom*, New York, NY: Knopf, 1999.
13. Ernst & Young, *Worldwide Index of Women as Public Sector Leaders: Opening Doors for Women Working in Government*, Ernst & Young, 2013, http://www.ey.com/gl/en/industries/worldwidewomeninpublicsector—worldwide-index-of-women-as-public-sector-leaders
14. *Women on Boards* (Report), February 2011, www.gov.uk/government/uploads/system/uploads/attachment_data/file/31480/11-745-women-on-boards.pdf

15. Inter-Parliamentary Union, *Women in National Parliaments, table,* Inter-Parliamentary Union (IPU), 2016, www.ipu.org/wmn-e/arc/classif280210.htm
16. UNFPA, *State of World Population 2005* (Report), UNFPA, 2005, www.unfpa.org/publications/state-world-population-2005
17. *OECD Economic Surveys: India,* 2014, DOI:10.1787/eco_surveys-ind-2014-
18. Sorsa, P., Raising the Economic Participation of Women in India: A New Growth Engine? OECD Economics Department Working Paper No. 1185, Paris: OECD Publishing, http://www.keepeek.com/Digital-Asset-Management/oecd/economics/raising-the-economic-participation-of-women-in-india_5js6g5kvpd6j-en#.WVEiCZKGNdg
19. World Economic Forum, *Global Gender Gap Report 2015,* Cologny/Geneva: World Economic Forum, 2015, http://www3.weforum.org/docs/GGGR2015/cover.pdf
20. UN Women, *Progress of the World's Women: In Pursuit of Justice* (Report), UN Women, 2011, www.unwomen.org/en/digital-library/publications/2011/7/progress-of-the-world-s-women-in-pursuit-of-justice
21. Speech of Justice Gita Mittal on the inauguration of the Vulnerable Witness Court Room at Tis Hazari Court, Delhi, on April 26, 2017.
22. McKinsey, 'A CEO's Guide to Gender Equality', *McKinsey Quarterly,* November 2015, http://www.mckinsey.com/global-themes/leadership/a-ceos-guide-to-gender-equality (accessed on February 2, 2016).
23. Keswani, Sumeet, 'It's 2016 and Only 7% of Directors Are Women. It's Time To Do Something: Freida Pinto', New Delhi: *Sunday Times of India,* May 15, 2016, http://timesofindia.indiatimes.com/home/sunday-times/all-that-matters/Its-2016-and-only-7-of-directors-are-women-Its-time-to-do-somet (accessed on June 25, 2017).
24. PTI, 'Keira Knightley: I Have Turned Down a Role Due to Pay Gap', *Times of India,* New Delhi: January 29, 2017, http://timesofindia.indiatimes.com/entertainment/english/hollywood/news/Keira-Knightley-Have-turned-down-role-due-to-pay-gap/articles (accessed on June 26, 2017).
25. *The Hindu,* 'Regional Newspapers More Eager to Address Women's Issues', *The Hindu,* February 23, 2005, www.thehindu.com/2005/02/21/stories/2005022102771300.htm
26. World Economic Forum, *The Future of Jobs: Employment, Skills and Workforce Strategy for the Fourth Industrial Revolution,* Global Challenge Insight Report, Cologny/Geneva: World Economic Forum, 2016.
27. Lagarde, Christine, 'Delivering on the Promise of 2025 Keynote Address' at the International Monetary Fund W-20 Summit, September 6, 2015, Ankara, Turkey (IMF Staff Discussion Note, Women, Work, and the Economy: Macroeconomic Gains from Gender Equity).
28. Bhattacharyya, Ricca, 'Tata Steel Pushes for Gender Diversity; To Increase Female Staff to 18% from 9% in 4 years', *Economic Times,* New Delhi: November 10, 2015, p. 12.

29. *Business Today*, 'Proactive Recruitment: Mercer and *Business Today* Research', *Business Today*, January 2006.
30. Graves, L., P. Ohlott, and M. Ruderman, 'Parents Hear This: Your Family Commitments Can Help You at Work', *Journal of Applied Psychology*, January 2007.
31. Khosla, Varuni, 'GSK Consumer Healthcare raises maternity and adoption leave to 6 months', *Economic Times*, New Delhi, April 4, 2016, http://economictimes.indiatimes.com/jobs/gsk-consumer-healthcare-raises-maternity-and-adoption-leave-to-6-months/articleshow/516402 (accessed on June 26, 2017).
32. Dasgupta, Brinda and Sreeradha D. Basu, 'Companies Roll Out New Initiatives for Young Mothers', New Delhi: *Economic Times*, February 16, 2016, http://economictimes.indiatimes.com/jobs/companies-roll-out-new-initiatives-for-young-mothers/articleshow/51002697.cms (accessed on June 26, 2017).
33. ABA (American Bar Association), *Commission on Women in the Profession: Recruitment, Retention, and Success of Women Lawyers*, Chicago, IL: ABA, 2000.
34. Dasgupta, Brinda, 'Now, Sick Leave for Fertility Treatment at Godrej Industries', Bengaluru, *Economic Times*, July 22, 2016, http://economictimes.indiatimes.com/jobs/sick-leave-for-fertility-treatment-at-godrej-industries/articleshow/53329351.cms (accessed on June 28, 2017).
35. Airy, Anupama, 'Genderbenders', *Sunday Hindustan Times*, New Delhi: November 3, 2013, p. 12.
36. Dreher, G. F., 'Breaking the Glass Ceiling: The Effects of Sex Ratios and Work-Life Programs on Female Leadership at the Top', *Human Relations*, 56 (2003), 541–62.
37. IBM, IBM Exite Camp, 2016, http://www.clarendon.vic.edu.au/wp-content/uploads/IBM-EXITE-Camp-2016-Information-1.pdf
38. NES Global Talent, *Attracting and Retaining Women in Oil and Gas Engineering: A Survey Examining the Gender Talent Gap*, 2015, https://www.nesglobaltalent.com/sites/default/files/images/women-in-engineering-report-single_final.pdf
39. *The Times of India*, 'Come Back, It is Better the Second Time', *The Times of India*, New Delhi: June 10, 2014, p. 14.
40. Hewlett, S. A., L. Buck, and C. West, 'Leadership in Your Midst: Tapping the Hidden Strengths of Minority Executives', *Harvard Business Review* 83, no. 11 (2005): 74–82.
41. Corporate Executive Board, *Four Imperatives to Increase Representation of Women in Leadership Positions*, Arlington, VA: Corporate Executive Board (CEB), 2014.
42. Chartered Institute of Personnel and Development, *Flexible Working Provision and Uptake*, London: Chartered Institute of Personnel and Development (CIPD), 2012.
43. Schwartz, Felice N., 'Management, Women and the New Facts of Life', *Harvard Business Review* January–February, 1989, https://hbr.org/1989/01/management-women-and-the-new-facts-of-life (accessed June 28, 2017).

44. Hewlett, S. A. and Ripa Rashid, *Winning the War for Talent in Emerging Markets: Why Women Are the Solution*, Harvard Business Review Press, 2011.
45. Crossby, F. J., A. Iyer, and S. Sincharoen, 'Understanding Affirmative Action', *Annual Review of Psychology* no. 57 (2006): 585–611.
46. *Guidelines on Corporate Social Responsibility and Sustainability for Central Public Sector Enterprises*, 2013, www.dpemou.nic.in/MOUFiles/Revised_CSR_Guidelines.pdf
47. Hewlett and Rashid, *Winning the War for Talent in Emerging Markets*.
48. Krivkovich, Alexis, Eric Kutcher, and Lareina Yee, 'Breaking Down the Gender Challenge', *McKinsey Quarterly*, March 2016, http://www.mckinsey.com/business-functions/organization/our-insights/breaking-down-the-gender-challenge (accessed on June 28, 2017).
49. Hewlett and Rashid, *Winning the War for Talent in Emerging Markets*, Boston, MA.
50. Basu, Sreeradha, 'IIM-B, Goldman to Handhold Women into Entrepreneurship', Mumbai: *Economic Times*, November 15, 2016, http://epaperbeta.timesofindia.com/Article.aspx?eid=31818&articlexml=IIM-B-Goldman-to-Handhold-Women-into-Entrepreneurship-15112016020007 (accessed on June 28, 2017).
51. Sethi, Atul, 'Be a Man and Share Responsibilities', *Times of India*, October 16, 2011.
52. Jejeebhoy, S. J., and K. G. Santhya, *Enabling Adolescent Boys to Adopt Attitudes That Espouse Gender Equality and Oppose Violence Against Women and Girls: Evidence from Rural Bihar—Policy Brief*, New Delhi: Population Council, 2017.
53. McKinsey, 'CEO's Guide', *McKinsey Quarterly*.
54. Steinem, Gloria, 'Revving Up for the Next 25 Years', in *The Fabric of the Future*, edited by M. J. Ryan Berkeley, CA: Conari Press, 1998.
55. McKinsey and Company, *Reinventing the Workplace to Unlock the Potential of Gender Diversity*, McKinsey and Company, 2016.
56. World Bank, *World Development Report 2012: Gender Equality and Development*, Washington, DC: World Bank, 2012.
57. Eswaran, M., B. Ramasamy, and W. Wadhwa, 'Status, Caste, and Time Allocation of Women in Rural India', *Economic Development and Cultural Change* 61, no. 2 (2013).

# Index

ability development, 153–55
academic institutions, 280
accountability, 139
All India Survey on Higher Education, 34
ambition, 94–97
   analysis, 100–101
   expectations, living up to, 97–100
ambivalence, 201–3
   America, polls in, 202
   in attitudes, 201
   gender roles, 203–4
      communication, 206–7
      delegate, 205
      growth/roadblock, facilitating, 204–5
      work for, 204
   leading headhunters, 201
anger, emotion, 40–41, 180, 182
*ardhanarisvara*, 26
Asia-Pacific region, 63
assertiveness, 37, 39, 51, 87, 99, 158, 159, 200, 213
authenticity, 27, 162, 163

being different, 30, 71,
Best Enterprise Award, 117
Big Five personality tests, 39
biological cycles, misconceptions, 41
Bradley, Margaret, 191
BRIC countries, 43, 48, 53, 68, 226
Brooks, Alison Wood, 86

Bureau of Public Enterprises, 110
business enterprises, 279
business/private sector
   career-path alternatives, 309–10
   corporate commitment development, 306–7
   CSR program, 313–15
   ensuring conducive environment, 303–4
   EXITE camp program, 307
   flexible schedules, 308–9
   former employees, linkage with, 310–11
   human resource, segment of, 301–2
   parenting leave, 309
   part-time employment, 309
   recruitment/training, maximum ROI on, 304–5
   reform backlash, stem, 312–13
   stigma remove, 307
   talent pool, equal distribution of, 300–301
   treating women's issues, 302–3
   voluntary work and community service, 311–12

Canadian International Development Agency, 212
career, 91–92
   career-focused group, 44–45, 86
   proactive management, lack of, 93–94

stepping stones, 92
transitions, 174
Center for Creative Leadership (CCL), 302
Center for Work-Life Policy, 43
Central Public Sector Enterprises (CPSEs), 314
change agents, 22, 136, 212, 243, 280
child-bearing phases, 47
child-rearing phases, 47
civil service/public sector institutional reforms, 287
Clinton, Hillary, 51
coaching, 173–74
   five signature themes
      ability, deal with trouble, 188–91
      managing emotions, 178–83
      overcommitment, 191–94
      standing up to be counted, 183–88
      strategic mindset, developing, 194–97
   leadership transitions, 175–78
commitment, 194
communication, 75, 167, 206–7, 214
companies, 60, 64
   assumption, 143
   boards, women on, 220, 227–29
   categories of, 218
   culture, 225
   and organizations, 31
   significant number of, 219
   Women Matter, 68
Companies Act, 218
competence, 211–12
computer science programs, 56
Confederation of Indian Industry (CII), 60
conflict management, 188
conscious bias, 72
conscious stereotypes, 76
constructive feedback, success, 150–51
depersonalize, 151–52
message from messenger, separation, 152–53
corporate America, 70, 244
corporate boardrooms, 23
corporate performance, 55
   succession planning, 74–76
   talent acquisition and placement, 55–60
   talent development and utilization, 64–65
      challenging assignments, 66–68
      limited developmental exposure, 66
      nomination on executive committees, 68–69
      world of science, 69
   talent maintenance/retention
      conflict between work and family obligations, 62–63
      excessively long hours, 63–64
   talent recognition and evaluation, 70–73
corporate simulation, 1, 2
Corporate Social Responsibility (CSR), 313–15
cream, being pushed to the top, 143–45
creative recruitment techniques, 62
cross-gender relationships, 149
crying, 40
C-Suite, 222
"Culture Meter" program, 269
culture, 146–47
   change, 138
   stereotypes, 46
Customer Service, 146

delegation, 194
Department of Personnel, 120
Department of Public Enterprises, 118, 120
descriptive stereotype, 35, 55

Index 331

difficult conversation, 190
diversity, 12, 224–29
diversity and inclusion (D&I), 256–57, 268–69
Diversity and Women's Network (DAWN), 271
Dow Jones Sustainability Index (DJSI), 258
dream, 104
  gender bias, develop understanding of, 104–5
  homemaker and professional, discarding, 105–6
  never too late to fulfill, 106–7
  personal goals, 104
Dr Lawrence Summers, 36
dual-career relationships, 48

effectiveness, 7, 13, 64, 115, 166, 201, 301
efficiency, 291
emotions, 41, 178–83
employers' organizations, 297–300
empowerment, ecosystem of, 276–78
  business/private sector role, 300–15
  civil society, 322–23
  consciously choose careers, 319
  emerging markets, multinational corporations in, 315–16
  employers' organizations, 297–300
  five-sector partnership model, 281–83
  gender equity, 283–93
  gender-sensitive press and media, 295–97
  influencers, act as, 321–22
  judicial/legal provisions, 293–95
  mandating quotas of women, 288–90
  multi-sectoral gender institutional architecture, 281
  multi-sectoral solution, 323–25

NGOs, 317–19
nurturing women entrepreneurs, 317
opportunities, confluence of, 278–80
own gender assumptions, 321
principal actor, 280
public bodies, 286–88
sensitive parenting, 321
sensitizing men, 320
shifting gender roles of men, 320–21
skill, 161–62
universities/educational institutions, partnering with, 316–17
Equal Pay Act, 15
equality, with difference
  assumptions, 7
  complex scenario with vast contradictions, 8–12
  models, 13–26
  redefining leadership, 27
Equality and Human Rights Commission (EHRC), 219
"equals" sign, 13
equity, 24, 119, 166, 245, 283–85
Europe, 16, 223, 224, 235, 269, 282
executive committees, nomination on, 68–69
EXITE camp program, 308
Export Processing Zones, 124

Factories Act, 122–27
family focused group, 45
feeling, emotion, 41, 180
female labor participation, 287–88
femininity, 26, 96, 204
Fifth National Meet, 117
*First Step: India Overview*, 63
first-line leaders, 175
Flexible Work Arrangement Program (FWA), 316
*Fortune*, 85

Forum of Women in Public Sector, 110, 112, 113, 117, 209
Fourth World Conference, 8
Frase-Blunt, Martha, 74
Fundamental Right and Directive Principle, 283

gender
  bias, 54, 104–5, 250, 278
  blindness, 14
  differences, 13, 105, 150, 200, 238
  diversity, 139, 224, 254–55
  gender-blind society, 22
  gender equality bias, 116
  gender neutrality, 14
  gender-responsive organizations, 229
  gender stereotypes, 30–31, 71, 77
  gender-sensitive budgets, 291
  gender-sensitive press and media, 295–97
  gender-sensitive programs, 243–44
Gender Empowerment Measure (GEM), 290
gender equity
  integrated policy interventions, 283–85
  social and economic indicators
    Gender Empowerment Measure, 290
    Gender-Related Development Index, 290
    gender-sensitive budgets, 291
    tax incentives, 291, 292
    WEF gender gap study, 292–93
Gender-Related Development Index (GDI), 290
glass ceiling, 31–33, 87, 119
glass wall, 32
Global Board of Directors Survey, 219
*Global Gender Gap Report 2015*, 292–93

Harkness, Susan, 15
Harmonizing Diversity, 243
Herzberg, Frederick, 42
Hewlett, S. A., 48
Hinduja Global Solutions, 57
Hindustan Unilever (HUL), 311
Hochschild, Arlie Russell, 95
Human resources (HR), 61, 90, 107
  course of action, 57
  policies, 60, 269–70

ICICI Bank, 258–59
  diversity, business case for, 259–60
  functional bias, 261
  gender neutral organizational culture, 260
  iWork@home, 261–62
  track accountability, mechanism to, 262–63
inequality, 9, 10, 69, 324
influencing skills, honing, 158–61
innate abilities, 142
intelligence, 25, 36–39
intercorporate network, 132–35
  formation of, 135–37
International Labor Organization (ILO), 233
International Personnel Association (IPA), 48
Inter-Parliamentary Union, 8
interpersonal relationships, stereotype, 35
invisible barriers, 84–89, 102
  ambition, 94–97
    analysis, 100–101
    expectations, living up to, 97–100
  career, 91–92
    proactive management, lack of, 93–94
    stepping stones, 92

dream, 104
  gender bias, develop understanding of, 104–5
  homemaker and professional, discarding, 105–6
  never too late to fulfill, 106–7
  personal goals, 104
  organizational culture, 89–91
  tightrope circus, 102–3
  IT-enabled service organizations, 57

Kagan, Jerome, 96

Lagarde, Christine, 18
leadership, 18, 19, 49–52, 84, 85
  brand, 216–18
  program, demographics of, 174
  identity, 215–16
  redefining, 26–27
  transitions, 175–78
leaking pipeline, 60
LeanIn.org, 74
liberation movements, 126
limited developmental exposure, 66
Lyness, K. S., 66

male role model, 41
masculinity, 26, 319, 322
McKinsey, 70, 74
mentorships, 149
Michael Page India, 46
middle-level leaders, 175–76
Miller, Eric J., 99
Ministry of Commerce, 124
Ministry of Labor, 120, 122, 124
Ministry of Petroleum and Natural Gas (MoPNG), 136
mobility, issue of, 47
monocultural paradigm, 14
Morrison, Toni, 198
*Mothers and Daughters of Invention* (Stanley), 73
Myths, woman, 34–39

barriers, to women's advancement, 53
women and leadership do not go together, 49–52
women cannot deal with tough feedback, 39–41
women do not like to travel, relocate/take international assignments, 46–48
women do not value achievement, promotion, and meaningful work, 42–46

National Academy of Sciences, 85
National Convention, 111
National Council of Educational Research and Training (NCERT), 37
National governments, 279
National Meets, 114, 115
National Network, 110
National Organization for Women (NOW), 16
National Petroleum Management Program (NPMP), 132, 200
National Research Council (NRC), 150
National Stock Exchange (NSE)
  dual-ladder career policy, 266
  ensuring safe commute, 267–68
  equal opportunity employer policy, 264
  executive coaching, 266
  people philosophy, 265
  talent acquisition, 265
  talent management, 265
  work initiatives, best place to, 267
  work–life balance, 267
negotiation, 159–61
Nehru Centenary Celebrations Committee, 109
Nemilov, Anton, 69
NES Global Talent Survey, 71
network, 107
  collaboration with agencies, 120–27

formative years, reflections on, 114–15
fundamental interventions
best enterprise award creation, 117
entry level, reservation on opinion poll, 118–20
sensitization, 117
systematic database, creation of, 115–17
intercorporate initiative, lessons from, 137–40
intercorporate network, 132–37
relationships, 113
sustainability, struggle for fund-raising issues, 128–29
office bearers, selection of, 129
organizational issues, 127–28
vision development, 130–32
not-for-profit organizations, 279

Oil India Limited, 29, 57
old boys networks, 219
Open House Session, 110
open-door policy, 168
organization, 34, 156, 246
assertiveness, 37
companies and, 31
culture, 43, 89–91, 142–43, 146–47
good bosses, 200
HR leaders in, 61
issues, 127–28
leadership teams in, 74
men in, 239–40
politics, 147
pyramid, 32
strokes for, 248–53
overcommitment, 191–94, 205
overseas training, 65

parliament, women in, 289–90
pay gap, 54, 98
performance appraisal, 144
performance management, 190

periodic assessment, 139
personal effectiveness, 166
personal goals, dreams, 104
personal relationship, 148
petroleum industry, 132–34
physiological differences, equality, 19
pipeline myth, 144
policy development, 139
Pound, Ezra, 224
power, women's perception of, 85
prescriptive stereotype, 55
probability, 42
professional quality, 71
professional technology, 228
program evaluation, 3
progressive companies, 64
psychological glass ceiling, 88
public sector enterprises (PSEs), 116, 128, 135

Rashid, R., 48
recognition, skill, 96
resiliency, building, 156–57
ripple effect, 120

sanctuaries creation, in workplaces
aspiring managers, men for, 252
best men in organization, 239–40
business case, making
corporate governance, 247–48
customer focus, 244–45
diversity, strategic importance of, 246–47
ethical values, 248
higher financial returns, 245–46
risk management, 247
talent retention, 246
career ladder
CEOs, men for, 252
difference, assumption of, 250
in emerging markets, 235
equality, assumption of, 249–50
gender differences, 238
ICICI Bank, 258–63

## Index

International Labor Organization, 233
National Stock Exchange, 264–68
playing field, 240–41
senior leaders, men for, 252
small change strategy, 242–44
Tata Consultancy Services, 268–72
Wipro, 254–58
women are equal but different, 251
women-owned businesses, 233–34
women's departments, 232
work–life balance, 236
Second Career Internship Program (SCIP), 310
second shift, 95
selection committee, 72
self-disclosures, 162–63
Self-Help Groups (SHGs), 286
self-promotion, 36, 160–162, 186, 187
senior-level leaders, 176–77
sensitization, 117, 269, 296, 313
service industries, 9
sex differences, 18
Sixth National Meet, 118
skill, 142
   building/development, 145
   cream, being pushed to the top, 143–45
   success
     being yourself, dealing with challenge, 161–64
     building resiliency and change readiness, 156–57
     constructive feedback, 150–53
     developing ability, 153–55
     honing influencing skills, 158–61
     meaning and definition of, 145
     organization culture and politics of, 146–47
     organization seeking mentors and role models, 147–50
     strategies for, 145–46
     work–life balance, 164–71

socialization, 91, 93, 94, 96, 154
Springboard Women's Development Program, 120
Standing Conference of Public Enterprises (SCOPE), 110, 111, 122, 124
Stanley, Autumn, 73
Steinem, Gloria, 106
stereotype, 4, 29–30, 40
   glass ceilings and walls, encountering, 31–33
   implications and consequences, 78
   kinds of, 55
   myths, woman, 34–39
     barriers to women's advancement, 53
     women and leadership do not go together, 49–52
     women cannot deal with tough feedback, 39–41
     women do not like to travel, relocate/take international assignments, 46–48
     women do not value achievement, promotion, and meaningful work, 42–46
   women's careers, impact on, 30–31
strategic mindset, 194–97
stress, 41, 86, 167, 252
success
   being yourself, dealing with challenge, 161–64
   building resiliency and change readiness, 156–57
   constructive feedback, 150–53
   developing ability, 153–55
   honing influencing skills, 158–61
   meaning and definition of, 145
   organization
     culture and politics of, 146–47
     seeking mentors and role models, 147–50
   work–life balance, 164–71
succession planning, 74–76

Sur, Abha, 69
sustainability, struggle for
   fund-raising issues, 128–29
   office bearers, selection of, 129
   organizational issues, 127–28
   vision development, 130–32
   systematic database, 115–17

taboo, 137, 144
talent
   acquisition and placement, 55–60
   development and utilization, 64–65
      challenging assignments, 66–68
      limited developmental exposure, 66
      nomination on executive committees, 68–69
      world of science, 69
   maintenance/retention
      conflict between work and family obligations, 62–63
      excessively long hours, 63–64
      recognition and evaluation, 70–73
Tata Consultancy Services (TCS)
   customers and markets, responsiveness to, 270
   diversity and inclusion, 268–69
   enabling work environment, 269
   every level, programs for, 270–71
   HR policies, 269–70
   iExcel, 271–72
Tata Institute of Social Sciences, 109
tax incentives, 291, 292
technical support, 148
"think leader, think male" phenomenon, 49
Thompson, D. E., 66
tightrope circus, 102–3
tokenism, 220–23
Trade Related Entrepreneurship Assistance and Development Scheme for Women (TREAD), 285
transformation, 92, 130, 131, 141, 277
transitions, 174, 175

UAE, 43, 48
"up or out" promotion system, 72
unconscious stereotypes, 76
UNESCO, 69
unfamiliar behaviors, 155
United States, 16–17, 31, 36
US Department of Labor in Washington, 6
US Presidential Elections, 51

visibility, 187, 188, 226

wage gap, 15, 296
Waldfogel, Jane, 15
*Wall Street Journal*, 31
widespread assumptions, 44
Wipro
   diversity and inclusion, 256–57
   gender diversity, life stage-based approach, 254–55
   nurtures talent, culture that, 254
   raise awareness, 255–56
   women's empowerment principles, 257–58
woman boss, 199–201
   ambivalence, 201–3
   America, polls in, 202
   in attitudes, 201
   gender roles, 203–7
   leading headhunters, 201
   boardrooms, 223–24
   companies, 218–20
   crystallizing leadership identity, 215–16
   diversity, boards, 224–29
   leadership
      authority and expertise, resistance, 209–12
      brand, development, 216–18
      power and authority, 212–14
      tokenism, 221–23
women entrepreneurs, nurturing, 317
Women in Leadership, 84, 88
Women in Public Sector (WIPS), 112, 116–18, 209

Women's associations, 280
Women's inheritance rights, 294–95
Women's Issues at Workplaces, 6
work–life balance, 164–67
    building support networks, 169–70
    multiple roles and emerging role stress, managing, 167
    number of roles, review and reducing, 168
    relationships professional, 170–71
    time management, 168–69
    workshops, 154
World Development Report, 46
World Economic Forum (WEF) gender gap study, 292–93